The map opposite appears in James Anderson's *Account of the Present State of the Hebrides and Western Coasts of Scotland* ... (Edinburgh 1785). Various proposed roads and canals are shown, including a road from Fort William to Erribol and thence to Thurso (see p. 84). The following description, headed REMARKS, is printed alongside the map:

1. AMONG the Hebrides, and all along the West Coasts of Scotland, the tide of flood sets to the N. and ebbs to the S.; and there, especially in narrow sounds, the tide flows with very great rapidity; forming at one place in particular (the Connel in Loch-Etive) a cascade of salt-water, where, at certain times of tide, the water falls at once five or six feet, where ships a few hours afterwards may sail in perfect safety. To those who are strangers to the different phenomena produced by the tides, the navigation of those seas would be troublesome and hazardous; but seamen who are acquainted, and who know how to avail themselves of those strong tides, find they often prove of very great service; as they can by the aid of them, on many occasions, go quickly forward even with a brisk gale a-head.

2. The navigation in those seas would be rendered still more safe and easy, if light-houses were erected on the following places, viz, 1. On the Mull of Cantire---2. On the island of Scalpa in Harris---3. On North Ronalshaw in Orkney---and, 4. On Kinnaird's head, Aberdeenshire.

3. The natural harbours among the Western Islands and narrow channels are excellent, and so numerous as to be in almost every case of difficulty within reach. But these harbours are at present known only to a few fishermen who annually visit those seas in the herring-busses, and by smugglers. The first class of these men, being unable to buy expensive charts, have no opportunity of discovering the errors of those charts that exist, and smugglers do not wish to give others information in regard to these particulars. A set of small charts of those coasts that could be used in little vessels, and that might be procured at a moderate expence, is much wanted.

4. The seas among the Hebrides abound every-where, at the proper seasons, with astonishing quantities of cod, ling, herrings, and a vast variety of other kinds of fish. The herrings frequently fill the lochs and harbours, so that inconceivable quantities are or might be caught in them. Into these lochs, however, the coming of the herring is uncertain, and by consequence the fishery in these lochs is precarious. But, in the open sea on those coasts, both on the east and on the west of Scotland, the herrings abound every season, and *there* might be carried on a much more steady fishing than the lochs afford, were they looked after.

5. The finest cod are found in strong currents, about head-lands, where the tide flows with uncommon rapidity; and in these places the fish are said never to be out of season. There the fishing must be carried on with handlines, at the turn of the tides only. On banks, where little current prevails, they are filled for with long lines, and on these banks they are in season only a part of the year; and when at the best, they are much inferior to the stream-cod, though greatly superior in quality to those from Newfoundland. It is only of late that the value of stream-cod has come to be known, and no extensive fishery of that kind is as yet established. Orkney bids fair to excel in this kind of fishery. Cod are found on banks from 10 to 40 fathom; ling on banks from 10 to 200 fathom water. No chart has ever yet been made of the proper fishing-banks on the west coast, nor are these banks well known by the natives. Such fishing-charts are very much wanted.

6. The Western Isles and adjacent coasts are known to contain many valuable articles belonging to the mineral kingdom. Besides coals which have been discovered in Bute, Islay, Mull, Cannay, Morven, and very lately near Dunstaffnage, there is found in Islay, lead, copper, quicksilver, emery, marble, and pure chrystalline sand, fit for making the finest glass. Lead is found also near Loch-Sunart---beautiful marble at Tiree, of a kind *sui generis*----statuary marble in Skye, and in many places in Ross-shire and Sutherland. Limestone, marle, and shelly sand, abound in the greatest profusion. Black lead is found near Loch-Urn; and manganese has been of late discovered in Ross-shire.

7. Mull, Staffa, Cannay, and Egg, exhibit abundance of basaltic columns of the most perfect kinds, arranged into forms stupenduously magnificent; and other volcanic productions, that might admit of being converted into glass at a very moderate expence, also abound. Fine free-stone is found in Arran, Islay and Mull; and great plenty of a strong coarse kind is found all along the adjacent coasts. The sheep of Coll, Barra, Uist, Harris, &c. are chiefly flesh - coloured, mixed with black, of a wool exceedingly firm, and free from hairs.

8. The native sheep of all the Northern Islands carry a wool that exceeds all others known in Europe for its fineness and peculiar silky softness. The cattle are small, but beautiful, and highly valued in every part of Britain. In many places, large flocks of red deer are yet found wild in the mountains. Black game, woodcock, plover, and snipe, abound on the lower grounds, grouse in the higher fields, and ptarmegin in the mountains. The lakes in the low islands swarm during the winter season, with innumerable quantities of water-fowl of various sorts.

9. In many places are found extensive forests of oak and fir-wood, which, if properly cared for, might soon furnish masts and timber for the Royal Navy of Britain; but these for some time past have not obtained the attention that their great importance deserves.

10. The hills upon the West Coast rise from the sea with a bold front, and appear rugged, but are not of a very great height; as these hills do not rise by a gradual continued ascent as you recede from the sea. The country may be said to be upon the whole, a plane surface furrowed with many deep and abrupt excavations: Hence, valleys are found to extend backwards very far into the country, with scarce any rise above the level of the sea; along which valleys, level roads may be carried, or canals for internal navigation might be opened in many places at a very moderate expence. This would be much facilitated by the numerous, long, and narrow lochs which usually occupy a great part of these level valleys in their present state. Such roads and canals would tend greatly to facilitate commerce, were that country properly attended to: And the small rivers that descend from the steep mountains on each side of those valleys, by the great fall that might always be commanded, would have such a power on machinery, as would give great advantages for various sorts of manufactures.

11. Among the Hebrides the soil is in many places extremely fertile, and the climate much more favourable than is generally imagined. But, from the want of markets, and because the rents arising from revenue the tenants are necessarily allowed to remain in a state of nature nearly. The people, though numerous, patient, and industrious, are allowed to remain in a hopeless state of things, have it not in their power, by any exertions of their own, either to prove useful to the State, or in any sensible degree to benefit themselves.

After the
Forty-Five

A.J.YOUNGSON

---

to my friends
Frank Davidson
and
Jack Miller

After the Forty-Five

The Economic Impact on the Scottish Highlands

A.J.YOUNGSON

EDINBURGH
UNIVERSITY
PRESS

© A.J.Youngson 1973

EDINBURGH UNIVERSITY PRESS
22 George Square, Edinburgh

ISBN 0 85224 226 3

North America
Aldine·Atherton, Inc.
529 South Wabash Avenue, Chicago

Library of Congress
Catalog Card Number 72-79288

Printed in Great Britain
by W & J Mackay Limited, Chatham

Preface

On the shelves of a famous American university there is a handful of books concerning Scotland. Of these, approximately three-fifths are about Mary, Queen of Scots, and the remainder are about Bonnie Prince Charlie. This impression that almost everything interesting in Scottish history occurred before the end of 1746 is one for which the Scots themselves are largely responsible. But it is not correct. And it is even less correct to suppose that by that date everything important had happened. Most of what is truly important for modern Scotland has probably happened since 1746.

This book is an attempt to explain what was proposed to be done and what was done in the Highlands after the Forty-five. It was begun largely as the result of a comment by that great American scholar, Jacob Viner, to the effect that it was strange that Adam Smith made no proposals regarding the Highlands; but once begun, the life of the clans, and the struggle between their ways and the ways of the expanding commercial world, became of absorbing interest. It is not only instructive, it is fascinating, even dramatic, to see a civilisation fight for its life—and lose. And there is contemporary significance in this struggle which took place in the Highlands over a period of about eighty years—it is, of course, just arguable that it is still going on—because in country after country of the modern world there are plans for economic development—modernisation plans— which are not altogether unlike those of the eighteenth century, and which encounter the same sort of difficulties as were encountered in the Highlands between one and two hundred years ago.

I have tried to write this book without that intense emotional involvement which characterises so much that is written about the Highlands. Such understanding as is possible will not be reached on the basis of uncritical admiration for the work of the 'improvers', but neither will it be founded on depicting them as unscrupulous self-seekers and their opponents as saints and martyrs. The 'clearances', in particular, are an emotional subject, but a subject which is basically economic and vastly complicated. Indeed, there is little prospect of a fair and well-informed assessment of this celebrated 'episode' until Mr Robin Adam's labours on the Sutherland Estate Papers are complete.

Preface

What I have written is to a considerable extent from the point of view of public policy. I have therefore relied a good deal on official records and reports. I have also relied on the contemporary writings of travellers, landowners, economists, agricultural experts, ministers of the Kirk and other observers who provided probably fuller information and sharper and abler contemporary analysis than is available for any other pre-nineteenth-century case of 'underdevelopment'. Modern writing I have not much depended upon, except for the admirable thesis 'The British Fisheries Society, 1786–1893' by Dr Jean Dunlop (Dr Jean Munro). I am much indebted to Dr Munro for permission to quote from this unpublished thesis.

Parts of the book were read by Mr Robin Adam, Professor Gordon Donaldson, and Mr George Richardson. I am indebted to each of them for valuable comments and suggestions, but what is now printed is of course my sole responsibility. I am also obliged to Mr Finlayson, of Edinburgh University Library, for friendly and expert guidance on innumerable occasions, to Miss Dickson, of the Edinburgh Public Library, for help in finding some of the illustrations, to the officials of the Scottish Record Office for their help and courtesy, and to numerous friends—not least my wife—for sharing with me a growing passion for the Highlands.

Writing this book was extraordinarily interesting. I hope it will likewise be found interesting to read.

A.J. YOUNGSON
Edinburgh, April 1972

Contents

Illustrations

ACKNOWLEDGEMENTS

The publishers are grateful to the Ordnance Survey for
permission to reproduce the map of Ullapool (plate 13, Crown
Copyright 1968); to the City Librarian, Edinburgh for plates
4, 6, and 7; to Professor A.J.Youngson for plate 20; and to
Edinburgh University Library for all the remaining plates.

I

The Highland Scene

Towards the end of 1764 a young man whose home was in Ayrshire arrived in the Calvinist city of Geneva. He had made many disagreeable journeys over bad roads, and had sometimes slept in his clothes on the floors of inns or private houses, or even in hay lofts. Like all his contemporaries he was accustomed to hard living and rough travelling; but he was a gentleman, with introductions to the rich and the famous, and now he was to visit Voltaire. From Geneva he took a coach to Ferney—it was the day before Christmas: 'the earth was covered with snow; I surveyed wild nature with a noble eye'—and in a short time he reached Voltaire's large and agreeable country house. With his host he talked of Scotland, mentioning that he and Dr Johnson intended one day to make a tour to the Hebrides; and Voltaire, he records, 'looked at me as if I had talked of going to the North Pole'.

Almost nine years were to pass before Boswell and Johnson actually set off for the west of Scotland, but in the 1770s their journey was only a little less remarkable than its proposal had seemed in the 1760s. For a man no longer young—Johnson celebrated, or rather refused to celebrate his sixty-fourth birthday in Skye—and decidedly overweight, the tour was extremely adventurous. Both men had to walk, ride, or sail every inch of the way, for once beyond Inverness they were in country, as Johnson himself put it, 'upon which, perhaps, no wheel has ever rolled'.[1] They lived in inns which were barbarous even by the standards of the eighteenth century, or in houses in which the supply of brandy, wine, tea, sugar, silks, and other items was entirely smuggled; and they were unable to speak to over nine-tenths of the population, who spoke only Gaelic. Johnson was indeed far from home, as he had expected. To penetrate beyond the fringes of the Highlands in those days was no light task, and very few educated men attempted it; to meet someone in society who had done so—not himself a highlander—was like meeting someone today who has just returned from Patagonia, or the rain forests of the Orinoco.

Johnson and Boswell crossed from Inverness to Skye and then returned southward *via* Mull and Inveraray in the autumn of 1773; and Johnson's

Journey was published at the beginning of 1775. Those who preceded them, travellers in the Highlands from curiosity or out of a sense of adventure, were very few. One of the most interesting accounts of life in the Highlands in the first half of the eighteenth century was written not by a traveller but by a visiting government employee, Edward Burt. Burt, variously described as an engineer officer who served with General Wade in Scotland in the 1720s, as an army contractor, and as an illiterate hack-writer, was certainly living in or near Inverness about the year 1725. His *Letters from a Gentleman in the North of Scotland* were first published in 1754, and they provide an interesting and often entertaining account—with 'some few strokes that savour a little of the satirical'—of the life and manners of the people at that time. In 1750 another visitor, most likely a government agent, made an extensive tour, probably at some risk to his life, with a view, evidently, to collecting information about the condition and political loyalties of the clans, especially those whose members had been 'out' in the recent rebellion. His report was naturally not published at the time. But over a hundred years later it was brought to light by Andrew Lang and published in 1898. It is a storehouse of first-hand, picturesque, but by no means unprejudiced information. Ten years later, in 1760, Bishop Pococke spent six months in touring Scotland. Pococke, a churchman 'of mild manners and primitive simplicity', had already seen a good deal of the world. He had made tours in France, Italy and other parts of Europe, had travelled in Egypt, and had visited Jerusalem and the marvellous ruins at Baalbek. His tour of the Highlands was remarkably extensive. Beginning at Inveraray, he travelled via Iona and Inverness as far north as Loch Eriboll and Tongue, returning through Dornoch and Tain to the shores of the Moray Firth. Concerned chiefly with place-names and antiquities, the letters in which Pococke described his tour are of rather limited interest.

Much the most important of those who travelled and wrote before Dr Johnson was Thomas Pennant. Like Pococke, Pennant was an experienced traveller. He was moreover a naturalist of repute, who corresponded with Linnaeus, and who published, along with a good deal else, two well-known scientific books, *British Zoology* and *A History of Quadrupeds*, works which were regarded with respect by Buffon. Pennant records that in 1769 he had 'the hardihood to venture on a journey to the remotest part of North Britain'.[2] This journey included crossing the hills from Blair Atholl to Deeside, riding up the coast from Inverness to Duncansby Head and back, and then down the Great Glen from Inverness to Fort William and on to Inveraray. Returning in 1772 he sailed up the west coast as far as Loch Broom, visiting several islands of the Inner Hebrides, and, intending to reach the north coast, rode north into Assynt; but here he turned back because, he tell us, 'we were informed that the way was impassable for horses, and that even an highland foot-messenger must avoid part of the hills by crossing an arm of the sea'.[3] His accounts of his journeys were published in 1771 and 1774-6. Dr Johnson admired his work: 'he's the best traveller I ever read; he observes more things than any one else does'.[4]

Pennant's highland tours, which were the most extensive recorded up to that time, involved well over 1,000 miles of riding and sailing. Yet it is notable how much of the Highlands Pennant did not see. He did not visit the Outer Hebrides; was scarcely at all in Sutherland and not very much in Perthshire; crossed from coast to coast only once; was never in the Spey Valley, Applecross, Knoydart, Morar, Moidart or Ardnamurchan; and north of the Great Glen saw almost nothing that was not within a few miles of the coast. To say this is not to belittle his achievement, which was remarkable. But it reflects the disloacted, scattered, extensive and inaccessible character of highland geography. What attracted travellers to the Highlands in the eighteenth century was their strangeness and remoteness; what defeated them, at least to some extent, was the multiplicity of half-isolated areas of which they were, and still are, composed.

The idea of regions and sub-regions within the Highlands was not one with which the eighteenth century was familiar. Travellers noted, in a general way, the different kinds of scenery through which they passed. They would comment on the fertile country which they saw in Perthshire or Caithness, on the wild, black heath of Rannoch, on the craggy, vast mountains of Glencoe or Sutherland. But on the whole it was those more commonplace features of Highland scenery which are repeated so often, in so many districts, but which are not to be found elsewhere, that struck them most; for this is what makes up the grandeur and remoteness of the Highlands. Mountains, sea-lochs, moorland; fast flowing streams and rivers running over stony beds; pine trees and larches, little patches of green fields, scattered villages, islands beyond islands—this is far more grand and lonely than the fertile, populated country further south. The facts of geology, climate and social custom require that Scotland be thought of as consisting of two regions, Highlands and Lowlands, and the distinction was examined with growing interest as the eighteenth century drew to a close.[5]

There was nothing novel in the idea. 'The Kingdom of Scotland', wrote a French traveller in 1661, 'is ordinarily divided into two parts, which are on this side and beyond the river Tay';[6] 'Scotland', according to an Englishman writing a few years later, 'is distinguished into High-lands and Low-lands....'[7] No doubt the contrast between these two regions has been drawn in a different way by each generation, aspects stressed at one time being less noticeable, or less noticed, at another; but it persists. The modern Scot, although not so deeply as his ancestors, is for the most part very much aware of his identity as a Highlander or Lowlander. It is true that other contrasts may be drawn, particularly between those who live on the west coast, in and around Glasgow, and those who live on the east coast, in and around Edinburgh. But this distinction, and others like it, while real and often important, is less substantial and far-reaching than that between Highland and Lowland.

In surveying the two regions many contrasts and comparisons can be made. But it is important to realize how deep-seated some of the differences are. Obviously a good deal stems from the nature of the country, and in this respect it might be thought sufficient simply to look at a map. Are not the Highlands there shown as the area of peculiarly mountainous country stretching up into the latitudes of southern Norway, dividing the cold North Sea from the almost equally cold Atlantic, the ultimate and therefore the most isolated projection of north-west Europe? But this is a superficial and inaccurate observation. It is true that north of the Highland Border Fault, a sharp geological division which stretches north-eastwards from the mouth of the River Clyde to Stonehaven, there is much high land and more truly mountainous country than anywhere else in Great Britain. Especially between the Highland Border Fault and the Great Glen which runs from Fort William to Inverness there is a very much higher proportion than elsewhere of ground above 2,000 feet. But this is a matter of degree. In the south of Scotland, for example, and in the north of England, there is a great deal of land above the 600 foot contour, and much of these regions also—although not quite as much—could truly be described as mountainous.

What really distinguishes the Highlands from all other parts of Great Britain is not shown on an ordinary map, for it consists of the physical constitution and properties of the land itself. These are a direct consequence of geological history. What is fundamentally unique about the Highlands is their geology. A map showing the predominant types of rock brings this out particularly clearly. The whole of Britain is made up largely of chalk, friable sandstone, clays, slates, shales and mudstones—except the Highlands. There, these rock types are almost completely absent. Instead, there is a good proportion of gneiss, hardly to be seen elsewhere in Britain; there is much more granite; and above all, the greater part of the area consists of a mixture of hard sandstone, quartzose rocks, limestone, gneiss, and schists of various sorts. Precisely from the Highland Border Fault northward this kind of country begins. It is an exaggeration, although perhaps a pardonable one, to say that the Highlands could scarcely be more geologically different from the rest of Great Britain if they were part of another continent; and in some areas, such as north-west Sutherland, they look as if they might be part of another planet.

These differences are not mere curiosities of geology, for it is largely upon them that there depend both the immediate fertility of the soil and the general habitability and improveability of the country; that is to say, its capacity to encourage and support an energetic and prosperous agricultural population. And it is in these respects that the potential of the Highlands seems from the outset decidedly limited. The amount of rock which easily breaks down to form soil is small—less than one per cent over extensive parts of the Highlands. Consequently, large areas are either useless for agriculture or are of very limited use. The Cairngorms and the Ben Nevis *massif*, for example, form extensive alpine plateaux at a height of three and a half to four thousand feet, solid ground but cold, granite and uncultivable. From Skye to Loch Eriboll there runs the Moine Overthrust, a barren strip of rocky chaotic country, consisting in Wester Ross and Sutherland

'of a myriad little hills of great steepness, with little glens running hither and thither among them. The lochans are seemingly countless and most of them have a floor of peat. The gneiss hills themselves are like rock buns, looking as if they had risen in some giant oven and set into their rough shapes. This ground holds up the water in pockets in the rock and allows the formation of cotton sedge bogs and such very shallow lochans as grow water lobelia and water lillies. . . .

The gneiss is difficult country to walk through: by keeping to the little glens it is impossible to steer a straight course for any distance and no one would attempt to go in a straight line over the hills. On the upper gneiss country where many detours are necessary round rock faces and soft spots, a speed of one mile an hour is quite good going. It is also quite easy to lose one's self, for these little round hills are all very much alike.

The crofting townships on the gneiss are strictly coastal. . . .'[8]

But the geography of the Highlands defies generalisation. Even in some of the most barren and desolate areas there occur tiny pockets of relatively good soil. Travelling north from Kylesku, one comes suddenly upon the green fields of Scourie, walled and cultivated in an undulating hollow less than a mile square set in a world of rock and wetness. Similar patches occur elsewhere—at Eriboll, for example, there is a tiny area of cultivable land set amid the rocks and beside the sea, where the traveller is surprised by the sight of something not seen for perhaps fifty miles—a good-sized green field. Sudden transitions from one kind of country to another are, on a larger scale, no less surprising. So abrupt are the changes of altitude and of rock form that in a few miles one can pass from luxuriant woodland to tundra; from mild oceanic conditions to the severity of a sub-arctic climate; from flat, placid pasture land to country inhabited only by ptarmigan and eagles.

Early writers on the Highlands often failed to appreciate the diversity of the region they were dealing with, or were baffled by it, and then failed to grasp its principal characteristics. This was partly because knowledge was so fragmentary, travellers so few. The Highlands were not a trade route. They were remarkably inaccessible, and in the first half of the eighteenth century the civil and even the military authorities were far from being able to exercise complete control. There are few accounts of life in the Highlands before 1780, and large parts of the area then remained, as Knox said in 1787, 'an almost undescribed country'.[9] Those few who visited the Highlands to extend their knowledge and then to pass on their discoveries to the polite world were chiefly interested in manners, political allegiances, flora and fauna, or—too often—the authenticity of the poems of Ossian. None was very interested in the economic activities of the Highlanders, and none attempted to provide a brief sketch of the economic geography of the whole area. But there was one traveller, no less remarkable than Dr Johnson himself, who presumably visited the region only briefly and who left no extensive account, but who did attend to the physical characteristics of the country as a whole, and to its economy, and who wrote a brief description which many a literary man might envy: James Watt, engineer. In 1776 Watt was instructed to prepare a report on the possibility of constructing a canal from Fort William to Inverness. He surveyed the scene, and wrote as follows:

'The Highland Mountains, which commence at the *Firth* of *Clyde*, extend upon the West Side of the Country to the Northernmost Parts of Scotland, in general they begin close at the Sea Shore; they are intersected by deep but narrow Vallies; the Quantity of Arable Land is exceeding small, and its Produce greatly lessened by the prodigious Rains that fall upon that Coast. The Tops of the Mountains are craggy, and their Sides are steep, but they produce a Grass very proper for breeding small Black Cattle, and in some Places for feeding Sheep.

The Sea Coast is exceeding rugged and rocky, and abounds with great Inlets, which are excellent Harbours. It is sheltered by many Islands, which, like the Main Land, are generally mountainous and rocky, but rather more fertile.

The Salt Water Loughs or Arms of the Sea, are Nurseries for Fish, of which many Kinds are found in Plenty in the Seas upon these Coasts, the Herrings, the Cod, and Ling, are those which are taken in greatest Quantities, and exported to Foreign Parts; but there are other Species, which may perhaps become Subjects of Trade.

The Shores produce in Abundance the *Alga Marina*, or Sea Weed, which being burnt, makes the Alkaline Salt called Kelp. The Quantities of the Commodity made and consumed of late Years are immense, and the Rents paid for the Kelp of some Shores, have borne a great Proportion to that of the Land they surrounded.

There are in many Parts of the Country considerable Coppice Woods of Oak and other Timber. The Oak Woods have been greatly hurt by the destructive Practice of cutting them for their Bark, the Timber being often left to rot upon the Spot.

The East Coast of *Scotland* exhibits a very different Prospect. The high Mountains are several Miles distant from the Sea Coast, the intermediate Space consists of Arable Lands intermixed with Hills of a moderate Size and Height. In many Places, great Tracts of level Ground are in a very advanced State of Cultivation, but the Country in general will admit Improvements, and the Spirit of making them seems to be daily increasing. Although the Sea Ports are in general inconvenient, and the Coast no Way sheltered, yet [south of Inverness] it is lined with Towns, the Inhabitants of which are industrious. In many Places they subsist by fishing, though the Fish upon that Coast are not to be compared, either for Plenty or Size, to those upon the West Side of the Country.'[10]

This excellent description of the region, and of the use then made of it, brings out several important points, including the considerable difference between the east and the west Highlands—a difference which is the result, as Watt could not know, of glacial action.

Millions of years ago when the Highlands were under ice, there was ice-flow east and west from a central area located south and east of the Great Glen. The ice which flowed westward, across the western Highlands, carved out steeper hillsides and sharper peaks than in the east, denuded the country to a greater extent and left less glacial drift. The net effect is a significant difference in the suitability of east and west for agricultural activity and, for that matter, for human habitation. The land in the west Highlands varies from peat bogs and wet moors on ill-drained flats and flood-plains to fairly dry grassy moors and alpine screes on the steep higher slopes. Tree cover is almost confined to small patches on the coast, and agricultural land is mostly found in small pockets, again chiefly near the coast. The eastern Highlands, on the other hand, contain some considerable stretches of good agricultural land as well as much sandy, gravelly soil, particularly favourable to the growth of heather and conifers. The Spey Valley, along with Deeside and some parts of Perthshire, is probably the best location in Scotland for pines, firs and larches. In other parts of the eastern Highlands, such as Caithness and the Black Isle (if these can be called Highland at all), the land is lower in altitude than in the west, undulating and fertile. Also, the principal valleys in the east open northward to the Moray Firth, or east and south-east towards Aberdeenshire and Angus, and thus offer relatively easy communication with lowland Scotland.

Climate reinforces these differences. If a line is drawn northward from approximately the eastern end of Loch Katrine to Loch Eriboll, it will be found that the greater part of the country to the east has a rainfall of be-tween 30 and 60 inches per annum, whereas to the west of this line—and this includes the whole of Argyll, most of Ross and Cromarty, about half of Inverness-shire and a third of Sutherland—rainfall exceeds 60 inches per annum; the average precipitation at Fort William is almost 80 inches, while on a good deal of the high ground in south-western Ross and Cromarty, western Inverness-shire and northern Argyll, rainfall exceeds 100 inches per annum. There are, of course, great variations. The country between Loch Broom and Loch Maree mostly receives less than 50 inches per year, as does most of the island of Lewis; Islay has a similar rainfall, and far to the west Tiree—once known as 'the granary of the isles'—has an enviable and jus-tifiable reputation for sunshine and moderate rainfall. But it is only the im-mediately coastal areas on the west-mainland (and this applies particularly to those which reach out into the Atlantic) that enjoy a drier and sunnier climate than the higher, rain-soaked ground further inland.

This heavier rainfall in the west, coupled with the steeper slopes of the hills west of the Great Glen, means that more water flows faster down western hillsides than hillsides in the east. The greater velocity of flow very much increases the carrying power of the water, and hence the soil in the west is much more washed away than on the drier, easier slopes further east. This process of denudation has been going on for millennia, and it further increases the relative natural poverty of the western areas.

With respect to other climatic factors the differences between east and west are less marked but are still significant. Severe gales are commonly experienced throughout the Highlands, as anyone who has lived there can testify. Destruction of woodlands is not uncommon in Speyside and on the eastern slopes of the Grampians; but wind velocities are greater in the west, particularly along the coasts and on high ground; the west coasts of Ross and Cromarty and of Sutherland are probably the most windswept areas in Europe. Severe gales, although most common in winter, are not con-fined to the winter months but blow frequently in the summer as well. Leafy vegetation is battered by the wind and, anywhere along an exposed coast, subject to salt spray. Its growth is thus reduced or destroyed. The tree-line on the west coast—where there is a tree-line—may be no more than 200 feet, whereas it is 1,800 feet on the western side of the Cairngorms. (But again, generalisations cannot be correct. There are sheltered areas in the west, along the shores of Loch Broom or Loch Sunart, for example, where rhododendrons and azaleas grow beneath tall, unspoilt larches, firs and wellingtonia.)

As regards temperatures, the west coast is certainly no worse off than the eastern highlands. Owing to the large number of sea lochs in the west which penetrate many miles inland, a greater amount of land is close to water than might at first appear and, due to the relative warmth of the sea water along the west coast, especially south of Skye, this makes for a milder and more equable climate than in the east. The summers are less warm, but the winters are less cold. The west coast is relatively snow-free and frost-free;[11] and it enjoys a mean annual temperature whi ch is exceeded in Britain only in west Wales and along the south coast of England. These favourable conditions, however, are again confined to small areas of land close to water: the hills in the west tend to rise steeply almost from the water's edge (many peaks over 3,000 feet are within five miles of the sea; Ben Nevis, the highest hill in Scotland, is only about three miles distant from salt water) and at a height of only a few hundred feet above sea level mean temperatures are far lower.[12] All ground above 2,000 feet, whether in east or west highlands, has a sub-Arctic climate with mean monthly temperatures below freezing point for seven months of the year, and the average temperatures for July do not often exceed 50°F. This means that above 2,000 feet the highland climate corresponds to that of the arctic tundra. It is partly for this reason that villages and clachans in the west are to be found almost exclusively along the sea or on the margin of a sea loch.

The final distinction between east and west Highlands lies in the character of the coastlines themselves and of the seas that break upon them. The east coast is open to the North Sea. There are three firths, two of them providing excellent anchorages, and most of the coastline consists of smooth cliff or sand dunes. The west coast, on the other hand, is indented by innumerable sea-lochs; is mountainous to the sea's edge; and off the coast lie literally thousands of islands. Some of these islands are tiny, perhaps nothing more than a rock awash at high tide, or an islet where there are sea birds and a few sheep can graze in summer; others, like Skye or Lewis and Harris, are several hundred square miles in extent and have a present population of a few thousand people. Some again, are close to the mainland, hardly more than a stone's throw off; others, like the Flannan Isles, St Kilda, the Monach Isles, Mingulay, lie from 60 to over 100 miles from the mainland. Between all these islands there are thousands of sounds and channels. The tides and currents which run through these passages[13] make navigation difficult—to say nothing of the frequent gales and bad visibility. As a result, human settlement is in a large number of small, scattered communities, either on islands or along the mainland shore, possibly within the entrance to a sea loch. These scattered communities are joined by the sea; but because it is often rough and dangerous, and always unpredictable,[14] and because travel overland is exceptionally difficult due to high mountains and the consequent need to travel long distances through glens or along the coast, villages, even when not far apart, have tended to remain surprisingly isolated. Steam navigation greatly altered the situation. But before its advent in the

1820s, the west Highlands and islands were at a severe disadvantage. To travel along the east coast was a simple matter, to sail along it was usually uncomfortable but not excessively difficult; in the west, on the other hand, particularly north of Skye, communities possessed no easy and reliable access either to one another or to the outside world.

Extending from Loch Long to Duncansby Head and from the Braes of Angus to Cape Wrath and the Outer Hebrides—in area a half of Scotland, a fifth of Great Britain—the Highlands (and the way of life of the inhabitants) were by 1750 or thereabouts little altered from their primeval state. It was a land of ancient settlement. In neolithic times, small groups of settlers had found patches of arable land and pasture free of the predominant oak wood and thorny scrub which then covered Western Europe, and in these 'areas of easy settlement' neolithic sites and groups of collective tombs are numerous. Population gradually increased, but as man extended his capacity to subdue the forest the lowland became a more attractive area for settlement than the north. By the time of the Dark Ages, Scotland was already divided into a Highland and a Lowland zone, and the efforts of the Lowland zone to establish its political authority over the northern and western districts continued sporadically through the medieval and into the modern period.

The struggle effectively began after the Battle of Largs in 1263, fought by Alexander III against the 'occupying' Norwegians. Victory made the Western Isles a part of the Kingdom of Scotland, but the government had little effective control over these remote and inaccessible areas, and fighting, raiding and stealing became the established order. In the fourteenth century a branch of the MacDonalds set themselves up as Lords of the Isles; the lordship, held in conjunction with the earldom of Ross, embracing territory on the mainland almost as far east as Inverness, as well as the islands. This lordship had strong pretensions to autonomy, and the Lords of the Isles were allied at various times to Edward IV and Henry VIII, in active opposition to the Scottish crown. In 1411, Donald, Lord of the Isles, after burning Inverness, advanced as far east as Aberdeenshire with the intention of sacking Aberdeen itself, and there fought, and lost, the murderous battle of Harlaw against the Earl of Mar. And there were innumerable other disturbances and conflicts. In 1390 one of the younger sons of Robert II, enjoying the picturesque and well-earned title of 'the wolf of Badenoch', attacked and burned the towns of Forres and Elgin—by no stretch of the imagination in the Highland zone—and, for good measure, burned Elgin cathedral as well; a few years later, in 1396, there was fought the famous 'judicial combat' between thirty men of the Clan Chattan and thirty of the Clan Kay on the Inch of Perth, a savage attempt, immortalised in *The Fair*

Maid of Perth, to achieve justice by the sword and to put an end to at any rate one Highland feud. Thus it was that the Highlands were ruled, or not ruled, in the middle ages. But at last in James IV Scotland found a renaissance king, 'a strong and energetic king who endeavoured to hold the law to his people',[15] and in the 1490s, as a consequence of several expeditions, James destroyed the power of the chiefs of Clan Donald, the Lords of the Isles, and put an end to their virtually independent authority in the west. For the next two hundred and fifty years the government in Edinburgh (or London) exercised a remote and partial control, unable and perhaps hardly seeking to prevent internecine warfare within the Highlands, content if they could prevent or minimise highland excursions into the lowlands. The lowlander's idea of the highlander as 'a wild man dwelling in the woods and mountains, and a born thief'[16] came to maturity early in this period—it was a court poet of the sixteenth century who, after describing how God made a highlander out of a lump of horse manure, put the view in a nutshell:

Quoth God to the Helandman—Quhair wilt thou now?

I will doun to the lowland, Lord, and thair steill a kow.

Power rested on the military strong-points of Dumbarton and Inverness at either end of the Highland Line, and, in the eighteenth century, on a handful of troops strung out along it.[17] Inverness was for long a frontier town, 'surrounded', in the words of James VI, 'on all sides by most aggresive and rebellious tribes, *the clans.*'[18]

The lowland Scot in the eighteenth century likewise disapproved of the clans, although there is not much evidence that he commonly understood them. The clan was both a unit of military organisation and a social system. The origins of the clan system are obscure. It is possible that organisation by clans had arisen in a remote past when lawlessness and sporadic warfare drove poor men to seek masters who would protect them and gave men of property a motive to surround themselves with servants and dependants who would fight on their behalf. The men of property were landowners by definition and military leaders by necessity, and in the course of time their status became that of chiefs and their relations and followers became the clan. Whatever the truth of this matter, the authority of the chief became, as Dr Johnson observed, absolute. The chief, he wrote, being the owner of the land, was one

'whose natural power must be very great, where no man lives but by agriculture; and where the produce of the land is not conveyed through the labyrinths of traffick, but passes directly, from the hand that gathers it, to the mouth that eats it. The laird has all those in his power that live upon his farms.'[19]

All were held together by the need for military strength in a world of poverty and sporadic warfare. But the association was not merely one of necessity, a military-economic marriage of desperate convenience. For, as Dr Johnson also observed, the power of the chief 'was yet strengthened by the kindness of consanguinity and the reverence of patriarchal authority. The laird was the father of the clan. . . . Every duty, moral or political, was absorbed in affection and adherence to the chief.'[20] John Home made the same point in a different way: 'The most sacred oath to a Highlander, was to swear by the hand of his chief. The constant exclamation, upon any sudden accident, was, may God be with the chief, or, may the chief be uppermost. Ready at all times to die for the head of the kindred, Highlanders have been known to interpose their bodies between the pointed musket, and their chief, and to receive the shot which was aimed at him.'[21] Loyalty, both to the clan and to the chief who symbolised its unity, was the master principle of the clan system. The clan was first and foremost a social group where chief and people 'lived on the footing of familiarity which nowadays would be considered as mean and unbecoming',[22] albeit a group organised for agricultural production and for war.

Next to the chief in economic and social importance and authority stood the tacksmen. The tacksmen were usually close relations of the chief, and their holdings, sometimes considerable, were, or were regarded as, hereditary. They were simultaneously 'the middle-men in a military organisation'[23] and the directors of agricultural activities on the chief's estate. The tenurial system was outlined by Walker in the following words:

'The possessors of land, over the Highlands in general, are of three different kinds; tacksmen, tenants, and subtenants. The tacksmen hold their land of the proprietor, by lease; the tenants hold their farms, without any lease, at the will of the landlord; the subtenants have small possessions of land, let out to them from year to year, by the tacksmen and tenants.

The tacksmen are a superior order of people in the community. They are generally relations to the proprietor, and often men of education and of considerable endowments. In the year 1764, the farms they possessed, generally ran from twenty to fifty-five pounds a year. The tenants again, are of a lower class, and their possessions are usually from five to twenty pounds per annum. The subtenants have small parcels of land let to them by the tacksmen and tenants, from fifteen shillings to forty shillings of yearly value, and resemble what are called cottars of crofters, in some other parts of Scotland.

A farm of thirty pounds a year, will have ten such subtenants upon it. Each of these has a family. The tacksman, besides his wife and children, has eight men servants, six women and two boys. The whole amounts to about seventy-one persons. Such a number of people, living by agriculture, upon so small a property, is not to be found any where else.'[24]

1. The breacan, or plaid, consisted of six to twelve yards of tartan, reaching to the knees, often fastened round the middle with a belt.

T. Jefferys sculp.

T. Jefferys sculp.

The evidence is that the tacksmen were poor farmers; 'Although some of them acquired a taste for, and knowledge of, the breeding of cattle . . . very few of them were agricultural improvers. . . .'[25] But this criticism, certainly insofar as it relates to the period before 1750, is hardly to the point. The clan system was not devised for—and in the end it turned out that it could not be adapted to—raising the standard of living. The tacksmen were the subordinate commanders, under the chief, in the military expeditions of the clan. 'This was their employment; and neither their own dispositions, nor the situation of the country, inclined them to engage in the drudgery of agriculture.'[26] Their objectives were to maintain themselves and their families in a customary way of life, and to be able to come to the assistance of their chief, whenever required, with a body of fighting men drawn from their holdings. Both these purposes were served by letting their lands in small portions to lesser men, who helped the tacksman to work his retained land by rendering labour services, and who followed him and the chief in war. In such a system, the tacksman, and through him the chief of the clan, was very much concerned to have a large number of dependents; 'the value of landed property was, in these times, to be reckoned, not by the rent it produced, but by the men whom it could send into the field. It is mentioned indeed of one of the chieftains, that being questioned by a stranger as to the rent of his estate, he answered, that it could raise 500 men.'[27]

It follows that the tenants and the subtenants likewise lived with a view to war. They too were concerned only to maintain a customary way of life; they too were uninterested in agricultural improvement. Because of the nature of their agricultural operations,

'periods of labour were short; and they could devote the intermediate time to indolence, or to amusement, unless when their assistance was required for the defence of their chief and of their families, or for attacking some neighbouring clan. Prowess on these occasions was the most valuable quality they could possess, and that on which their pride was founded; warlike achievements engrossed their thoughts; and the amusements of their leisure hours generally consisted of active exercises, or displays of strength and agility, calculated to enhance their estimation as warriors.'[28]

Or, as Ramsey of Ochtertyre put it in a single pregnant sentence: 'every person wished to be thought a soldier'.[29]

It is possible to view such an existence as ideal. Adam Ferguson, himself a highlander and a Gaelic speaker, wrote in his *Essay on the History of Civil Society* with understanding and admiration of the 'barbarian' state in which subordination of ranks is coupled with social and intellectual equality, in which ceaseless warfare, demanding loyalty and self-sacrifice, strengthens

2. A highland 'toun'. 'The petty tenants, and labouring peasants, live in miserable cabins, which afford them little more than shelter from the storms.' (Johnson).

the bonds of society, in which work is no virtue; the situation of
> 'a people regardless of commercial arts; profuse of their own lives, and
> of those of others; vehement in their attachment to one society, and
> implacable in their antipathy to another.'[30]

Such, according to Ferguson, was the state of the Greeks and the Romans
'in a great and shining part of their history', and it is reasonable to infer, as
Duncan Forbes has suggested,[31] that Ferguson viewed the clan system in
the same way and with equal sympathy. But this is not how most eighteenth-century writers saw the clans. Especially to the political economists
of the second half of the century, the clan was little more than a vehicle for
securing tenurial arrangements—bad ones at that. The clan system was
supposed by these writers to be responsible for three fundamental obstacles
to progress: uneconomically small holdings: insecurity of tenure; and
labour services which were both excessive and uncertain.

To some extent this view rested on failure to realise the importance of
the social aspects of clan organisation. Within its limits, however, it had
some justification in the second half of the century when the clan system
was under new pressures and was beginning to operate in a different way.
But it is unlikely that the above-mentioned defects were at all serious
before the 1750s—even supposing that the clansmen had put a much
higher value on economic progress than they did. Units of land-holding
were often small, but there is no evidence that population was increasing
so as to press upon the means of subsistence more seriously than before;
besides, there were still possibilities, at least in some parts of the Highlands,
of increasing the area of grazing and of cultivation. That the subtenants,
the great majority of the population, were tenants at will, and therefore
enjoyed no security of tenure, is certainly true. But in an age when landowners were anxious to keep and to accumulate men, and when the clan of
which all were members was still held together by bonds of duty and
friendship, the chances of arbitrary eviction, while real enough, remained
small. For similar reasons it is unlikely that services repressed enterprise or
were felt to be a burden. The tenants were obliged to plow and harrow
their superior's land, to provide labour at harvest time, to build dykes, cut
and lead peats, weed the fields and thatch the houses. Services were various
and numerous, and extended 'to every sort of labour that must be executed
upon a farm.'[32] But as long as money rents were unimportant, and while
the tenants depended on the chief and the tacksmen of military leadership
and security, the system as a whole was one of mutual advantage.

The technological counterpart of these political and socio-economic
arrangements was a primitive agriculture. As is usual in mountainous
regions, the most profitable use that could be made of the land was to rear
animals—mostly cattle, in the Highlands—in part for home consumption

but principally for sale to farmers in more fertile districts, to be fattened for slaughter. Crops were grown—usually oats, sometimes mixed with barley, and a little hay—but these were only for local consumption or to support the stock. It was on the sale of cattle that the highlanders depended largely for their subsistence and entirely for their comfort. Cattle were 'the only article upon the farm which affords money to the tenant, and payment to the landlord',[33] and farms were frequently valued according to the number of black cattle that they could carry; almost every article of luxury or of war that came to the Highlands came in exchange for what live-stock the highlanders could spare to the south or to Ireland. And what could be spared from this great natural grazing area was not a little. Winding their way down the great droving routes that led from Skye and the north-west, from easter Ross and the far north, from Perthshire and the central Highlands to Crieff, and in later years to Falkirk came thousands of animals every year. The total number cannot be known, but according to Pennant in 1772, 4,000 animals crossed at Kyle Rhea annually; these came from Skye and the outer Hebrides and were only a fraction of the whole supply. The cattle traffic was the great business of the Highlands, a trade which made the highlander regard the rearing of cattle not only as an object of primary consideration, but as an indispensable necessity.

Cattle-rearing, although predominant, was only a part of the general pattern of agricultural activity. Other animals were kept and some crops were grown. Land usage varied between different parts of the Highlands and changed gradually over time, but the following description of farms in the central highlands, although published as late as 1792, may be taken, without very much modification, as a fair and particularly clear statement of eighteenth-century practice in general.

'The vallies, especially the larger ones, are separated from the hills by a stone fence, called the "head dyke" (or by an imaginary line of partition answering to it), running along the brae or slope . . . the more productive, or the greener surface, being included within it; the black heathy brows of the hills being left out as "muir".

The vally lands, contained within these head dykes, are laid out, or have grown fortuitously, into arable land, meadow, and pasture.

The ARABLE LANDS have a two-fold distinction: a portion of them laying near the "steading" or homestall, and generally the best soiled part, is termed INFIELD; is kept, and has been time immemorially kept, in tillage; and upon this description of lands, all the manure which the country has afforded for ages, together with earth and thatch of demolished hut, etc. etc. has been laid. The other portion of the arable lands, namely, such plots of the bottoms, or lower parts of the vallies, as are sufficiently level, and sufficiently free from wood and stones, to be plowed, are termed OUTFIELD, and are kept in corn and natural ley or weedy wastes alternately, without receiving the smallest return of manure; except that, formerly, cattle were folded upon these outfield lands. . . .

Such patches as lie intermixed among plots, or "fields", of arable land, and are either too wet, too woody, or too stoney, to be plowed, are termed MEADOW, and are kept perpetually under the sithe and sickle, for a scanty supply of hay; being every year shaven to the quick, and seldom, if ever, manured.

The faces of the braes, the roots of the hills, the woody or rough stoney wastes of the bottom; with a small plot near the house, termed "door land" (for baiting horses upon at meal times, teddering a cow, etc.), are kept as PASTURE, for cattle in summer, and sheep in winter; the sheep, and generally the horses, being kept during summer, above the head dyke, upon the muir lands.

These hill lands, or MUIR, are laid out, or distributed, as a train of fortuitous circumstances, as tumults and retaliation, as connexions, intrigue and accommodation, have brought about.

In general, each farm reaches across half the valley, namely, from the river or burn to the head dyke, and has generally some portion of muir immediately above it, contiguous to the green pasture grounds. In some cases, however, these contiguous muirs are inconsiderable; and in others, are in a state of commonage, between two or more farms; and are always so among the petty tenants of the same farm.

When the contiguous muir is not sufficient for the maintenance of the hill stock in summer, a portion of hill, lying perhaps several miles from the residence of the occupier, and perhaps common to the stock of several farms, makes up the deficiency.

In these DETACHED GRAZINGS and distant sheelings are involved a train of evils: the drift of the stock; the driving across intermediate grazings; the inconveniencies and danger of having stock at a distance; the never-ceasing disputes with the occupiers of the surrounding lands. . . .'[34]

Subordinate to this system of land division was the practice of run-rig. This occurred when, as was customary, there were a number of tenants on the same farm, living in groups of five or six families together, having a common pasture for their cattle, and the arable land being divided among them 'by ridge and ridge alternately', each cultivator looking after his own collection of scattered strips. Originally, the re-allocation of strips every year, or every second or third year, had perhaps been normal. This custom declined after 1750, fastest in the central highlands, more slowly in the west and in the islands; but even at the end of the eighteenth century periodic re-allocation was still common.

3. View of the Hebrides from Appin;
Castle Stalker, Mull, Lismore, Jura, etc.

P. Sandby, pinxt R.A.

Earl of BREADALBANE'S Seat at KILLING.

Pub.d as the Act directs by G. Kearsly in Fleet Street 1 Aug.t 1778.

Productivity was wretchedly low. Growing potatoes was a novelty in the 1740s,[35] and hay, oats and barley were raised with unvarying repetition. This would have kept yields down even if the techniques of cultivation had been much better than they were. Seaweed was used occasionally as a manure, with at least temporary benefit to the barley crops; but it is very doubtful if the value of sea shells or shell sand, known in the north of Ireland about the end of the seventeenth century, was appreciated anywhere in the Highlands even a hundred years later, although by that time a flourishing export trade in sea shells had been built up from Creetown to other places in Galloway, to Ayrshire, Dumfriesshire, Cumberland, and even to Ireland. The instruments of cultivation were in no better a state than the practice of manuring, and were fairly described as belonging to 'a very early and unimproved age of the world'.[36] The highland plow, made sometimes with two handles but more often with only one, was a small instrument with an ineffective mold-board, which required four horses and three men for its operation. Where plowing was impossible, use was made of the cascrome, or crooked spade. This tool was about six feet long, with a thick flat wooden head tipped with a sharp narrow piece of iron. The length of the shaft, and the strength of the head, made it a lever of considerable power. It was a crude but useful instrument in a country where arable ground was often in very small pockets, or was so encumbered with boulders and loose stones as to make plowing impossible. Its supporters claimed that a highlander with a cascrome could open more ground in a day than three men using ordinary spades; and it is easy to believe that the land dug with the cascrome yielded, on average, a much better return than plowed land. It is sometimes argued that the labour cost of cultivation by cascrome must have been unduly high; but it is not clear that it was higher per unit of output, and in any case such calculations are irrelevant if—as seems usually to have been the case—there was no alternative use for the labour thus employed.

Crops came up with an enormous admixture of rank strong weeds, such as wild carrot, mustard and thistle. This made harvesting a difficult problem, and the solution sometimes adopted was to pull everything up by the roots. The straw was then either burned, or used for thatch. In winter, the cattle were free to roam through the fields, no doubt accompanied by the ubiquitous goats, of which there were large and numerous flocks. Absence of winter herding, of manuring, of rotations, of seed selection, of drainage, of cultivation of the growing crop, of shelter belts, of anything that could be described as even average agricultural practice by the modest standards of the middle of the eighteenth century meant that both man and beast lived, at times, close to starvation:

'In the latter end of April, and the early part of May, the country exhi-

4. The Earl of Breadalbane's seat at Killin, west end of Loch Tay.

bited the most desolate and distressing picture. Not the faintest appearance of greenness, nor even a blade of pasturable herbage to be detected, except in the parks and paddocks of men of fortune . . . nothing to be seen but stone and dry blades of couch grass or other pallid remains of unpasturable herbage; the pasture and meadow lands gnawed to the quick . . . The cattle . . . in a starving state; some actually starved; others barely able to crawl out of the way of the passenger . . .'[37]

This description refers to the end of the century, and the writer acknowledges that the season (1793) had been 'more than usually severe'; but there is no reason to suppose that conditions fifty years earlier had been any better. As for the people, life was much the same for them. Although actual famines seem to have been more frequent and severe after 1750 than before, food shortage was endemic in the Highlands, and every few years in the eighteenth century there occurred, at least in some locality, the horrors of starvation.

Poverty and the clan system were the mutual suports of war; and war reinforced the clan system and deepened poverty. The geography of the Highlands made an even spread of population impossible. The clans existed in pockets of settlement, isolated from one another by the natural barriers of lochs, moors and mountains. Isolation and ignorance bred suspicion; independence bred rivalry; and rivalry and suspicion readily degenerated into quarrels, rapacity and enmity. Insecurity was the dominating feature of Highland life. In wild country, remote from central government, the clans engaged in sporadic warfare and supplemented their meagre resources by acts of more or less organised plunder. In Knoidart, 'a perfect Den of Thieves and Robbers' according to a government agent who travelled through the Highlands in 1750, Coll McDonald of Barrisdale,

'entered into a Confederacy with McDonald of Lochgarry and the Camerons of Loch Arkeg with some other as great Villains in Rannoch, a part of Perthshire. This famous Company had the Honour to Methodize Theft into a Regular Trade, they kept a number of Savages in Dependance upon them for this purpose whom they Out-hounded upon the Sutherlands, Rosses, Munroes, and McKenzies to the North, the Frasers, McIntoshes, Grants, Roses of Kilravock, Brodies, Gordons, Farquharsons, Forbeses, and Ogilvies to the East; and the Shires of Perth, Stirling, Dunbarton, and Argyle to the South. When the Thieves were Successful these Gentlemen had a Dividend of the Spoil of their own making; but if they returned Empty handed the fellows were at no Loss, as they forced their Provisions wherever they travelled, and every one who laid in their way thought himself very fortunate if they Required no more, for which reason they seldom failed to be plentifully Supplied

5. The cascrome was still widely used in the Western Highlands and Islands at the end of the nineteenth century.

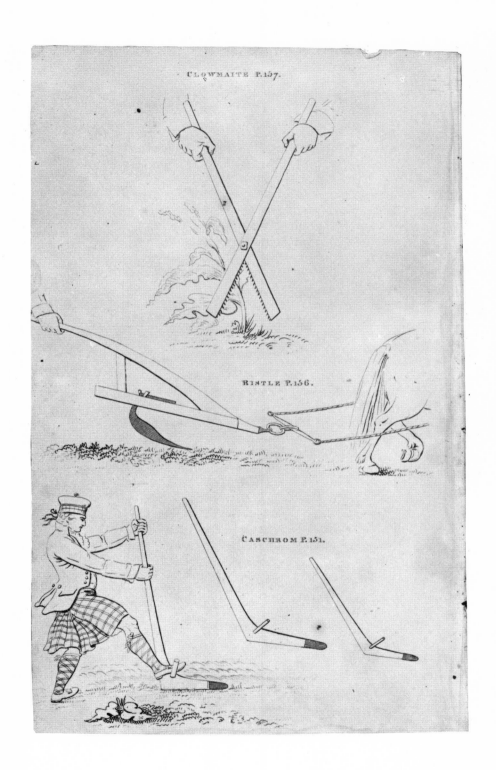

CLOWMAITE P.157.

RISTLE P.156.

CASCHROM P.151.

P. Sandby R.A. pinx.   T. Medland s.

VIEW of BEN-LOMOND from CAMERON WOOD.

Published as the Act directs, by G. Kearsly in Fleet Street, Aug.ˢᵗ, 1780.

with the best the Country afforded, and if at any time it happened that one of them met his Deserts at the Gallows by the Vigilance of the Neighbouring Clans, which very rarely happened, the whole Tribe to which the Thief belong'd never fail'd to Embrace the first Opportunity of having (as they term it) Blood for Blood.

I knew a Gentleman of the McIntoshes whom these Villains had Reduced almost to want: at last he determined to watch them with a Strong Party and accordingly apprehended some of them, and got two of them hang'd at Inverness; 15 years after a Son of this Gentleman's, who was a Merchant at Inverness, being called by Business to Fort William, set out not suspecting any thing; but he never arrived there or cou'd ever be heard of after.'[38]

Sometimes robbery with violence was replaced by what the twentieth century knows as 'the protection racket'. The same McDonald of Barrisdale 'offered 3 or 4 Years before the late Rebellion to be the Protector of so many Countries; by which means he Raised from Seaforth's Country, a part of Lord Lovat's, and the Chisholm's, with some other places in the Neighbourhood, above double their proportion of the Land Tax. Barrisdale by his former Trade and this Latter expedient lived at a very high Rate. . . . The other Arch Thief, McDonald of Lochgarry, took the same Trade in hand and became Protector of the Countries of Strathherrick Abertarfand and other places in their Neighbourhood. When any Gentleman of more Spirit than his Neighbours refused to Submit to such Imposition, these Villains set Thieves upon him till he was soon Convinced of the Necessity of his Compliance and Obedience. . . . The Thieves knew full well how easy it was for [their masters] to deliver any of them up at pleasure to the Civil Magistrate, or even of themselves to Hang them up without that Formality, for which Reason almost the whole Insurance Money was neat Profit. At last Cluny McPherson undertook to protect all the Countries to the South of Loch Ness and to the North of Dundee, for which purpose he had a good Company in Arms in the Years 1744 and 1745 . . .'[39]

In conditions of such disorder (even supposing the above account to contain an element of picturesque exaggeration) it is hardly to be wondered at that men did not find the details of agricultural improvement of absorbing interest, nor that tacksmen found it both easy and desirable to surround themselves with a crowd of dependents who were content with a bare subsistence, and who would fight when required. In land-holding and therefore in agricultural practice, as in clan life itself, 'we hear, as it were, always the sound of fighting—the atmosphere of war. If it was not always being actually waged, it was at least always in habitual contemplation.'[40]

It would be wrong to suggest that there was no sign of improvement

6. View of Ben Lomond from Cameron Wood.

before 1750, and that economic life was completely static and unchanging. A number of innovations, some of them quite important, were made in some districts of the Highlands during the first half of the eighteenth century, notably in the south and the south-west. In Mull, Iona, Morvern and Tiree, in 1732, lands began to be leased by the proprietor directly to small tenants, without the intervention of tacksmen. Leases were determined by competition among those who wished to rent the land, tenants were given reasonable security of tenure, and services—with a few relatively unimportant exceptions relating to the maintenance of harbours, roads and mill leads—were abolished. This amounted to an extensive and fairly drastic change of practice. Depriving the hereditary tacksmen of their great tacks was a notable step forward, as was the abolition of services. Even more significant was the elevation of subordinate tenants-at-will to the status of men who leased directly from the proprietor, and who were able to rely, and to make others rely, upon contractual engagements.

These departures from ancient tradition were the work of the second Duke of Argyll, the gross revenue of whose lands in Argyll rose from about £5,000 in 1703, when he succeeded to the dukedom, to £6,687 in 1743, when his brother succeeded him. By 1761 the gross revenue had reached nearly £10,000. 'Since feu-duties and teinds were relatively static, most of the increase is attributable to rents and domanial products.'[41] The new arrangements of the 1730s proved only moderately successful, and many of the new tenants became insolvent; but the old practices were not revived. The second Duke was not a solitary pioneer in the path of improvement. There were other lairds who began before 1745 to pursue efficiency in the management of their properties, such as Archibald Campbell of Knockbuy, 'who from about 1728 devoted much of his estate on Lochfyneside to the grazing of cattle for the market, went in for extensive cattle-dealing, and raised the rental to fourfold its earlier level in the sixty following years.'[42] Rent raising was probably widespread in the Highlands between the 'Fifteen and the 'Forty-five. On the Long Island, the McKenzies were alleged in 1750 to be 'frugal and industrious in their way, and Remarkably disposed to grow Rich. They have screwed their Rents to an extravagant Height (which they vitiously term improving their Estates) without putting the Tenant upon a proper way of improving the Ground to enable him to pay that Rent, which makes the Common People little better than Slaves and Beggars.'[43] On the other hand, the rise of Glasgow as an international trading centre was already having considerable economic effects upon the islands of the west coast of Scotland. Whereas the islanders had once traded chiefly with Inverness, landing their goods at Glenelg, and thence carrying them a long distance overland by horseback, by the 1720s they were using the far easier sea route to Glasgow, sending their hides, tallow, butter and cheese to the expanding metropolitan market, as well as driving black cattle south to Crieff. Likewise, in the far north, Caithness exported both corn and fish to ports on the east coast, even as far as London, and from Sutherland 2,500 head of cattle were going south in the 1760s, and it was a growing trade. It is therefore quite wrong to suppose that the highlanders were thirled throughout the first half of the eighteenth century, and for a couple of decades later, to a static subsistence economy which offered no scope for commercial enterprise, was everywhere the same, and which conducted its affairs without knowledge of or reference to developments beyond its borders. On the other hand, changes were never general, but were confined to particular places or groups of places. Development was never evenly spread. Caithness, much of Argyll and the lowland parts of Perthshire were always in advance of the rest of the Highlands.

It is equally a mistake to think that the rising of 1745 was a general revolt of the clans, a violent and spontaneous expression of hostility to lowland and more especially to Hanoverian domination, made by the generality of highlanders, all feeling and acting the same way in a common cause. This simple romantic idea is still entertained in some quarters, along with the even more unhistorical notion that the Scots people as a whole supported the rebellion. The truth is that the Scots people as a whole were emphatically opposed to it. 'The determining factor probably [in the failure of the rebellion] was the absolute opposition of the Church of Scotland, and indeed all presbyterians, to the restoration of a Roman Catholic sovereign.'[44] The influence of the Church of Scotland was enormous throughout Scotland, and no minister of the Church supported the Prince. Contemporaries judged that between two-thirds and nine-tenths of the people of Scotland were for the House of Hanover: George II had 'two-thirds of the country zealous for him on principle';[45] those 'zealous for Revolution principles' (i.e. the principles of the Revolution of 1688) were 'above three-fourths of our people';[46] 'nine parts of ten in Scotland'[47] were against the Prince and his followers.

Similarly, the highlanders were themselves divided. Those who fought for Prince Charles were usually referred to as 'the Highlanders'; but not all were highlanders—between ten and twenty per cent of the strength of the Jacobite army came from the substantially episcopalian shires of Aberdeen and Banff, although almost none at all from the counties farther south[48]—and not all highlanders who fought in the campaign fought with the Jacobites. Many of the clans either held aloof or were actively hostile to the rising: Campbell, Mackay, Munro, Macpherson, Grant and Fraser; and the McLeods, McLeans, MacNeills and MacDonalds of the Isles. Personal loyalties frequently played a vital part. Thus in 1745, when Independent Companies were being raised in the Highlands to oppose the Prince,

Mackenzie of Fairburn refused command of one of these companies, although remaining loyal to the king, 'because this small mealling I possess
was given my predecessor by King James v in free gift . . . the case is con-
science with me.'[49] Indeed, personal loyalties and the attitudes of a few
individuals swayed the course of affairs; the clan system was in action.
'The Highlanders who came out did so from a variety of motives, chiefly
feudal, sometimes ecclesiastical, seldom political, and occasionally only
under pressure from their chiefs.'[50] At the very start of the rebellion,
Cameron of Locheil judged that it could not succeed; but his loyalty to the
Stuarts overcame regard to his own interest. It was 'a point agreed among
the Highlanders that if Locheil had persisted in his refusal to take arms, the
other chiefs would not have joined the standard without him, and the
spark of rebellion must have instantly expired.'[51] On the other side stood
Duncan Forbes, born near Inverness, educated at Edinburgh and Leyden,
fifth laird of Culloden, and by 1745 Lord President. In the task of organising
and co-ordinating resistance to the Jacobites Forbes was both tireless and
indispensable. When he was at Inverness early in 1746 and the town seemed
likely to be taken by the rebels, Forbes received a letter giving an account
of the battle of Falkirk and the following information:

'As the scene is shifted nearer your quarter, you will know more than we.
I wish to God you may not know too much. We can see no help for
you, but shipping, in case they do come in a body; and we are not sure
that you have that at hand. We form many schemes for your safety, and
are very anxious; as, by their discourse here [Edinburgh], you were the
chief object of their resentment; especially when they came back from
England: for it was their fixed opinion, that with the McDonalds and
MacLeods of Skye, the McKenzies and Frazers, they might have been
masters of London, had all these joined them soon enough; the failing
of which they place to your Lordship's account.'[52]

Forbes was a highlander. Had he not been, his influence could never have
been so great. More than any one man, it has been said 'he preserved the
throne for the House of Hanover, chiefly at his own expense, and for no
reward but that which Charles Esmond found customary among princes.'[53]

In the final battle many Scotsmen fought against Prince Charles, including the officers and men of three Scottish regiments—the 1st Foot (Royal
Scots), 21st (Royal Scots Fusiliers) and 25th (King's Own Scottish Bor-
derers). The Independent Companies of the Black Watch, recruited entirely
in the Highlands and formed into a Regiment—the famous 42nd—in
1739, were not present at Culloden, as they were fighting in Flanders. But
the part played in the development of the Highlands by those who enlisted in
the 42nd, or in the fifty or so battalions raised mainly in the Highlands between 1740 and 1815, was to prove of considerable subsequent importance.

The battle of Culloden was one of the decisive battles of history. But neither its outcome nor the legislation which followed it could change the situation in the Highlands overnight, and when Duncan Forbes surveyed the position in 1746 he wrote, possibly for the guidance of government, a masterly description of the highlanders' way of life as it was and had been for many generations.

'The inhabitants of the mountains, unacquainted with industry and the fruits of it, and united in some degree by the similarity of dress and language, stick close to their antient idle way of life; retain their barbarous customs and maxims; depend generally on their Chiefs, as their sovereign Lords and masters; and being accustomed to the use of Arms, and inured to hard living, are dangerous to the public peace; and must continue to be so, until, being deprived of Arms for some years, they forget the use of them. From Perth to Inverness, which is above 100 measured miles, and from thence to the Western Sea, including the Western Islands, there is no town or village of any consequence, that could be the Seat of any Court of Justice the least considerable, except Dunkeld, which is within 10 computed miles of Perth; neither is there any sort of Inn or Accomodation for travellers, excepting a few that have been built on the King's Roads made by Marshall Wade. Of this large tract of land, no part is in any degree cultivated, except some spots here and there in Straths or Glens, by the sides of Rivers, brooks, or lakes, and on the Sea Coast and Western Islands. The Grounds that are cultivated yield small quantities of mean Corns, not sufficient to feed the Inhabitants, who depend for their nourishment on milk, butter, cheese, etc. the product of their Cattle. Their constant residence during the harvest, winter, and spring, is at their small farms, in houses made of turf; the roof, which is thatched, supported by timber. In the summer seasons, they drive flocks and herds many miles higher amongst the mountains, where they have made large ranges of coarse pasture. The whole family follow the cattle; the men to guard them, and to prevent them straying; the women to milk them, and to look after the butter and cheese, etc. The places in which they reside when thus employed they call shoelings, and their habitations are the most miserable huts that ever were seen.

[Because the clans] live by themselves, and possess different Straths, Glens, or districts, without any considerable mixture of Strangers, it has been for a great many years impracticable (and hardly thought safe to try it) to give the Law its course amongst the mountains. . . . The Want of Roads, excepting the King's Road already mentioned, the Want of Accommodation, the supposed ferocity of the inhabitants, and the difference of language, have proved hitherto a bar to all free intercourse between the high and low lands, and have left the High-

landers in possession of their own idle customs and extravagant maxims, absolute strangers to the advantages that must accrue from Industry, and to the Blessings of having those advantages protected by law'.[54]
This was the situation with which the government, having defeated the rebellion, had now to deal.

2

The Annexed Estates
and Emigration

The defeat of the rebellion in 1745 was decisive; but it had not been easy. 'The conclusion of this enterprise was such as most people both at home and abroad expected; but the progress of the rebels was what nobody expected; for they defeated more than once the king's troops; they over-ran one of the united kingdoms, and marched so far into the other, that the capital trembled at their approach, and during the tide of fortune, which had its ebbs and flows, there were moments when nothing seemed impossible; and, to say the truth, it was not easy to forecast, or imagine anything more unlikely, than what had already happened.'[1]

Moreover, the rebellion was the fourth attempt since the Revolution, starting in the Highlands, to restore the Stewarts to the throne. The King's ministers responded with stern and far-reaching measures. Over forty persons were attainted for their part in the rising, and a number of the leaders and rebellious clan chiefs were executed. For the longer term, the policy pursued was designed to weaken if not to destroy the clan system throughout the Highlands. An Act was passed prohibiting under severe penalties the wearing of the highland dress (except as a uniform in the Forces of the Crown). This Act was never carried systematically into effect, but it was nevertheless a damaging and keenly felt attack on the highlander's visible identity. Almost as much as the gaelic, it was the tartan, plaid and kilt which marked off the clansmen from other men—and which served, incidentally, as 'a ready-made uniform which created a community of feeling and a community of action that give the embattled clans the character of a regular army'.[2] Possibly even more important, the Disarming Act of 1716, which had been rather a dead letter,[3] and the chief result of which seems to have been that in 1745 'the loyal clans were without weapons while the disloyal were comparatively well armed',[4] was replaced by a new Act, more stringent in its terms, and rigidly enforced. Furthermore, the Heritable Jurisdictions—grants by the Crown of judicial power to individuals— were, with a few reservations, abolished. These hereditary privileges, when fully exercised, gave their possessor so much authority that he was like a king in his own domain, and could call his followers into the field. The power of the highland chiefs rested more on their patriarchal standing than on legal privileges, but the abolition of Heritable Jurisdictions weakened their position, and the simultaneous abolition of wardholding—an ancient system of tenure associated with personal and military service—further weakened it.

The ultimate aim of these Acts was the destruction of the political separateness of the Highlands. As Ramsay of Ochtertyre put it years later,

'The whole weight of government was employed to dissolve every tie between the chief and the clan, and to abolish all distinctions between the Highland and Lowland Scots. Even the gentry who had not been engaged in the rebellion found it expedient to drop some of their national customs, which either gave offence, or were prohibited by law. It was doubtless with reluctance that people advanced in life complied with these innovations. But these old-fashioned gentlemen being now mostly gone, their successors have no longer the same attachment either to their people or to ancient modes of life. They affect the manners of the Lowland gentry. . . .'[5]

From one point of view the policy of the government was well judged, for it attacked not only the direct ability of the clans to put armed men into the field, but also their morale. Not to be able to carry arms was, for a true highlander, a grave penalty; not to be free to dress so as to identify himself with his chief and his fellow clansmen was at least as bad, for it undermined his confidence and his spirit. On the other hand, it may be questioned whether these measures were necessary for the destruction of the political and military power of what is sometimes called Celtic Feudalism. The old way of life was already weakened by changing attitudes and changed social and economic relations. Roads, rents, contractual obligations—subsequently potatoes and sheep—did more than Parliament to make another 'Forty-five impossible. The clan system was a way of life for 300,000 people which could not be overturned by legislation. What destroyed it was contact with—and ultimately acceptance of—the economic usages and ambitions of a commercial society.

Prior to the Rebellion, the government had regarded the Highlands as an isolated region of which no good could be expected and from which little of value could be derived; the aim of policy had been to contain the military and political forces which existed there; nothing constructive was attempted. After 1745, the government's intention was to integrate the Highlands with the rest of Great Britain. At the political level this policy was pursued extensively and with determination. As far as economic activities were concerned, the government seems to have expected that economic change would be accelerated throughout the Highlands principally by the work of the Commissioners for the Annexed Estates.

After the collapse of the Rebellion, a large number of estates, most of them in the Highlands, were forfeit to the Crown through the attainder for treason of their owners. The Vesting Act of June 1747 authorised the Scottish Court of Exchequer, as guardian of Crown revenues in Scotland, to survey and value these estates, appoint factors, determine claims and pay creditors. In all, fifty-three estates were surveyed, and forty-one of these— the forfeited estates—were taken over by the Barons of Exchequer. Most forfeited estates were sold by public auction to pay creditors, but thirteen estates were inalienably annexed to the Crown by the Annexing Act of March 1752. This Act provided that the rent and profits arising from the estates were to be used solely

> 'for the Purposes of civilizing the Inhabitants upon the said Estates, and other Parts of the Highlands and Islands of Scotland, and promoting amongst them the Protestant Religion, good Government Industry and Manufactures, and the Principles of Duty and Loyalty to his Majesty, his Heirs and Successors, and to no other Use or Purpose whatsoever.'

Unpaid Commissioners, of whom there were at various times between twenty-eight and thirty-five, were appointed: crown officials, noblemen, judges, substantial lairds. First appointed in 1755, the Commissioners took over the estates of Barrisdale, Cromarty, Lovat, Perth, Struan and part of Kinlochmoidart, as well as Monaltry in Aberdeenshire and part of Arn-prior in Stirlingshire. The other estates were at first held of subject superiors, and then in 1770 the Crown purchased the superiorities and the Commissioners took over from the Barons of Exchequer the estates of Lochiel, Ardsheal, Callart, Lochgarry, Cluny, and those parts of Arnprior and Kinlochmoidart for which they were not already responsible. They thus came to manage, and to develop, eleven highland estates spread over thirty parishes—about fifteen per cent of all parishes in the Highlands—beginning their work in the later 1750s and continuing it for over a quarter of a century.[6] Estate management on such a scale, carried on for so long a period, was well calculated to have a profound effect on the economic life of the Highlands, both by its immediate impact and by the force of its example. Admittedly the Commissioners would not have made much of a mark had they fallen a prey to muddled policies with no clear objective. In fact, their policies were consistent, and their activities did much to help the commercial lowland economy to infiltrate the still feudal Highlands.

The Commissioners dealt with many aspects of life on the estates, notably agriculture, communications, education, manufactures and the establishing of new towns. Aware that the attitude of the highlanders towards work and progress was itself a difficulty, the Commissioners sought for a few years to influence those who already lived on the estates by settling among them soldiers and sailors returned from the Seven Years' War, who would prove, it was hoped, 'good Workmen for Carrying on the different improvements whose Example by raising a Spirit of Emulation among the present inhabitants may promote Industry which has hitherto been at the Lowest Ebb'.[7] This scheme was not a success. Although each man or family was provided with money, three acres of land and—after much delay—a house (of sorts), the settlers proved little apt for either farming or fishing, and soon drifted away. Many of them seem to have been an unruly lot. The land they were given was often poor, existing tenants objected to their presence, and skill, tools, manure and perseverence were all wanting. Although several hundred settlers were brought onto the estates, and well over £10,000 expended on the plan, of which much was expected, the principal effects of it seem to have been that some small patches of land were cleared and a number of houses built which by the 1790s were either deserted or occupied 'by a more industrious set of people'.[8] The Commissioners had more success with their parallel but far more modest scheme for 'King's Cottagers', day labourers and skilled men whom they wished to settle or retain upon the estates. These cottagers were lent money and given small plots of land, and their skill and industry probably helped some little settlements to survive, notably the new village founded by the Commissioners in the early 1760s at Kinloch Rannoch.

The introduction of new settlers among them was one way to combat the highlanders' attachment to their ancient way of life. Another was education. An increased provision of schools and schoolmasters was recommended by almost every writer on highland affairs in the eighteenth century as an important means of promoting economic development, and particular emphasis was usually placed on the learning of English. Gaelic and barbarism were regarded by many as synonymous, while it was argued that because of their inability to speak English

> 'the common people can carry on no Transactions with the more Southern parts of Great Britain, without the Intervention of their Superiors, who know the English language, and are thereby kept in that undue dependence and unacquaintance with the Arts of Life which have long been the Misery of these Countrys.'[9]

The parochial schools were too few to provide for a widely scattered population, especially in the west, and although their efforts were supplemented by those of numerous charity schools the situation remained unsatisfactory.[10] Conscious that the people in many parishes were anxious that their children should not remain uneducated, the Commissioners built schools, recruited schoolmasters, and in some cases paid the school fees of poor children. The schools were modest affairs—they rarely cost more than £20 to construct—and the remuneration of the teachers was usually between £10 and £20 per annum, although they also had a house, a garden, a few acres and a cow. All instruction was given in English. Probably few children learned more than to read and write but at least one schoolmaster thought that progress was being made:

> '. . . the people begin to have a greater relish both for knowledge and industry, many of them not only sending their children to School but even attainding themselves. . . .'[11]

Between 1760 and 1790 the proportion of highlanders who could not understand or speak English fell perceptibly.

In the matter of particular occupations the Commissioners' attention was directed chiefly to agriculture, concerning which they formulated general rules. In 1762 they set out their 'Rules and Articles for managing the Annexed Estates.'[12] These show the Commissioners 'desirious as soon as may be to free and relieve the Tennents of the annexed estates from the burden of Thirlage;' give them power to adjust boundaries, exchange land between tenants, and generally facilitate and carry on the process of enclosure—the tenants to pay 5 per cent of the cost after three years; and record their wish to 'aid and encourage' satisfactory tenants to build better 'houses and offices . . . properly covered with Thatch Fearn or heather sewed with Tarred Rope yarn or some better Matterials.' Tenants were to 'house and inclose' at night in winter 'their Horse, Black Cattle, Sheep and all other Bestial,' and there were detailed rules about rotations—tenants were 'bound to follow annually in a regular Course not under five Aikers of ground for each Plow kept by them upon their severall Farms and proportionally,' and were to have at least two acres each year in red clover, as well as two fifths of their enclosed arable land sown to grass. Tree planting was encouraged—the Commissioners themselves bought tens of thousands of trees as well as bushels of acorns—and tenants were to be compensated when vacating their farms for any planting which they had carried out. Not all the provisions, however, could have applied equally well to an estate in Norfolk; in 1765 there was added the rule, 'All tenants shall be obliged to pay their Proportion of the Fox and Eagle Hunters Wages, and of the Wages of Killers of other Vermin.' Likewise—for this is very typical of the thinking of the age—the Commissioners reserved the power 'to search for and work all mines and minerals.'

These rules cover a wide variety of important topics in a specific and practical way. Admittedly, it is not too difficult to draw up a list of desirable practices; but there was more to it than that. Not only did the Commissioners stick to the general line of policy which the rules specify,[13] there is also evidence that they made energetic efforts to have the rules adhered to. In the summer of 1762 they issued a set of 'Instructions for the Factors upon the annexed Estates,'[14] and they constantly insisted on receiving careful reports from the factors, upon which they commented, and as a result of which they sometimes asked for additional information or issued further instructions. Factors, in short, were kept up to the mark, and the Commissioners were well informed about the progress being made. What is particularly remarkable, besides the efficiency with which the Commissioners kept in touch with their scattered estates, is the combination of extensive views with a grasp of detail.[15] For example, in a paper entitled 'A Scheme for the Improvement of the Highlands'[16] there occur the following paragraphs:

> '3mo In the more mountainous parts it would be a most substantial improvement to introduce the Spade and hoe culture which will produce Crops of Corn turnips and grass much more Plentifull than can be produced by the rough method of the Plough this is a great object in those mountaneous Countrys whereas by ordinary culture there is not winter ffood for the half of the Cattle that are plentyfully fed in summer. There is another advantage of this method, which is to employ a number of hands who can find no other work, and the additional product will afford them very tolerable wages.
>
> 4mo Premiums for draining Lakes marshes and mosses will introduce a habit of Labour much wanted in thes Countries; and also tend to population. . . .'

The absence of trees in many areas, and the decay of woodland in others, also attracted the Commissioners' attention. The highland forests had been degenerating and diminishing for centuries. Proprietors seem to have been careless and tenants wasteful; no doubt the woods in those days seemed endless. There was little organised trade (the activities of the York Buildings Company in the Abernethy Forest in the early 1730s were exceptional)[17] and less efficiency—the mills on the Struan estate were 'perhaps the most Gothick thing of their kind in the World. The Saws are one fourth of an Inch thick, and at the most moderat Computation destroy at least one fifth part of all the Timber Manufactoured that way'[18]—and tenants cut trees with or without permission, and floated them down the rivers for sale to local merchants; or used them for fuel, for house-building or boat-building or, occasionally, to make agricultural implements. Others supplemented their incomes by stripping the bark from oak and birch trees and selling it to the tanners, leaving the standing trees to die and decay. And what was not destroyed by the clansmen was apt to be eaten by the goats. The Commissioners responded by appointing woodkeepers to control cutting, and by trying to enforce an Act of 1766 which carried severe penalties for stealing or destroying timber. They also encouraged their factors to plant new woods and enclose them, and large sums of money were spent in this way in the 1760s and 1770s. Thus the Commissioners laboured to inculcate habits of industry, to introduce new techniques—

with due regard for their suitability in different parts of the estates—to provide employment, and above all to set an example of enterprising and efficient management.

The Commissioners probably regarded the modernisation of agriculture as the basis of their plans for the development of the Highlands. But they were aware that agriculture alone was not enough. Another possibility was the herring fishing. For centuries fishermen in sea-going boats, or busses as they were called, had been coming from Holland, as well as from England and the Lowlands of Scotland, to catch herring along the north-west coast. Loch Hourn and Loch Broom especially were noted for the dense shoals which frequently appeared along their shores in the 1750s, and two of the forfeited estates—Cromarty and Barrisdale—were situated on these lochs. But the native highlanders were not much interested in fishing, except as a subsidiary, largely subsistence occupation: 'the Country People have neither Ability or Skill to fit out proper Vessels to Catch [the herring], and the Gentlemen do not concern themselves with it'.[19] The Commissioners decided to try to settle discharged soldiers and sailors at Inverie on Loch Hourn and at Ullapool, and to make arrangements for the provision of salt and casks, without which it was impossible to work for other than a local market. But neither of these ventures, begun in the 1760s, lasted for more than a few years. The men settled seem to have preferred farming to fishing, and in any case to have been disinclined to steady work; while the irregular appearance of the shoals in the 1760s caused disappointment and loss.

In the 1770s some progress was made. A Liverpool merchant obtained from the Commissioners permission to erect a building for stores and for curing herring on Isle Martin in Loch Broom. This investment is said to have reached £5,000, and it was successful, providing employment for local fishers and workmen. A similar business was begun in 1783 on Isle Tanera, one of the Summer Isles, by another established fish merchant, and perhaps as a result of the success of both of these undertakings a number of petitions for help in developing the herring fishing were received by the Commissioners in the early 1780s. But by this time the return of the estates to their former owners was imminent, and little could be done. In this direction, therefore, the achievement of the Commissioners was negligible, and herring fishing remained an occasional, largely a subsistence occupation in which only a small minority of highlanders was involved. Later efforts were to show how intractable the problems were.

The Commissioners also sought to encourage manufactures, and here the obvious subject was the linen industry. Back in the seventeenth century the Scots Parliament had tried to encourage the linen industry in Scotland and, starting in 1727, the important Board of Trustees for Manufactures had concentrated its extensive efforts on improving and enlarging the industry, with considerable success. In 1753 Parliament had allocated a sum of £3,000 annually for nine years to the Board of Trustees for the encouragement of the industry in the Highlands. Seed was distributed, instructors were recruited, and 'stations' were set up at Loch Carron, Loch Broom and in Glenmoriston. After 1760, the Commissioners continued the work themselves, concentrating their efforts on their new settlements at Beauly and Kinloch Rannoch, and at the established village of Callander, but not neglecting other areas. Spinning schools were established—there was a particularly successful one at Stornoway, begun in 1763—subsidies were given, sometimes on what seems a pretty generous scale—for example, £300 to Duncan Grant 'for enabling him to prosecute the linen manufacture in Badenoch, Strathspey, Braemurray and Strathdown, for one year'[20]—and skilled men and women were sent into the Highlands to conduct and teach their trade. The results were moderately encouraging. Between 1750 and the late 1770s the output of linen cloth in the Highlands seems to have multiplied about three fold, a rate of growth rather faster than that for Scotland as a whole. On the other hand, four-fifths of highland output came from Perthshire, much of it from the lowland parts of that county. One tenth came from Inverness-shire—there was an important spinning school in Inverness itself—and the rest came in small, scattered lots of poor quality from all the remaining counties. The difficulties of making progress in the remote districts were early apparent. When Ninian Jeffrey complained in 1767[21] that the Trustees for Manufactures had induced him ten years before to leave Kelso with his family and go to Lochcarron 'where neither Lint nor wheel was ever seen before' in order to 'introduce the Linen Manufacture into the remote Highlands,' and had then let him down, Lord Kames commented:

> 'we have learned by woful experience that these [Loch Broom and Loch Carron] are unfit places for carrying on any branch of the Linen Manufacture. The climate, the barrenness of the soil, the dearness of all sorts of provisions, even of oat meal, the distance from commerce, are all of them obstacles, which in conjunction are insurmountable.'[22]

But he thought that Jeffrey's proposal that he be invited to help to develop the herring and cod fisheries 'merits to be a subject of enquiry. Supposing the coast of Coygach to afford good stations for the herring fishery it would undoubtedly be a great benefit to the poor people upon the coast to provide them salt and Cask at prime cost.' Nothing seems to have come of this, and a few years later Jeffrey was recommending 'the Rearing of Sheep' and asking for a forty-one year lease of some lands near Ullapool 'as there is no perswading the Natives to follow any new Plan but what they see turn out to Advantage.'

7. Achray Bridge, north of Aberfoyle. Many structures of this type were built by the Commissioners for the Forfeited Estates in the 18th century

DUNKELD.

This instance of the way in which the Commissioners' attention was turned back to agriculture, even when they tried to interest themselves in other matters, is significant and not unusual. On the other hand, Kames's reference to dearness of provisions and distance from commerce indicates a line of policy which the Commissioners steadily pursued. They evidently believed that as well as stimulating agriculture and industry directly, by means of subsidies, skilled management, expert advice and so on, they could make an important indirect contribution to industrial and agricultural development by facilitating trade. This they sought to do both by improving communications and by establishing new or expanding existing towns and villages.

Communications in the eighteenth century were nowhere good, but they were probably nowhere worse than in the Highlands. The roads built by General Wade before 1745 were of only limited value. They were planned, as Telford observed, 'with other Views than promoting Commerce and Industry' and were therefore 'generally in such Directions, and so inconveniently steep, as to be nearly unfit for the Purposes of Civil Life'.[23] They were connecting roads between some principal centres of population, all south of the Great Glen, and did nothing to improve access to the glens which were off the main routes or to the wilder western districts. On the other hand, they were a stimulus to enterprise by others:

'The ease and convenience of these roads has induced several of the highland gentlemen to make good ways, at their own expence, from their homes to the main road; and where there were nothing but turf huts for one hundred miles together, there are now, at ten or twelve miles distance from each other, houses of stone and lime, for the accommodation of travellers. The English drovers, who used to attend the fairs of cattle on the borders of the highlands, now go into the heart of the country....'[24]

After 1745, Wade's successors gave more attention to subsidiary roads, but most of this important work was left to the landowners and the efforts of statute labour.

Early in the 1760s, the Commissioners began to help. At first, building bridges seems to have been their chief contribution towards solving the communications problem. In 1762 and 1763 alone, nineteen bridges were built at the Commissioners' expense, most of them in Perthshire. Some of these were very small affairs— £9 15s and a supply of free timber seems to have been all that was needed to build 'two timber bridges over the water of Tarrigag'[25] in the barony of Stratherrick. But £200 was wanted for a bridge at Kinloch Rannoch, and £350 for the bridge at Callander, where the Commissioners had particularly high hopes of successful development. In 1772 Smeaton submitted estimates for a bridge over the Beauly at Dumballoch at £2,244, for another over the Conan at Boat of Braan at £3,432,

8. Dunkeld, 'seated under and environed by crags, partly naked, partly wooded, with summits of a vast height.' (Pennant)

and for a 'Pier or Landing Place at Portleich on Cromarty Bay'[26] at £711. At the same time he warned that the estimation of costs was very difficult because of uncertainties regarding carriage and labour. Some bridges were built jointly by the Commissioners and interested landowners. A bridge over the Tay at Kenmore, helping to connect lowland Perthshire to the West coast was built partly by public subscription and partly by the Commissioners, and was opened in 1774, while the greatest of all the bridges, that over the Tay at Perth, was completed about 1770 at a cost of over £26,000, of which the Commissioners paid half. Road-building also attracted the Commissioners' attention, and they did particularly useful work in the west, where communications were notoriously bad:

'All these Countries viz. Knoydart, the Two Morirs, Moydart, and Arisag, are the most Rough Mountainous and impassable parts in all the Highlands of Scotland, and are commonly called by the Inhabitants of the Neighbouring Countries the Highlands of the Highlands. . . . The People of these Wild Countries could never believe that they were Accessible 'till the King's Forces Scoured them after the Battle of Culloden which was a prodigious Surprize to the Inhabitants.'[27]

'The Roads to and from this Country [Coigach] may be reckoned the worst in the highlands and no bridges upon the rivers, so that nothing but necessity makes people resort there. For a great part of the year this Country is inaccessible.'[28]

Roads were built by the Commissioners, or with their help, in Coigach and Rannoch in the 1770s, and in all the estates. Many were local roads, but a road between Lochbroom and Dingwall was opened about 1772, and towards the end of the decade the Commissioners were helping to complete a seventy-five mile stretch of road along the coast from Inveraray to Campbeltown. Roads and bridges constituted the largest item of the Commissioners' capital expenditure in the 1760s and 1770s. In Strathyre, for example, in the eighteen months from the spring of 1774, £2,012 was expended, of which £784 was for roads and bridges.

What was spent on town building is harder to trace. Inverness was the only town of any importance in the Highlands. It stood on the frontier—both English and Gaelic were commonly spoken in the streets—and it had frequently suffered attack by rebellious clans. With a population of possibly six or seven thousand in the 1750s it was an important trading centre for the Highlands, although it seems to have been in decline during the first half of the eighteenth century; contemporaries speak of ruinous houses and dilapidated and forsaken commercial buildings. It traded in corn, supplying malt to many districts, and in skins, providing the highlanders in return with malt, corn, dye-stuffs, coarse linen and iron. It served, moreover, as a link with France and the Low Countries. Leaving Inverness aside, there was scarcely even a village of any size in the Highlands, at least before the later 1760s. Campbeltown, in the extreme south west, was a small town, and Stornoway was just beginning its rise to prominence, also as a fishing port. Dunkeld, although a very small place, was perhaps as important as any on the central mainland; it boasted a small linen manufacture, and in the summer months even attracted a few visitors who sought to benefit by drinking goats' milk and whey. After these, the most important settlements were the trading towns or villages strung out along the highland frontier, where the produce of the glens and mountains could be exchanged for lowland goods:

> 'Highland Carriers and Pedlers brought . . . Skins of all kinds viz: Goat, Sheep, Kid and lamb Skins, Deer, Roe, fox, ottar and Martins Skins, some of which were dressed and Manufactured at Crieff, the Rest sold to advantage at other Markets particularly Perth; these Peddlers brought likewise great Quantities of Coarse Tartans and plaidings from the highlands, and in Return of all the above articles, they took . . . great Quantities of Linnen Cloth some thin stuffs for womens apparill, considerable quantities of all Materials for dying, Tobacco, soap, iron and diverse other kinds of Merchandise. . . .'[29]

This trade—very like that being conducted at the same time across the Appalachians—had been going on for centuries, and at first there was probably little scope for its extension. But the Commissioners were anxious to encourage towns and villages based on all kinds of economic activity, and the factors were never slow to put forward comments and ideas. As early as 1756 it was noted that the village of Callander showed particular promise as a trading centre. It was

> 'already begun upon a regular plan, and has made a considerable progress. . . . There were small feus given here to a number of people by the late James Drummond of Perth, and there are a great number of People now, artificers and others from different parts of the Kingdom desirous of having feus in that place. The Situation is extremely good . . . [there is] an easy access to be had to it from the Low Country and the Highlands . . . and now that there is a Communication opened that way betwixt the Highlands and the Low Country, there is the greater reason to expect that several Branches of Business Commerce and Manufactures might succeed in this place. . . .'[30]

In the following years the Commissioners did their best to encourage these activities. A village at Meikleport (ten miles from Crieff) was suggested, there being 'a considerable quantity of plain arable ground in it that would admit of many divisions to accommodate the supernumerary hands in the rest of the lands.'[31] There were plans for 'a Village to be built at the head of Loch Rannoch, for the Reception of King's Cottagers',[32] (plans which were implemented in the 1760s), while on the other side of the country there were proposals for 'a small village' at Beauly,

'an extreme proper place for erecting a village . . . a convenient little harbour could be made at a small expence, it lies in the centre of a very populous fine Country, of excellent Soil, but whereas the Inhabitants are strangers to the right method of agriculture Manufacturers and Industry, there are several yearly Fairs held in and about the place, a market cross in it and a great Collection of poor people, who live in hutts, and retail Ale and spiritous liquors to the people who resort thither . . . This place also lies commodious for a communication with a great part of Ross shire. . . .'[33]

There was also the suggestion of a village 'at a place called Ullapool', chosen chiefly because of the herring fishing ('particularly these two years past, the Success has been extraordinary')[34] a suggestion carried into effect some twenty years later by the British Fisheries Society.

What lay behind this enthusiasm for the enlargement of existing villages or the establishment of new ones? The answer has to be sought partly in the kind of statement quoted above, but further light is thrown on the problem by additional instructions which the Commissioners received from the government in 1771. These directed, *inter alia*, that the Commissioners

'shall have a particular attention (as far as conveniently may be done) to the Enlargement, or new erection of Towns and Villages, to the end that the Inhabitants by Neighbourhood and Mutual Commerce, may be the better enabled to assist each other in Agriculture and Manufactures, and in securing their property against theft and Rapine. . . .'

Furthermore, the general intention of the policy was stated to be

'effectually to Reclaim the Inhabitants of these Estates from their long habits of Sloth and inactivity and reconcile them to the love of Labour, Industry and Good order. . . .'[35]

That idleness was reprehensible, particularly among the poor, was standard eighteenth-century doctrine; this was a view which had been gaining ground since at least the days of John Knox. And there was certainly nothing new in the proposition that the highlanders were habitually idle. To some extent it was true. Primitive agriculture requires little exertion, for it involves not much more than sowing the seed in the springtime and reaping the crop in the autumn, along with the largely passive task of herding animals. Coupled with this, the highlanders were used to war and preparation for war, activities which may entail brief spells of great effort but which are certainly not synonymous with a life of steady toil. Lowlanders were therefore not altogether mistaken in depicting the highlander as an idle fellow, one who had more than his fair share of time for songs, or stories, or simply sitting at the cottage door. And it was an easy step to pass from this idea to the notion that what the highlander needed was instruction and discipline; above all, discipline. Left to themselves in the country the clansmen would remain idle, begging if they must, possibly stealing: 'great numbers . . . tho' not worth a Shilling, would be ashamed to be seen at any kind of labour though they think it no Shame to Steal.'[36] But the town, even the village, appealed to the eighteenth-century mind as a centre of order; as a place of organised activity where the pattern and style of progressive eighteenth-century life could be imposed; as the focus *par excellence* of civilizing influences. And this, progressive men believed, was what the Highlands wanted. Hence their anxiety to establish or enlarge villages, to have schools in these villages, to teach habits of industry and useful skills. The whole way of life was to be altered. Already the highlanders were forbidden to carry arms or to wear traditional dress. Now their language itself was attacked: 'In order to improve and civilise this part of the Highlands [estate of Lovat] I humbly apprehend that a particular attention to introduce the English language is of the greatest Consequence'.[37] And heavy emphasis was placed on the provision of public education for their children: 'All the tenants ought to be strictly tyed down by their tacks to keep their children at School under severe penalties.' It was a comprehensive programme, and it had aspects which must make us, blessed with hindsight, doubt its comprehensive wisdom. 'There are Crowds of little Girls here', wrote the factor at Crieff, 'that stroll about the Streets, playing at hand Ball and other such Employments and diversions, who might be usefully employed in Spinning'. Is labour the only proper business of life? Must everything be sacrificed in order to increase output? For a moment the orderliness, the discipline and the drudgery of the planned slums and factories of Victorian England seem not far away. But the Commissioners had a different vision before them, that of an industrious, prosperous, 'civilised' Highlands, and they thought they knew how to make the vision come true. Manufactures, schools, villages, communications— all were aspects of a single process of improvement.

How much was achieved it is hard to say. The Commissioners formed ambitious plans, sometimes very good plans; but the resources at their disposal, and the possibilities of influencing the behaviour of 300,000 people living for the most part remote from those 'civilizing' influences which the Commissioners represented, were very limited. Other improvers, admittedly, were at work. The fifth Duke of Argyll, 'ultimate owner of the greater part of a county of three thousand square miles,—beyond Argyll of all or part of the estates of chieftains like Clanranald and Glengarry',[38] besides a number of properties elsewhere, was a great reforming landlord from the time of his accession to the dukedom in 1761. He established a flax spinning factory on Tiree, and required his tenants there to grow flax as well as to pay a part of their rents in spun yarn;[39] put down ale-houses and distilling; built harbours, granted long leases, and encouraged if he did not actually introduce into some districts the growing of hay and potatoes. The third Earl of Breadalbane built a road along the north side of Loch Tay which connected to Inveraray, abolished feudal tenures, laid out the square of the village of Kenmore and built houses there, and encouraged flax spinning, the yarn being sold at periodic fairs at Taymouth. Commercial activity was probably increasing. The trade in cattle, which 'stretched from the remotest glens to the Lowlands and the south',[40] no doubt responded to the fact that between 1746 and 1770 prices rose from twenty-five shillings to three pounds a head—a remarkably rapid rate of increase, especially in a trade so long-established and traditional. Along the coasts the herring fishing was a growing industry. In some places there was afforestation, impressing travellers by 'the vast plantations that begin to cloath the hills,'[41] although the destruction of woodlands was probably more important. Pennant noted in 1769 that the pine forests 'are become very rare'.[42] This was partly the result of indiscriminate cutting by the highlanders themselves,[43] and partly because by the 1760s the woods were being cut for sale in the lowlands and England:

'Near these woods is a sawmill, which brings in about £180 per annum, the deal, which is the red sort, is sold in plank to different parts of the country, carried on horses' backs.'[44]

Also, there were one or two small charcoal furnaces at work, notably at Taynuilt in Argyllshire. And here and there might be found a rope-works, or a tannery or a bleachfield.

But these aspects of Highland life were exceptional; they were not what chiefly impressed visitors to the Highlands. The first thing that struck the traveller, after the general wildness, remoteness and grandeur of the country, seems to have been the atrocious standard of housing. Sod houses were the rule, usually without windows or chimneys, supported with a rough framework of tree branches, and thatched with broom or heather.

'My next care was to provide for myself; and to this end I entered the dwelling-house. There my landlady sat with a parcel of children about her, some quite and others almost naked, by a little peat fire in the middle of the hut. . . . The floor was common earth, very uneven, and nowhere dry, but near the fire, and in the corners, where no foot had carried the muddy dirt from without-doors'.[45]

The entrances were so small that it was sometimes necessary to crawl in on all fours, and a framework of small branches tied together served as a door. 'In order to prevent the pains of suffocation',[46] the smoke was allowed to escape through the door opening, or through a hole in the wall or roof.

9. Nine inhabitants—not counting the animals—meant a well-filled cottage. Quite incorrectly, the drawing suggests a roomy, spacious dwelling.

Grignion Sc.

Inside of a WEAVERS COTTAGE in ILAY

Sheelins in JURA and a distant View of the Paps.

A Cottage in ILAY.

On the Perth estates in 1766 such houses were described as 'little better than graves above ground, built only of the surface of the earth and the best soil the fields afford'.[47] There were stone-built houses near Invercauld, but the effect seems to have been no better:

'The houses of the common people in these parts are shocking to humanity, formed of loose stones, and covered with clods, which they term *devots*, or with heath, broom, or branches of fir: they look, at a distance, like so many black molehills'.[48]

At Inveraray, which was 'the focus of improvements of unprecedented splendour and expense'[49] and where the third Duke of Argyll had several years before begun to build his new town, Pennant cooly observed in 1769 that the old town was still 'composed of the most wretched hovels that can be imagined'.[50] Many years were to pass before better houses became the rule. This was partly because craftsmen and better materials were scarce in the Highlands. When the minister of Assynt set out to build a new manse in 1771, he hired a master mason outwith the district, and imported the heavy timber from Ross, dressed wood from Coigach, nails and glue from a merchant in Tain, glass from Inverness, and two wheelbarrows all the way from Edinburgh.[51]

Once inside the house, a stranger could rely on hospitality but not much else. Furniture was almost non-existent. As for food, in the 1760s and 1770s people lived on oatmeal, barley-cakes and potatoes; butter and cheese; occasionally 'the coagulated blood of their cattle spread on their bannocks';[52] and milk and whisky, the latter possibly sweetened with honey.[53] There are few factual accounts of everyday life in the Highlands in the second half of the eighteenth century, but Pennant—one of the earliest and most observant visitors—wrote a brief description of life on Upper Deeside which is worth quoting.

'The people live very poorly . . . The men are thin but strong; idle and lazy except when employed in the chace, or any thing that looks like amusement; are content with their hard fare, and will not exert themselves further than to get what they deem necessaries. The women are more industrious, spin their own husbands cloaths, and get money by knitting stockings, the great trade of the Country. The common women are in general most remarkably plain, and soon acquire an old look. . . .'[54]

His general impression of the Highlanders was that they were—with exceptions—'worn down with poverty'.[55] This view may be exaggerated, but numerous scraps of evidence tend to support it. Burt, in the 1720s, had been astonished at the poverty of the ordinary highlanders, noting their miserable houses, poor food, and the children running dirty and half-naked:

'I have often seen them come out from the huts early in a cold morning

10. Pennant visited the sheilings on Jura—'a grotesque group'—in 1771. 'In one of the little conic huts, I spied a little infant asleep, under the protection of a faithful dog.'

stark naked, and squat themselves down (if I might decently use the comparison) like dogs on a dunghill . . . '[56]

Gentlemen's children were little better off; there was a saying, 'that a gentleman's bearns are to be distinguished by their speaking English'. Food was often scarce. In the more prosperous areas, in the summer time, the lairds and tacksmen might dine on game, of which there was plenty; but more often a gentleman who was well attended by servants sat down to a diet of oatmeal or pickled herrings. Many districts could barely produce enough food for their needs even in a good year; when the crops failed, or were deficient, a local famine resulted; such famines seem to have been more common by the early 1770s than twenty years before. Almost all travellers commented unfavourably on the 'idleness' of the Highlanders— in Assynt Pennant found them 'almost torpid with idleness, and most wretched'[57] —but idleness was sometimes the simple product of scarcity of work; in 1770, on the Sutherland estates, afforestation was ordered 'to provide employment for those who needed it'.[58] All this suggests a growing pressure of population on resources—the kind of pressure lamented by the tenants themselves on Lochtayside in 1770: 'How difficult it is to maintain such a vast number of souls upon so small possessions as the memorialists have may very easily be conceived.'[59]

If the standard of living in the Highlands was not rising—was even falling—in the 1750s and 1760s, it might be argued that the Commissioners and the improving landlords were not doing enough. They should have redoubled their efforts. But in what directions? Should there have been more spinning schools, more afforestation, more new villages, more raising of rents, more free copies of Andrew Wight's *Present State of Husbandry* 'to testify [the Commissioners'] good opinion of you for giving an example to your brother farmers of good husbandry'? This question is not easily answered; and it raises another. How were the improvers to secure the co-operation of the Highlanders? Clan sentiment remained in some places extremely important. Landlords hesitated to grant long leases to tenants whose loyalty was questionable, and tenants among whom ties of kinship and clanship were still strong were usually resentful of change, reluctant to co-operate and suspicious of all improvements.[60] The old tenurial arrange-ments had been altered—in particular, many of the great tacksmen had been removed. But even where this had been done, as on Tiree,

'society continued patriarchal and semi-feudal to an unexpected degree. . . . Most of the farm towns were still populous, representing a variety of classes and occupations which sustained the tacksman and his dependents in some measure of self-sufficiency.'[61]

In other parts of the country straightforward oppression by tacksmen, including the exaction of burdensome services, continued undiminished, while in Caithness, according to Pennant, 'the common people are kept in great servitude, and most of their time is given to their Lairds'.[62] It is always a mistake to suppose that those changes will be universally welcomed which some people term improvement. The work of the improvers threatened the influence of some and the security of others; this was obvious where tenures were at stake. But nothing is neutral in a conflict between a commercial and a feudal society. When General Wade, back in the 1730s, built a bridge over the Spean two miles west of the present bridge, his work was 'at first very disagreeable to the old Chieftains . . . by admitting strangers among them, the clans were taught that the Lairds were not the first of men'.[63] But the clans were also to learn that their own way of life as well as the lairds' was threatened. Those who had apparently the least to lose clung most tenaciously to their old ways. The very poverty of the small tenants and cottars meant that they had nothing material to fall back on, and so the improvers often encountered their greatest difficulties in those regions where little was produced but the bare necessities of life.

Thus in the years between 1750 and 1780 it may be said that improvement had begun; but it had only begun. There were places where up-to-date practices were known, were even common: but these were pockets of modernity in a land still dominated by its historic background of feudal practice and feudal ideas. Visitors to the Highlands—there were few of them before 1770—found a country wild and remote, populated—they did not say over-populated—by men and women who were alien, indolent and poor. Of course, travellers were naturally inclined to see whatever was striking and strange; no one wants to find life in another land the same as life at home—especially if he is going to write a book about it. But the overwhelming impression given by all who reported, even casually and incidentally, on the Highlands around 1770 or 1780, is of a world quite different from their own; antique, savage, poor and picturesque; modernised only in patches and superficially, except on the fringes, where it was touched by the Lowlands or by the waters just north of the Firth of Clyde. Boswell was not mistaken in supposing in 1773 that on their projected visit to the Highlands he and Dr Johnson 'might there contemplate a system of life almost totally different from what we had been accustomed to see; and, to find simplicity and wildness, and all the circumstances of remote time or place'.[64]

Whether or not the improvers were sometimes assailed by doubts about the wisdom or ultimate success of their policies we do not know. But whatever their confidence in the future, they began to witness after some fifteen years an unexpected sequel to their labours; people started to leave the Highlands in unprecedented numbers.

It is impossible to say when emigration began or became important.

Certainly it was not significant before 1750. But in 1757 a new influence arose: the government began to extend the policy which had created the Black Watch in 1739, and raised two new Highland regiments. From then until 1815 the recruitment of highlanders into the British army was continuous, and large numbers of these men were sent to North America to fight first in the Seven Years' War and then in the War of American Independence. Some of them elected to remain in North America when the fighting was over, and of these a number were given grants of land by the government; others returned with news of what the colonies were like, no doubt some of it favourable. Thus men from every district of the Highlands began to learn about other parts of the world, other customs, other opportunities. At the same time, communications between the Highlands and the south were improving; and the effect was the same. The pull of the south, and of the American colonies, became increasingly felt, and increasingly effective, in the 1750s and 1760s.

Perhaps the earliest public reference to emigration from the Highlands appeared in the *Scots Magazine* in the summer of 1771.

'We are informed from the western isles, that upwards of 500 souls from Islay, and the adjacent islands, prepare to migrate next summer to America, under the conduct of a gentleman of wealth and merit . . . and that there is a large colony of the most wealthy and substantial people in Sky, making ready to [go] to the fertile and cheap lands on the other side of the Atlantic ocean.'[65]

In the autumn it was reported that 370 persons had left Skye 'in order to settle in North Carolina'.[66] A year later 'forty-eight families of poor people from Sutherland arrived at Edinburgh, on their way to Greenock, in order to imbark for North America';[67] and in August there was another departure for North Carolina, the *Adventure* sailing from Loch Erribol with 200 passengers; and it was at the same time stated that emigration from the Highlands had been going on 'since the year 1768'.[68] From this time onwards, emigration—to the south, to Ireland, most spectacularly to North America—was probably continuous. There is no systematic record of it, and such numbers as are sometimes quoted are quite untrustworthy, certainly for the earlier decades. We shall never know. Even if total numbers were available, they would tell us little, unless broken down by districts, or at least sub-regions. And the significance even of aggregate figures would not be clear without accurate information about the size and distribution of the highland population. And even here, there are problems.

How many people were living in the Highlands by the middle of the eighteenth century cannot be stated with any confidence. According to Alexander Webster's invaluable 'Account of the Number of People in Scotland in the Year 1755', the total population of the country was 1·25 million, and the population of the six highland counties was 337,000, made up as follows:

Argyll	66,286	Perth	120,116
Caithness	22,215	Ross and Cromarty	48,084
Inverness	59,563	Sutherland	20,774

It is usually thought that Webster's figures are if anything on the low side, especially as regards the remoter highland parishes where the ministers themselves—upon whom Webster relied—could not easily know how many were living in a parish of, say, 100 square miles with no roads worth mentioning, and who were probably particularly badly informed about the numbers of those in the parish who did not belong to the Kirk. Nevertheless, it is not unreasonable to accept Webster's 'Account' as the basis for calculation.[69] But for present purposes the figure of 337,000 has to be reduced. In the six counties there are numerous parishes which could not be reckoned as highland in any reasonable sense even in the eighteenth century; parishes practising a lowland style of agriculture and, because of their location, integrated into the lowland economy. The eastern and southern fringes of the county of Perth, for example, have to be subtracted, and also one or two parishes close to Inverness. At a conservative estimate, excluding in this way only eighteen parishes out of the total of one hundred and ninety eight, the figure for highland population around 1750 falls to about 300,000.

No independent check on this figure seems possible, but it is worth noticing how the question is treated in Walker's *Economical History of the Hebrides*. Walker made six journeys through the Highlands between 1760 and 1786, partly 'to enquire into the state of religion in the Highland countries' on behalf of the General Assembly of the Church of Scotland, and partly to enquire into economic problems, including the problem of population, for the Commissioners for the Forfeited Estates. Walker's two volumes provide an exceptionally thorough and careful account of the Highlands in his day. Besides quoting Webster's figures, Walker provides for the islands figures which, he says, 'seem to have been taken about, or within a few years before, the year 1750'.[70] Sometimes these figures and Webster's figures are identical; occasionally they are above Webster's figures; more often they are below. The totals are 49,485 for the 'Church Record' of 1750, 52,200 for Webster. It seems quite likely that Webster's figures are a correction and possibly an up-dating of the earlier set. More interesting is Walker's treatment of the mainland parishes. His method is to list the one hundred and thirty parishes 'in which the Gaelic language is either preached or spoken by the natives', and using Webster's figures this gives a total of 237,598.[71] Adding the islands and the mainland together we get a total of 290,198. This is slightly less than the figures in the preceding paragraph owing to the fact that Walker includes fewer mainland parishes; but his assessment of which parishes were and which were not Gaelic-speaking presumably relates to a period later than 1750 (his book was published in 1808), and this would make some difference, for Gaelic was steadily being replaced by English in the second half of the eighteenth century. A figure of 300,000 for the Highlands about 1750 thus seems reasonable, or about one quarter of the total population of Scotland.

Relative to this population, it is quite clear that the numbers emigrating in the 1760s and '70s were very small. But they were not to remain small—all the later history of the Highlands is dominated by the fact of emigration—and from the very beginning contemporaries were worried: 'It is to be dreaded that these migrations will prove hurtful to the mother-country; and therefore its friends ought to use every proper method to prevent them.'[72] But no effective steps can be taken to remedy an evil the causes of which are not understood. The preliminary question therefore arose, what was the cause of emigration from the Highlands?

Much has been written on this subject and there is little agreement. It is clear only that there was no single cause; there were causes—the spread of sheep-farming, a rise in rents, changing social status and economic ambitions, growing pressure on resources. All these are to be mentioned, but not all were equally important, or of the same importance in different areas. As early as 1772 it was stated that 'opulent graziers' in Sutherland were 'ingrassing the farms, and turning them into pasture'.[73] This happened; but in the 1770s sheep-farming was much more important in Perthshire than in Sutherland, and even in Perthshire was far from dominant—on Lochtayside, in 1769, where the sheep : cattle ratio was almost exactly 1 to 4, there was seemingly no great pressure to extend the area under cattle or sheep. However important sheep became later in reducing the population, they were not of widespread importance in the early 1770s. Higher rents, to which the spread of sheep-farming doubtless contributed, were another factor that is hard to assess. Allegations were made that rents had been 'doubled and trebled',[74] and that people 'long out of all habit of industry'[75] were unable to adjust their operations so as to meet the new demands: 'The rage of raising rents . . . begins to depopulate the country.'[76] But again there is very little evidence of a direct cause and effect connection, and what seems more likely is that altered social relations had as much to do with the matter as altered rents. Tenants who had worked and starved for a clan chief were unwilling to do the same for a landlord. It was less a matter of inability to pay raised rents than of unwillingness to work in a merely commercial context for chieftains or tacksmen who had grown alien or absentee, their attitudes and pleasures increasingly founded on the social life of Edinburgh or London. Money was taking the place of men as the object of accumulation. Chiefs pressed upon their tacksmen or got rid of them altogether; tacksmen, like Robert Gordon of Achness, oppressed their subtenants, 'most of whom on that account emigrated last year to America.'[77]

Some of this emigration had the appearance of necessity. Population was certainly rising between 1750 and the early 1770s,[78] and there was starvation in Sutherland, and perhaps more generally in the Highlands, in 1772. This, coupled with what one factor called 'dreams about America',[79] fed the stream of emigration:

> 'Numbers of the miserables of this country were now migrating: they wandered in a state of desperation; too poor to pay, they madly sell themselves for their passage, preferring a temporary bondage in a strange land, to starving for life in their native soil.'[80]

Matters were made worse by a fall in the price of cattle. As the payment of most money rents depended on the sale of cattle to the drovers, the inevitable result was an accumulation of arrears of rent, causing further difficulties for tenants and landlords alike. By the summer of 1772 it was reported that 'the Spirit of Emigration spreads like a Contagion over Ross and Caithness'.[81]

Yet although many may have been driven to emigration by necessity, contemporaries repeatedly noticed that men of means were involved as well: 'the people who have emigrated . . . have carried with them at least ten thousand pounds in specie.'[82] 'Several of them are people of property. . . .'[83] This is not difficult to explain. The organisers, leaders and financiers of emigration were in some cases, probably in many cases, tacksmen. Economic change in the Highlands was working against the tacksmen as much as against the tenants. Farms were now let to the highest bidder; chiefs saw that the services of tacksmen might in some cases be dispensed with; the privileges of subordinate chieftainship were almost a thing of the past. Tacksmen could respond in two ways: compete on equal terms and become commercial farmers, in which case they might well be willing to buy the stock of unsuccessful tenants who were thus put in funds for a departure to the south, or America; or disengage themselves from a system which had changed, in their view, very much for the worse, and depart, quite possibly taking tenants with them to work as farmers in a new community organised on traditional lines on the other side of the Atlantic.[84] Whichever of these courses tacksmen followed, they promoted emigration.

The movement, if such it can be called, was slowed if not halted by the outbreak of war in 1775. It is doubtful if many people had by that date left the Highlands. But strong feelings were aroused. Some said that emigration would leave the country depopulated, barren and defenceless, others that it got rid of 'the idle part of the lowest class . . . who have been (especially after a bad harvest) a dead weight on the tenant, who has been obliged to purchase meal for the maintenance of many such incumbents on his tenement, almost to his total ruin.'[85] Some said that North America offered liberty and plenty, others that emigration to America was organised solely for the benefit of the organisers, that the hopes of the emigrants were pure delusion, and that 'those who shall drub the American Agents, deserve the thanks and good will of all the Country'.[86] Population was not a subject which the eighteenth century took lightly. It was also deeply interested in agricultural improvement. And for twenty years a good deal of thought, effort and money had been devoted to 'civilising' the Highlands. Loss of population would have attracted notice in any circumstances. When it occurred in the wild but not to be neglected Highlands, and in conjunction with sustained efforts at improvement made by enlightened men, it was a problem, a portent and a challenge. Politicians and pamphleteers, critics and economists alike were anxious to understand this strange and serious phenomenon. The debate on economic policy, more lively in the 1760s and 1770s than ever before, was given a fresh intensity with the emergence of the highland problem.

3

Aims and Principles of
Economic Policy

When he cast about for an example of a market so limited that the division of labour could scarcely be practised in it, Adam Smith selected the Highlands of Scotland: 'In the lone houses and very small villages which are scattered about in so desert a country as the Highlands of Scotland, every farmer must be butcher, baker and brewer for his own family'.[1] In discussing the effects of poverty on marriage and the growth of population, Smith again exemplified his argument by reference to the Highlands:

'A half-starved Highland woman frequently bears more than twenty children, while a pampered fine lady is often incapable of bearing any. . . . But poverty, though it does not prevent the generation, is extremely unfavourable to the rearing of children. . . . It is not uncommon, I have been frequently told, in the Highlands of Scotland for a mother who has borne twenty children not to have two alive.'[2]

Thus the Highlands were recognised in the eighteenth century—and not only by Adam Smith—as a region of poverty.

Strenuous efforts were made to change the economic situation in the Highlands in the decades before and after 1800, and it is natural to suppose that the intention was, in the first place, to reduce poverty. But this would be to attribute motives and scales of value to the eighteenth century which are inappropriate. Those who observed the situation in the Highlands and who sought to alter it were guided in what they did, and in what they tried to achieve, by the political and economic ideas which were current at the time. If we are to understand their policies, we must know not only how these men acted, but why they acted as they did.

Writers on economics before 1800 discussed a wider range of questions than modern economists. Thus Davenant, in his *Discourses on the Public Revenues* thought it proper to emphasise that welfare was founded upon morality:

'The Welfare of all countries in the World, depends upon the Morals of their People.

For tho' a Nation may gather Riches by Trade, Thrift, Industry, and from the Benefit of its Soil and Situation; and tho' a People may attain to great Wealth and Power, either by Force of Arms, or by the Sagacity of their Councils; yet, when their Manners are deprav'd, they will decline insensibly, and at last come to utter Distruction.

When a Country is grown vitious, Industry decays, the People become effeminate and unfit for Labour. To maintain Luxury, the Great Ones must oppress the Meaner Sort; and to avoid Oppression, the Meaner Sort are often compell'd to Seditious Tumults, or open Rebellion.'[3]

The moral, economic and political aspects of the social situation were thus viewed together. And this was not merely because these writers had not yet achieved an intellectual division of labour, assigning moral problems to the philosopher, economic problems to the economist, and political problems to the political scientist, but because they viewed society, and the welfare of society, in a unified way.

Nowadays, we tend to assume that economic growth is one of the main objectives of a rational economic policy, perhaps the main objective; that economic growth is possible for as far into the future as need concern us; and that it consists of raising the capacity of the population per head to dispose of goods and services. But the eighteenth century did not think of its economic plans for the future in this way. In particular, writers on economic questions before Adam Smith, almost without exception, thought of welfare and progress primarily in terms of the welfare and progress of the nation or state; that is to say, of society as a whole. They were not concerned about the welfare of individuals except in the sense that society was made up of individuals. It is almost impossible today to state this point of view clearly and simply because the very words 'individual' and 'society' have for us a meaning, a significance which is slightly different from what they had in the seventeenth and eighteenth centuries. For us, the individual is always at the centre of the picture; his rights and happiness, if not absolute, are certainly primary. The eighteenth century looked at things the other way round. They were much less concerned with the welfare of the individual, and much more with that of society as a whole. Their discussion of the provision of employment illustrates this point. Time and again it is stated to be one of the duties of government to provide employment. This looks modern, until one realises that the purpose was not so much to help the unemployed as to benefit the nation. The poor, Child complained, 'remain in a languishing, nasty, and useless condition, uncomfortable to themselves, and unprofitable to the Kingdom, this is confessed and lamented by all men.'[4] Davenant likewise thought unemployment 'a defect in our constitution', for the following reason:

'If all hands in the Kingdom that are able were employ'd in useful Labour, our Manufactures would be so increas'd that the Commonwealth would be thereby greatly enriched and the Poor . . . would be a benefit to the Kingdom.'[5]

Employment was not a right, it was a duty. To these writers, social relations, properly arranged, were not only productive of individual happiness; they were also good in themselves, and productive of a higher good. The problem was to guide or direct the interactions of individuals so as to create a pattern and degree of social welfare which was valuable over and above the sum of the welfare enjoyed by individuals, considered in isolation.

This non-individualist way of thinking sprang to some extent from a pre-utilitarian philosophical position, and was in harmony with important aspects of the thought of writers as diverse as Hobbes and Shaftesbury. But it is equally understandable as a response to the circumstances of the times. Before 1750, men thought of the welfare of the nation rather than of the welfare of the individuals within it because of the dangerous international situation in which they were placed. Theirs was a world in which all matters economic and political were arranged to meet the fact that 'warres may chance'. Their thinking and their policy were governed by the knowledge that they were living in independent nation-states afraid of their neighbours. These states had been painfully created out of a world of fragmentation and poverty, and the men who lived in them were prepared to sacrifice a great deal in the pursuit of national unification, economic and political power. It was their policies which Adam Smith contemptuously described as the 'mean and malignant expedients of the mercantile system'.[6]

Unity and power were required in the first place for self-defence, and in the second place for attacking others. But they were also needed because of a widespread opinion that trade, like wealth, is not something to be created but something to be found. Behind the arguments and convictions of writers like Mun and Davenant, Child, Pollexfen, Sir Dudley North and dozens of others, there is an idea, ill-defined and sometimes partially contradicted, of an economic world without growth. Output per man, like output per acre, could not be raised. Exchange, although it could in principle be mutually profitable, seldom was so. Hence, trade and wealth could be increased only by seizure from another, by peaceful means or by force. From this there follows Colbertism, the old colonial system, and the perpetual commercial wars of the later seventeenth century and the eighteenth century. These were all attempts at securing something at the expense of someone else. The aim of policy was possession, and the aim of trade was monopoly.

Thus political power was the determining factor in human affairs, not the free play of markets. The political ambitions of princes required wealth, and wealth itself was to be gained largely through the exercise of political power. Therefore, economic activity was or ought to be in the service of the state:

'Trade and Manufactures are the instruments by which kingdoms arrive at power and consequence; by which individuals arrive at wealth and independence. They enable us to keep up fleets and armies, equal, if not superior to any power in Europe; by which we check the insolence and humble the pride of our natural or avowed enemies.'[7]

Hence the eighteenth century's enthusiasm for 'subscribing liberally towards the support' of new enterprises: 'every individual seems to vie with his neighbour who shall best promote the happiness and welfare of his country. This is public spirit; this is real patriotism. . . .'[8] Politics, morals and economics were a single field of thought and action, and the happiness of individuals was subordinate to the nation's needs.

Such opinions were still very much to the fore in the 1770s. Naturally, different writers wrote with a different emphasis, and there was, on the whole, a gradual move away from attributing value to the welfare of the state almost independently of the welfare of the citizens who composed that state. Hume was among the first to incline to what we would call a 'rational' or 'modern' view, putting more emphasis on the individual's standard of living (and therefore on the distribution of income), distinguishing more sharply between strictly economic and other considerations, and casting doubt on the wisdom of any policy 'which aggrandises the public by the poverty of individuals'.[9] But Hume, although he strongly influenced did not dominate opinion. In 1777 James Anderson, in the Preface to his *Observations on the Means of Exciting a Spirit of National Industry*, provided an unusually thoughtful, comprehensive, and explicit statement of the aims of policy, a statement basically traditional in its outlook, but modified by 'enlightened' views on the importance of individual liberty. Paradoxically, his book was published one year later than the *Wealth of Nations*, in which Adam Smith had set the current of thought on a new course and, in effect, changed everything by adopting a wholly egoistic and utilitarian approach as the basis for economic debate.

It is chiefly Anderson's attitude to man and society which makes his work significant, coupled with the fact that he played a prominent part in the subsequent debate on highland policy. He approaches the problem of economic development in a typical eighteenth-century way by analysing 'the progress of Civil Society' by means of 'a retrospective survey of the changes that have taken place in Europe'[10] in respect of social ambitions and ideals. Anderson's general line is that when in the course of time the British constitution was secured upon the broad and stable base of universal liberty, then security of property was assured—'every man could sit under the shade of his own fig-tree, and eat the fruit of his own vine'. But the result of this was that men 'forgetting the care of *defending*, became only studious to *enjoy*.' This meant that self became the object of attention (neighbours are viewed 'in the disgusting light of *rivals*') and money, which indirectly enables man to satisfy most of his wants, 'becomes universally prized as the highest good on earth'. Thus the social affections give way to the selfish.

Anderson goes on to admit that 'all mankind wish to attain happiness'. But man by himself is helpless. He becomes rich and powerful only through co-operation in society. If he tries to ignore others, he will not only be poor, he will also be miserable:

'Happiness, the great object of his wishes, perpetually eludes his grasp; and he feels, that in the possession of *millions* no enjoyment affords un-mixed delight'.

Everyone wants happiness; but 'disinterested beneficence is the only pos-sible mean [sic] of attaining it'.

This is partly a call to his fellow-countrymen to give active support to Anderson's own schemes for national improvement; a typical old-fashioned appeal to patriotism. But the Preface also includes a restatement in a general way of the accepted view of the overall purposes of economic policy. And at the same time it indicates several important factors which were believed at the time to promote 'progress' or 'improvement'. For one thing, it emphasises that social welfare involves order and liberty. This was always regarded as fundamental, and it was seldom taken for granted.

There is also the point that the development of 'industry' (the word was used in a very wide sense) and orderly government are mutually support-ing. Neither one could be expected to prosper in the absence of the other. This was put very clearly by Hume:

'This industry is much promoted by the knowledge inseparable from ages of art and refinement; as, on the other hand, this knowledge enables the public to make the best advantage of the industry of its subjects. Laws, order, police, discipline; these can never be carried to any degree of perfection, before human reason has refined itself by exercise, and by an application to the more vulgar arts, at least, of commerce and manu-facture. Can we expect, that a government will be well modelled by a people, who know not how to make a spinning-wheel, or to employ a loom to advantage?'[11]

Liberty and personal independence were likewise recognised—increasingly in the later decades of the century—as being both valuable and useful, and the knowledge that these could affect economic developments, and be affected by them, was not lost sight of.

Given that economic change had thus to take its place and be valued along with many other changes, what significance did these writers attach to our basic notion of a rising standard of living? The answer is 'not much', because they usually took the view that it was undesirable that the standard of living of the mass of the people should rise.

There were at least two reasons for this. One was the widespread idea
that most men naturally prefer idleness to work. Picturesquely stated by
Arthur Young—'Every one but an idiot knows that the lower classes must
be kept poor or they will never be industrious'—this important opinion
was stated almost as an axiom by the great majority of writers on economic
problems from Petty onwards.

> 'It is observed by Clothiers, and others, who employ great numbers of
> poor people, that when Corn is extremely plentiful, that the Labour of
> the poor is proportionably dear: And scarce to be had at all (so licentious
> are they who labour only to eat, or rather to drink)'.[12]

The same was said by Child ('the most widely read of seventeenth-century
English economic writers'),[13] by Pollexfen: 'the advance of wages hath
proved an incentive to idleness',[14] by Farquier: 'if the price of labour in any
country is so great that the poor by working part of the week, can maintain themselves and family the whole week, 't is an evil to that country',[15]
by Tucker: 'if the price of labour is continually beat down, it is greatly for
the public good',[16] by North, Fielding, Townsend and many others. This
is the well-known 'doctrine of the utility of poverty' as Furniss called
it;[17] and although it is possible to quote eighteenth-century writers who
denied that men were motivated in such a way,[18] and others who argued
that the response to low prices (or high wages) would not be the same in
the long run as it appeared to be in the short,[19] nevertheless much the
commonest opinion was that 'men will not labour while they have the
means of idleness in their power.'[20] Wealth and greatness required that
the poor be industrious; therefore a rising standard of living for the mass
of the people could not be desirable.

The second reason for remaining satisfied with a generally low standard
of living was acceptance of the balance-of-trade theory of national wealth.
As Sir William Mildmay put it in 1765:

> 'Trade takes its rise from numbers of people employed in cultivating and
> improving the first production of nature for common use and conven-
> iency; from whence all nations, according to their skill and industry and
> the different effects of their soil and climate, endeavour to support their
> own interest by mutually supplying each other with what the one wants
> and the other has in too great abundance; and when the value of what is
> exported and sold abroad is greater than the value of what is imported
> and consumed at home, the difference upon the balance must be returned
> in money, the circulation of which, and the employment of the people,
> conjointly compose the national wealth of every country.'[21]

If it was accepted that the national wealth was made up in this way, it
became a matter of importance to maintain as far as possible the competitive strength of domestic production. The main way to do this, it was

thought, was to keep down wages. The naïve view that the international competitiveness of goods exported was principally or solely determined by the wage-cost of production at home was extremely common in the seventeenth and eighteenth centuries. Writing of Ireland, Davenant put the argument as crudely as possible:

"'T is an undeniable truth that the common provision of life is one half cheaper there than here. 'T is likewise as plain . . . these advantages of living must enable them to afford the same commodity cheaper than we can do'.[22]

Child said the same:

'Our fuel and victual is cheaper in remote parts from London and consequently our manufactures can do work cheaper than the Dutch'.[23]

These statements imply both a wages theory of value and a subsistence theory of wages. Cary made the latter explicit when he wrote:

'Nor can the people of England live on such low wages as they do in other countries; for we must consider that wages bear a rate in all countries according to the price of provisions.'[24]

This was the common view, although few writers seem to have believed that wages were always at subsistence level, or that in no circumstances should anything be done to raise the standard of living of working people. On these points, as on so many others, there was neither perfect clarity nor perfect consistency.[25]

This belief in the desirability of low, possibly of subsistence wages, coupled no doubt with very limited expectations of ever being able to increase output per head, as well as with the indifference bred of long familiarity with poverty, prevented most writers from wasting much time on sympathising with the poor. It is only in the occasional passage that the relief of poverty is presented as an aim of major importance, one to be pursued for its own sake; and these passages are almost all to be found in the later authors. Thus Anderson wrote with sympathy of 'the lower class of people [in north and west Scotland] . . . so abject in their behaviour, so mean in their apparel, so dejected and melancholy in appearance, and so thin and emaciated in their looks,'[26] and declared his anxiety, at the start of his *Observations on . . . National Industry*, to discover the causes of 'the numberless nameless hardships they have to struggle with; which so powerfully tend to repress every active exertion of the mind, and to produce that sorrowful melancholy appearance for which they are so remarkable.'[27] Similarly Knox, in his *View of the British Empire*, emphasised

'the hard lot of the great body of the people who inhabit a fifth part of our island . . . cut off, during most part of the year, by impassable mountains, and impracticable navigations, from the seats of commerce, industry, and plenty. . . . Upon the whole, the Highlands of Scotland, some few estates excepted, are the seats of oppression, poverty, famine, anguish, and wild despair, exciting the pity of every traveller, while the virtues of the inhabitants attract his admiration.'[28]

Both these writers were concerned with a specific problem, namely, the lack of development in the Highlands, and it is always harder to withhold sympathy in a particular case than to be unsympathetic in general on grounds of principle. Hume was exceptional in urging that feelings of humanity should not be overborne by commercial principles, although he acknowledged the truth of those in vogue, at least up to a point:

'It is true, the English feel some disadvantages in foreign trade by the high price of labour, which is in part the effect of the riches of their artisans, as of the plenty of money: But as foreign trade is not the most material circumstance, it is not to be put in competition with the happiness of so many millions.'[29]

This, however, was very advanced thinking for the eighteenth century. The general view was that the mass of the people were poor and would remain so. Development, or progress, was simply not envisaged in terms of a general raising of the standard of living.

But if writers of the seventeenth and eighteenth centuries hardly ever spoke about raising the standard of living, they hardly ever refrained from mentioning population and the growth of population. With astonishing unanimity, they were in favour of a large population. Numberless examples of this view could be produced, but two quotations, almost a century apart, will suffice. In 1699 Davenant wrote as follows:

'The people being the first matter of power and wealth, by whose labour and industry the nation must be the gainers in the balance, their increase or decrease must be carefully observed by the government that designs to thrive; that is, their increase must be promoted by good conduct and wholesome laws, and if they have been decreased by war or by any other accident, the breach is to be made up as soon as possible, for it is a maim to the body politic affecting all its parts.'[30]

Anderson, in 1777, said the same:

'For if it be allowed, that the numbers of people constitute the real strength of every state, it will be acknowledged, that that strength can only be augmented by such means as tend to promote the vigour and energy, the happiness, and consequent fecundity of these people. Every aim of sound policy therefore ought to be directed towards that end.'[31]

But why, the reader is bound to ask, are people 'the real strength of every state', why are they 'the first matter of power and wealth'? Is it only because 'plenty of people must also cause cheapness of wages; which will cause cheapness of manufacture'?[32] Or is this another metaphysical assertion, another aspect of the glorification of the state as something above and beyond the sum of those composing it?

To some extent it is, for it regards people as a means to some national end. It was the 'great quantity of People' in Holland, according to Sir William Temple, who 'make their Greatness and Riches'.[33] This idea of 'Greatness' is to be found in all writers before Adam Smith. Few defined it, but it is clear enough that what they meant was a combination of wealth and political power. These went together then as now. Temple himself put the matter as clearly as anyone in the seventeenth century at the very start of his book; he wrote, he explained, because he had

'lately seen the state of the United Provinces, after a prodigious growth in Riches, Beauty, extent of Commerce, and number of Inhabitants, arrived at length to such a height, (by the strength of their Navies, their fortified Towns, and standing-Forces, with a constant Revenue, proportion'd to the support of all this Greatness,) as made them the Envy of some, the Fear of others, and the Wonder of all their neighbours.'[34]

It is a compendious idea, in which the number of inhabitants is both an element in and a support of the 'greatness' of the state. The search for safety and security needed men, as much in the later eighteenth century as in the early seventeenth: 'a powerful, well-appointed fleet, and a proportionate number of men, always in readiness, will ever be necessary, both in peace and war.'[35] But men were also a source of wealth; the greater the population, the wealthier the state. It was declared to be self-evident

'that most Nations in the civilised Parts of the World, are more or less rich or poor, proportionably to the paucity or plenty of their people . . . The seven united Provinces are certainly the most populous tract of land in Christendom, and for their bigness, undoubtedly the richest . . . England . . . I hope is yet a more populous Country that France, and consequently richer.'[36]

Child was content to support this proposition with an appeal to what he called 'matter of fact'. Some writers were a little more subtle. Mun, for example, took notice of the fact that technology, as well as population, must have something to do with the 'strength and riches of both king and kingdom; for where the people are many and the arts good, there the traffic will be great and the country rich'.[37] To bring 'the arts' into it was at any rate an improvement. But most writers were content to assume—understandably enough, considering the circumstances of the times—an unchanging technology, and few offered much of an explanation of how technology and population produced power and riches.

Yet the mechanism of economic development did not lie entirely unexplored until the publication of the *Wealth of Nations*. The idea that there is a dynamic connection between the growth of population and something at any rate similar to what we would call economic growth—changes, that is to say, in the complexity as well as in the volume of production—seems first to have been developed in a systematic way by Sir William Temple in his *Observations upon the United Provinces of the Netherlands*. This small book was published in 1673 'to give some account of the Rise and Progress of this Commonwealth, the Causes of their Greatness, And the steps towards their Fall'.[38] The arrangement of Temple's book is itself significant. He starts with a long historical chapter which traces the progress of the Low Countries from before Charlemagne; this is by far the longest chapter in the book. It is followed by chapters on government, geography, 'People and Dispositions', religion, and then trade. Discussion of the specifically economic factors is thus founded on prior consideration of matters which Temple clearly regarded as of more fundamental importance—factors, moreover, which he was not prepared to take for granted. This is on the whole very much the sort of approach which one would expect from a seventeenth-century writer, although he is unusual—at any rate for a writer on economic questions—in finding in the political history of the country so much that he deemed essential for an understanding of the current situation, stressing particularly the advantages of a prolonged struggle for survival ('no State was ever born with stronger Throws, or nurst up with harder fare, or inur'd to greater Labours or Dangers in the whole course of its Youth')[39], and of responsible and efficient government.[40]

Having outlined the political and social scene, Temple sets out in the sixth chapter to explain how it is that a small country, almost devoid of harbours, having scarcely 'any thing properly of their own growth, that is considerable either for their own necessary use, or for Traffick with their Neighbours, besides Butter, Cheese, and Earthen Wares',[41] could become a great and prosperous trading nation. The problem is stated in the same terms as by Petty, and Temple's general answer—that Dutch success depends on shipping, on close attention to demand in foreign markets, and on manufacture based on imported goods and raw materials—is also the same as Petty's. But it is in offering a systematic and general explanation of the process of economic development that Temple is, at this stage in the history of thought, unique:

'I conceive the true original and ground of Trade, to be, great multitude of people crowded into small compass of Land, whereby all things necessary to life become dear, and all Men, who have possessions, are induced to Parsimony; but those who have none, are forced to industry and labour, or else to want. Bodies that are vigorous, fall to labour; Such as are not, supply that defect by some sort of Inventions or Ingenuity. These Customs arise first from Necessity, but encrease by Imitation, and grow in time to be habitual in a Country; And wherever they are so, if it lies upon the Sea, they naturally break out into Trade, both because, whatever they want of their own, that is necessary to so many Mens Lives, must be supply'd from abroad; and because, by the multitude of people, and smalness of Country, Land grows so dear, that the Improvement of Money, that way, is inconsiderable, and so turns to Sea, where the greatness of the Profit makes amends for the Venture.

This cannot be better illustrated, than by its contrary, which appears no where more than in *Ireland*; Where, by the largeness and plenty of the Soil, and scarcity of People, all things necessary to Life are so cheap, that an industrious Man, by two days labour, may gain enough to feed him the rest of the week; Which I take to be a very plain ground of the laziness attributed to the People: For Men naturally prefer Ease before Labour, and will not take pains, if they can live idle; though, when, by necessity, they have been inured to it, they cannot leave it, being grown a custom necessary to their Health, and to their very Entertainment: Nor perhaps is the change harder, from constant Ease to Labour, than from constant Labour to Ease.'[42]

This passage, and indeed the whole of the chapter in which it occurs, surely has a good claim to be regarded as one of the earliest tolerably complete statements of how economic growth may take place.

The argument that Temple puts forward raises the historically antecedent question, if 'great multitude of people crowded into small compass of Land' is the cause of prosperity, what causes density of population in the first place? Or as Temple himself puts it, 'the best account that can be given of [Dutch trade], will be, by considering the Causes and Accidents, that have served to force or invite so vast a confluence of People into their Country.'[43] His answer is, that war, religious persecution and other oppression outside Holland 'served to encrease the swarm in this Country, not only by such as were persecuted at home, but by great numbers of peaceable Men, who came here to seek for quiet in their Lives, and safety in their Possessions or Trades.'[44] At the same time he emphasises that Holland offered many positive attractions to immigrants: the safety of their towns, the liberty which could be enjoyed under their constitution, the excellence of their banking system, 'the Wisdom and Conduct of their State . . . that could not be shaken by any common Accidents',[45] and finally 'the great Beauty of their Country (forced in time, and by the improvements of Industry, in speight of Nature) which draws every day such numbers of curious and idle persons to see their Provinces, though not to inhabit them.'[46] Temple thus anticipates the modern approach to migration problems by analysing both the 'push' and the 'pull' factors. He goes on to enumerate many aspects of economic policy which he considers important— 'lowness of their Customs, and easiness of paying them', for example—

but soon returns to his main theme, namely, that the progress of the United Provinces can be understood only in terms of 'a great concurrence of Circumstances, a long course of Time, force of Orders and Method.'[47]

This brief but brilliant analysis of the Dutch achievement could be dismissed as of no significance for the history of economic ideas or the evolution of public policy, were it not that the ideas which Temple put forward were developed and added to by Hume and then restated in an expanded form by Sir James Steuart.

Hume's view of economic development is rooted in his view of human nature. 'Human happiness', he wrote, '. . . seems to consist in three ingredients; action, pleasure, and indolence'.[48] But he also believed that 'Avarice, or the desire of gain, is an universal passion, which operates at all times, in all places, and upon all persons.'[49] Although having some sympathy with the cruder view that only necessity makes men work—in several editions of his *Essays* he included a statement of it, without actually endorsing it[50]—Hume is far more subtle and sympathetic in his approach. According to him, people do not wholly dislike work (because it is action, a source of happiness) and, being avaricious, are not wholly indifferent to increases of income. Moreover, 'lucrative employment' offers a unique attraction which becomes stronger the more it is experienced:

> 'Give him a more harmless way of employing his mind or body, he is satisfied, and feels no longer that insatiable thirst after pleasure. But if the employment you give him be lucrative, especially if the profit be attached to every particular exertion of industry, he has gain so often in his eye, that he acquires, by degrees, a passion for it, and knows no such pleasure as that of seeing the daily encrease of his fortune.'[51]

Here Hume is depicting the emergence of commercially-minded man; not the simple peasant with his limited horizons and attachment to an established routine and scale of living, but a person trained to labour and motivated by commercial ambition. Probably he observed the spread of these habits and ambitions in the England, Scotland and France of his day; just as Sir William Temple had observed and commented upon them in seventeenth-century Holland[52]:

Having a view of human behaviour similar to Sir William Temple's, it is not surprising to find that Hume refers with approval to Temple's views on economic development. He notes that Temple 'ascribes the industry of the Dutch entirely to necessity, proceeding from their natural disadvantages', and then quotes the 'striking comparison' which Temple makes between Holland and Ireland.[53] In another essay Hume writes; 'Multitudes of people, necessity and liberty, have begotten commerce in Holland'[54]—an obvious restatement of Temple's analysis. In other places, not referring to

Holland, he adopts the general proposition that natural disadvantages are favourable to economic development. In the tropics, for example, 'warmth and equality of weather' make clothes and houses 'less requisite . . . and thereby remove, in part, that necessity, which is the great spur to industry and invention.'[55] In France, Italy and Spain 'the superior riches of the soil and happiness of the climate' contribute to 'the poverty of the common people'; in England, on the other hand, where 'the land is rich, but coarse; must be cultivated at a great expense; and produces slender crops, when not carefully managed, and by a method which gives not the full profit but in a course of several years', men look for, and achieve, 'profits proportionable to their expense and hazard'.[56] In other ways, too, Hume's views are reminiscent of Sir William Temple's;[57] and it is surely significant that Temple is the only English writer on economic matters whom Hume quotes in all his eleven economic essays.[58]

But of course Hume does much more than repeat ideas previously put forward. The originality of his contribution lies partly in his method of analysis, which is general in the sense that it relates not to a particular economy but to a typical, imaginary economy—the 'bulk of every state'; and lies partly in the novel and important ideas which he puts forward of a two-sector economy, the work force being thought of as divided into husbandmen and manufacturers on the one hand, and 'superflous hands' on the other. The argument runs as follows.[59] As soon as men 'quit their savage state' they are occupied either as husbandmen or as agriculturalists, principally the latter. As agricultural technology improves, it becomes possible to maintain an output sufficient to support the population at a modest level of consumption without employing the whole of the available labour force. Those not employed are the 'superflous hands'. For them there are three possibilities. They can be employed in fleets and armies; or they can remain idle; or they can use and develop their skill and industry so as to produce 'superfluities', the production and exchange of which will constitute a rise in the community's standard of living. These superfluities are luxuries, and the superflous hands are therefore engaged in 'the arts of luxury'. But this is not to be lamented, because—and this is what Hume is chiefly concerned to show—the superflous hands, when employed in manufactures of this kind, 'encrease the power of the state only as they store up so much labour, and that of a kind to which the public may lay claim, without depriving anyone of the necessaries of life'[60]—that is to say, the nation's productive capacity over and above the maintenance of a basic standard of living is an important form of wealth because it can be utilised, when occasion arises, for 'the public service'. But the point is also made that economic development—the growth of productive capacity—depends on the cultivation of 'manufactures and mechanic arts' which will produce

goods to be exchanged against the surplus of foodstuffs that the husbandmen are capable of producing but which, if there are no 'luxury' items against
which this agricultural surplus can be exchanged, will not actually be produced. The purpose of the argument is to defend luxury, to show that 'the
greatness of the sovereign and the happiness of the state are, in a great
measure, united with regard to trade and manufactures'. But it involves an
analysis of how luxury is possible, and how economic development pro-
motes further development:

> 'When a nation abounds in manufactures and mechanic arts, the pro-
> prietors of land, as well as the farmers, study agriculture as a science, and
> redouble their industry and attention. The superfluity, which arises from
> their labour, is not lost; but is exchanged with manufactures for those
> commodities, which men's luxury now makes them covet.'[61]

It certainly is a dynamic system, although it is put forward almost casually
and with that Baconian economy of language which is characteristic of
Hume's writing and which makes it easy to miss the significance of what is
being said.[62]

Briefly stated as it was, Hume's 'model' was not lost sight of, but was re-
produced at length a few years later by one of the most verbose and awk-
ward writers in the history of economic thought: Sir James Steuart.
Steuart begins by considering what would happen to population growth
if there were no agricultural improvement, and produces a straightforward
Malthusian answer:

> 'The generative faculty resembles a spring loaded with a weight, which
> always exerts itself in proportion to the diminution of resistance: when
> food has remained some time without augmentation or diminution,
> generation will carry numbers as high as possible; if then food come to be
> diminished, the spring is over-powered; the force of it becomes less than
> nothing. Inhabitants will diminish, at least, in proportion to the over-
> charge. If, upon the other hand, food be increased, the spring which
> stood as O, will begin to exert itself in proportion as resistance dimini-
> shes; people will begin to be better fed; they will multiply, and, in
> proportion as they increase in numbers, the food will become scarce
> again.'[63]

But suppose that man decides 'to add his labour and industry to the natural
activity of the soil'? Steuart sets off to answer this question by adopting
Hume's two-sector model. He points out that the additional food, except
for a small initial amount, will have to be exchanged 'so as to relieve the
wants of the most necessitous' if it is to continue to be produced:

> 'Otherwise, the plenty produced, remaining in the hands of those who
> produced it, will become to them an absolute superfluity; which, had
> they any trade with a neighbouring state, they would sell, or exchange,

and leave their fellow-citizens to starve. And as we suppose no trade at all, this superfluity will perish like their cherries, in a year of plenty; and consequently the farmers will immediately give over working.'[64]

It follows that the problem is to provide the farmers with a motive to continue production. This can be done if there can be contrived

'different employments for the hands of the necessitous, that, by their labour, they may produce an equivalent which may be acceptable to the farmers, in lieu of this superfluity; for these last certainly will not raise it, if they cannot dispose of it; nor will they dispose of it, but for a proper equivalent.'[65]

This equivalent is 'the spring of the whole machine', and those who produce it are 'free hands'. These free hands consist of 'a certain number of the whole [inhabitants], proportional to such superfluity of nourishment produced, [who] will apply themselves to industry and to the supplying of other wants'. Their occupation, Steuart explains, is hard to define, because theirs being 'a labour adapted to the wants of the society', it 'may vary according to these wants, and these again according to the spirit of the times'.[66]

Emphasising more than Hume had done the difficulties of maintaining a balance between the two sectors, Steuart next introduces money, 'the best equivalent of all',[67] which facilitates and stimulates economic activity, and then turns to consider why progress is not equally smooth, rapid and indeed identical in all countries. The answer is that in different places there are different resources, morals, governments and manners. The principles of development are the same everywhere; but they operate 'in concurrence' with many circumstances which affect the outcome. It is one thing to make simplifying assumptions: 'We have supposed a country capable of improvement, a laborious people, a taste for refinement and luxury in the rich, an ambition to become so, and an application to labour and ingenuity in the lower classes of men;'[68] it is another to study the real world where there are complicating factors, especially of soil and climate. The familiar idea that natural disadvantages are favourable to economic development reappears:

'If the soil be vastly rich, situated in a warm climate, and naturally watered, the productions of the earth will be almost spontaneous: This will make the inhabitants lazy. Laziness is the greatest of all obstacles to labour and industry. Manufactures will never flourish here. . . . It is not therefore in the most fruitful countries of the world, nor in those which are the best calculated for nourishing great multitudes, that we find the most inhabitants. It is in climates less favoured by nature, and where the soil produces to those only who labour, and in proportion to the industry of every one, where we may expect to find great multitudes; and

even these multitudes will be found greater or less in proportion as the turn of the inhabitants is directed to ingenuity and industry.'[69]
Steuart thus superimposes upon his model the more familiar and orthodox psychological/natural resources explanation of economic development.

All this is as different from so-called 'mercantilist' pattern of thought as could be. Yet, although his analysis of growth is so modern, Steuart seems to have accepted the old aims. He disapproves of indolence; wants to promote economic activity at least partly on the ground that it 'creates reciprocal relations and dependencies' between citizens (and extends this idea to international trade which, for the same reason, 'has an evident tendency towards the improvement of the world in general') ;[70] above all, wants to increase population, for 'the increase of numbers in a state shows youth and vigour. . . . Depopulation is as certain a mark of political disease as wasting is of the human body'.[71] Holland, once more, is cited as a country where trade has had the satisfactory effect of increasing numbers.

Steuart's *Principles of Political Oeconomy* was published in 1767. It was much the largest, the most realistic, the most analytical, the most general, the most comprehensive, and altogether the best treatise on economics published in English before Smith published his *Wealth of Nations* nine years later. It restated, at length, and further elaborated a number of accepted ideas as to how economic development was to be understood. It held the stage in the early 1770s, and probably for most of the decade, because it must have taken a few years for even so remarkable and well-written a work as Adam Smith's to supersede old and well-developed ideas, especially in the formulation of public policy. The debate on the future of the Highlands began in the 1770s. The framework for that debate must have been, to begin with, the Temple/Hume/Steuart theory; fragments of it are to be found scattered throughout the work of Anderson, Loch, Knox and others.

By the 1780s, opinion was becoming influenced, to some extent, by the *Wealth of Nations*. Smith's book, published in 1776, was soon established as the new great general work on economics. It did not deal in particular with Highland problems—there are only a handful of scattered references to the Highlands—but it established a radically new general framework for the discussion of economic problems, not least for problems of economic development. Yet, because of the nature of Adam Smith's views his influence in matters of regional development was probably not as great as his overall authority would suggest.

As Adam Smith himself saw it, an important feature of the *Wealth of Nations* was 'the very violent attack' which it made on the existing system of governmental restrictions and regulations. Most readers went further: the impression of successive generations was that Smith's book constituted a strong and almost unanswerable plea for *laisser faire*. Certainly, Smith inclined in this direction. His views, which were far from simple, may be summarised with least injustice in the following way. Provided that law and order are maintained—'commerce and manufactures . . . can seldom flourish in any state in which there is not a certain degree of confidence in the justice of government'[72]—and provided that the allocation of resources is not distorted from its 'natural' pattern by public policy, then there will take place 'the natural progress of opulence'—a course of development which, it is implied, is in some sense optimal. Put in this way, the many refinements and qualifications of Smith's discussion are omitted. But it was some such simplified version which struck the public mind; and whether it is or is not what Adam Smith intended to convey, it could not be of much interest to those trying to frame a regional policy. Any regional policy consists of restriction or stimuli of some kind. Insofar as the *Wealth of Nations* condemned these, it was, to the makers of regional policy, at best unhelpful.

On the other hand, Smith put forward a number of positive arguments and suggestions which may well have affected the debate on the future of the Highlands. First and foremost, there was the emphasis he placed—the converse of his arguments about regulations—on the liberty of the individual. This was in line with much contemporary thinking and was prominent in the work of James Anderson, who was one of the chief participants in the Highland debate. Smith also, like Steuart, emphasized the importance of transport—'the greatest of all improvements'[73]—condemned the tax on sea-borne coals, which affected the Highlands—'Where they are naturally cheap, they are consumed duty free: where they are naturally dear, they are loaded with a heavy duty'[74]—and argued at some length that the accumulation of capital was a prerequisite of progress:

'The annual produce of the land and labour of any nation can be increased in its value by no other means, but by increasing either the number of its productive labourers, or the productive powers of those labourers who had before been employed. The number of its productive labourers, it is evident, can never be much increased, but in consequence of an increase of capital, or of the funds destined for maintaining them. The productive powers of the same number of labourers cannot be increased, but in consequence either of some addition and improvement to those machines and instruments which facilitate and abridge labour; or of a more proper division and distribution of employment. In either case an additional capital is almost always required . . . When we compare, therefore, the state of a nation at two different periods, and find, that the annual produce of its land and labour is evidently greater at the latter than at the former, that its lands are better cultivated, its manufactures more numerous and more flourishing, and its trade more extensive, we may be assured that its capital must have increased during the interval between those two periods, and that more must have been added to it by the good conduct of some, than had been taken from it either by the private mis-conduct of others, or by the public extravagance of government.'[75]

This suggests, although it does not absolutely require, that economic pro-gress depends on the activities of men of capital, and that, if the nation (or region) is to become wealthier it must submit to those technological changes which the accumulation of capital is almost sure to bring with it. This argument seems unlikely to have had much influence on the forma-tion of policy, but it may have been important later, in shaping men's atti-tudes to the great changes in agriculture which swept over the Highlands in the decades after 1770.

Two other aspects of Smith's thought are also of importance. First, he argued that the employment of capital in agriculture was, of all ways of em-ploying capital, 'by far the most advantageous to the society', and attributed the rapid progress of the American colonies to the fact that 'almost their whole capitals have hitherto been employed in agriculture'.[76] Meaning by agriculture the production of 'rude produce', this argument could be taken to include fishing, and to support those who saw Highland development in terms of increasing primary production without very much emphasis on manufacturing industry. Secondly, Adam Smith emphasised the impor-tance of villages and towns in promoting economic development. 'The town', he wrote, 'is a continual fair or market, to which the inhabitants of the country resort, in order to exchange their rude for manufactured pro-duce'.[77] The country supplies the town with its food and raw materials, the town generates a demand which encourages the cultivation of the country and at the same time supplies some of the tools and services which facilitate that cultivation, as well as the goods which a prosperous peasantry cannot provide for itself:

'Smiths, carpenters, wheel-wrights . . . are people, whose service the farmer has frequent occasion for. Such artificers too stand, occasionally, in need of the assistance of one another . . . they naturally settle in the neighbourhood of one another, and thus form a small town or village. The butcher, the brewer, and the baker, soon join them, together with many other artificers and retailers, necessary or useful for supplying their occasional wants, and who contribute still further to augment the town. The inhabitants of the town and those of the country are mutually the servants of one another.'[78]

This trade, Adam Smith argued, was 'the great commerce of every civi-lized society,'[79] and it followed that policies designed to provide it—if there were to be policies—might be of major importance.

What Adam Smith said about towns and villages—and he was not the only one to say it—recurs in the pages of Anderson, Knox and others who struggled to bring prosperity to the Highlands. Some other points to be found in the *Wealth of Nations* are also to be found in these later writings. But on the whole the debate about the Highlands was not conducted in what could be called Smithian terms. It was the traditional view which mattered, modified a little, supported and supplemented here and there by what was to be found in Adam Smith's work, but not overturned by it.

In two ways the traditional view was especially important in the Highlands debate. First, it encouraged faith in the possibilities of Highland development, because of the idea that natural disadvantages—in which the Highlands abounded, and abound—were not a bar to improvement; rather the contrary. The Highlands were not well known, and writers had to depend on their own observations. They could not disguise the fact that the Highlands were remote, poor and inaccessible, but according to the theory there was no need for them to do so. Nevertheless they tended, as if not quite convinced by the theoretical arguments, to take an optimistic view about the plentifulness of resources there. This inclination to err on the side of optimism was well established. A work published in 1740 pictured the Highlands as rich in lead, copper and iron, capable of growing large amounts of grain and potatoes and of supporting large herds of cattle, and declared that the region could easily be made accessible to the rest of the country by a system of canals.[80] A good deal of this was terrible rubbish by an old-style projector; but the author had a good deal of experience in the area, and some of his ideas were not unreasonable. Later writers agreed that the number of cattle and sheep which the region carried could be greatly increased[81] (this was correct) and that potatoes and other foodstuffs could be grown almost throughout the Highlands. Anderson (along with Knox the best-informed and most cautious of these writers) wrote as follows:

'. . . beef and mutton could at all times be had in prodigious abundance. . . . Potatoes and garden-stuffs of all sorts could be reared to the greatest perfection, and in great abundance, at a small expence; the soil, although steep, being in many places exceeding fertile. . . . The neighbouring seas and lochs swarm with the finest fish, of all sorts, which could be caught at all seasons. . . .'[82]

But this is almost entirely misleading. It results from assuming that conditions to be found in a few places or for one or two seasons were completely general throughout the Highlands. Writers simply deluded themselves about the availability of good soil and favourable growing conditions.[83] Even Knox, more careful than most, who wrote about the possibility of improving 'the more fertile parts'[84] of the Highlands, could declare that 'Roots, vegetables, salads, and common fruits, being less hurt by the rains, can be raised in any quantity'.[85] The availability of water power was also mentioned as an important asset, giving 'a convenient opportunity of erecting whatever kind of mills may be necessary',[86] and Anderson, in discussing the natural advantages of different regions for the manufacture of cloth, went so far as to compare the parish of Halifax with the Highlands of Scotland, very much to the disadvantage of the former. Stress was also laid on the possibilities of forestry as an alternative to agriculture; growing a great variety of trees, the Highlands 'will become an immense forest, enriching the landlords, and giving employment to the hitherto starved commonality.'[87] Most surprising of all, communications were frequently said to represent no great difficulty, because of the way in which the lochs and firths stretched 'the conveniency of a level road'[88] into the heart of the country.

The point of all this is that it is not altogether absurd. Writers were perfectly correct when they pointed out that black cattle were successfully bred in the Highlands, that sheep farming could be extended, that Caithness exported grain, that excellent timber grew in Perthshire, that potatoes flourished in several districts, that herring were plentiful on the west coast, that many lochs and straths ran far inland, that there was lead, copper, kelp, ample water power and cheap labour. But they imagined that these advantages were more important and—except for the last—more generally available than they really were, and in any case they did not believe that the natural disadvantages of the area were fundamentally prejudicial to development.

Secondly, the essential aim of policy—including regional policy—was still the old aim: national greatness. This meant a drive for population, and for a fully employed population. What distressed the men of the 1770s was not so much that the Highlanders were poor as that they were idle, not contributing, or contributing very little, to the power of the state. The aim of regional policy was to *use* the Highlands, to bring more people and resources into action for the good of all. It followed that emigration was an evil. Everyone wrote against it. According to Child, 'whatever tends to the depopulating of a Kingdom, tends to the impoverishment of it';[89] Anderson, precisely a hundred years later, said the same.[90]

Breed, and prosper; prosper, and breed. Whichever way they looked at it, these men could see nothing but good in the growth of population, nothing but evil in the reverse. Their goal was clear. They knew what they wanted, and in the Highlands they found a region going needlessly to waste, where the maxims of an enlightened political economy, judiciously applied, could write a new page in the progress of civil society.

4

Policy Proposals

The most remarkable intellectual event of the 1770s was Adam Smith's publication of the *Wealth of Nations*. A hundred years later, Walter Bagehot could write, 'The life of almost everyone in England—perhaps of everyone—is different and better in consequence of it. . . . No other form of political philosophy has ever had one thousandth part of its influence upon us. . . . Adam Smith wrote in an extinct world, and one of the objects always before him was to destroy now extinct superstitions.'[1]

But the revolutionary impact of the *Wealth of Nations* is scarcely more noteworthy than the fact that a distinguished philosopher chose to write such a book at that time. Economics was not then established as a separate branch of learning; Adam Smith established it. He was able and interested to do so because, in the first place, commerce had become an honourable occupation. During the seventeenth century, Englishmen and Scotsmen had fought to protect their property and profits; both were now secure, and men's acquisitive instincts—including that 'natural propensity to truck, barter, and exchange one thing for another', which Adam Smith set forth as a fundamental human characteristic at the very start of his great book—were now free, or it was increasingly felt that they should be free, to operate without the application of any comprehensive controlling view of the ultimate purposes of society:

Thus God and Nature fixed the general frame,
And bade self-love and social be the same.

And secondly, the fundamental belief of the Enlightenment, that men by taking thought could renew the life of the world, restoring its original purity, energy and justice, coincided with an improved understanding of how markets work and with significant increases in the stock of technical knowledge. It was thus possible, as never before, to think of devising policies, and policies which had some chance of being adopted, for securing a better economic outcome.

In working out their prescriptions for policy, the economists of the eighteenth century were inevitably, because of their basic philosophical beliefs, on the side of liberty, although this preference was by no means so strong as to commit them to supporting freedom of individual economic action in any and every case. Also, and for the same reasons, they were inclined to treat the interests of all men as equal. This should have given them a natural concern for the rights of the under-privileged, and to some extent it did. But their attitude to the poor differed a good deal from our own. They were disposed to argue—none more readily than Adam Smith—that poverty was not very important, and that it was not a major cause of unhappiness. Those occupying a subordinate station in life, according to Smith himself,

> 'enjoy their share of all that [the earth] produces. In what constitutes the real happiness of human life, they are in no respect inferior to those who would seem so much above them. In ease of the body and peace of the mind, all the different ranks of life are nearly upon a level, and the beggar, who suns himself by the side of the highway, possesses that security which kings are fighting for.'[2]

One may question whether this is a very realistic picture of how the good things of life were shared in the eighteenth century, or a very reasonable attitude to poverty. But it was quite common, at any rate in Scotland. Adam Ferguson said much the same, and even Burns directed his anger not against the rich, or the inequalities of the system, but against the paid officials who stood between the rich and the poor and who abused their authority.

This notion of some kind of equality between rich and poor, of similarity or at least comparability of experience, was founded on several aspects of Scottish life. Scotland was a nation unified and to some extent informed by its church and its universities; having a zeal for self-improvement backed up by a nation-wide educational system which would be the envy of many developing countries of the present day; and led by a relatively large aristocratic class whose ties of kinship extended widely throughout society. The resulting close relationship between people of widely differing ranks was further strengthened by the neighbourliness of life in eighteenth-century Scotland, especially of urban life. In Edinburgh lords, philosophers and fishwives rubbed shoulders—sometimes quite literally—on the stairs of tenements and in the narrow closes of the Old Town. Edinburgh was a capital city, but the structure of its life was personal, and in that sense provincial. People knew one another and one another's business in a way that is now difficult even in a small market town. Moreover, questions of philosophy and of national policy were not regarded as the preserve of a few. Intellectual activity, to an extent probably without parallel in Europe at that time, was a shared experience. As George Davie has put it, 'the ideas argued over at the dinner tables of Charlotte Square . . . were eagerly overheard and assimilated throughout Scotland, and freely commented on and criticized by persons of the most varied backgrounds.'[3]

Given the social structure, and given the background of ideas that the Enlightenment supplied, it was almost inevitable that Scots reformers of the later eighteenth century should put their trust in the virtues and energies and good sense of the individual, and show a corresponding distrust of official control. Of this latter there was a good deal—'tight regulation of foreign trade, wide-ranging though somewhat haphazard intervention by government in domestic economic matters'[4]—and the Highlands, as we shall see, had their share. The salt laws and the coal duties were especially conspicuous, and almost all writers agreed in deploring their effects. In this Anderson went furthest, declaring that if there was to be development of the fisheries, and thence any more general economic development in the Highlands, free trade in salt had to be established: 'Unless this is to be done, here we may stop.'[5] Knox was almost equally emphatic as regards the effects of the coal duties—'To the want of coals has been owing, in a great measure, the slow improvements in agriculture and manufactures in the northern parts of Scotland, and the isles ... the most valuable national purposes have been suspended during a course of eighty years, for the shadow of a trifle'[6]—and he added the point that as far as the salt duties were concerned, their reduction would have a direct effect in raising the standard of living of people who, as things stood, were frequently on the verge of starvation:

> 'Having no towns or stores where [salt] can be retailed out at a moderate price, these poor people are forced to live, through the winter and spring, upon half putrified fish, that have been dried without salt, the effects of which are severely felt by thousands in that miserable bad country.'[7]

Almost thirty years later, when the duty had been reduced but was still high enough approximately to equal the prime cost of production, the point was made in the Appendix to Sir John Sinclair's *General Report of Scotland* that the salt duty was 'absolutely ruinous' to the remoter areas of the Highlands because it made the salting of beef impossible and thus put the grazier in a weak position in a distant market:

> 'Cattle, and not corn, are the natural produce of these districts. For this produce they have no market at hand. In most cases, cattle must be driven a hundred, or sometimes two hundred miles. And what adds tenfold to this calamity is, that this market often fails; so that the tenant is under the dire necessity of driving his cattle home again, and to return pennyless, with his stock greatly reduced in value.'[8]

In advocating 'a perfect Freedom in buying and selling' fish, salt and other articles of commerce Anderson and Knox were proponents of what might be called internal free trade. This policy they did not back up with a theoretical analysis as Adam Smith had done; instead they appealed to the evident defects of the existing arrangements of control and intervention, defects about which almost everyone was agreed. They did, however, strengthen the argument for reform in two ways. First, Anderson in particular based his policies upon the philosophical as well as the practical advantages of independence. All men, he believed, were born equal or nearly so—'Every good man must be sensible that Heaven has endowed all ranks of people with talents nearly equal'[9]—and it was therefore both right and possible that the advantages of freedom should be fully enjoyed by everyone. On this topic he wrote with an enthusiasm which is in striking contrast to the studious moderation of so many of his contemporaries, comparing 'the nerveless abasement of that dependent thing which crawls upon the dust, and licks the courtier's feet' with 'the celestial energy of that mind, which [is] animated with a consciousness of independence.'[10] For this celestial energy there would be practical applications, however. Innovations and improvements in agriculture and the mechanical arts were naturally to be expected from those 'whose minds have been accustomed to that animating fervour which a spirit of independence most naturally inspires',[11] provided that ignorance and prejudice were overcome by education. Anderson was indeed outstandingly sympathetic to the problems and motivation of the poor. Observing that gentlemen, not least in the Highlands, were apt 'too harshly to complain of the indolence, and other bad qualities, they think they perceive in these poor people', he argued that the pattern of behaviour of poor tenants was formed by prejudices 'which ought to be respected' and by habits which, 'we all know, can only be overcome by slow and almost imperceptible degrees.'[12] What was wanted was 'a calm benevolence of mind', a willingness among those who had the good fortune to be already educated to help those whose talents were still buried under a load of ignorance and whose skills and responses remained feeble and rudimentary. Nor was it—and this was the third link in the chain of argument—entirely a matter of benevolence. Poor tenants, said Anderson, made poor landlords:

'A man who is poor, can never pay a rent: a man who is dependent upon the will of another for his subsistence, can never be actuated by that energetic spirit which alone can stimulate to arduous undertakings.—If, therefore, you hope to thrive yourselves, strive to make your inferiors rich; and if you hope to make them rich, first make them independent. . . .

All essential improvements must ever be carried on by the lower ranks of people;—but a dependent mind will never attempt to make any improvement, nor be brought to adopt one however plainly it may be pointed out.—Let your attention, therefore, be turned chiefly towards those in the lowest ranks in society;—free them not only from depen-

dence on yourself but protect them also from the rod of others.—
Cherish them in thy bosom with lenient tenderness,—they will soon
abundantly requite you for all your pains.'[13]
Happy discovery, that to do that which was benevolent and right was also
the quickest way to raise the value of landed property!

These arguments might be regarded as no more than an elaboration of
the popular doctrine that tenures ought not to be short and uncertain. But
they helped to promote that doctrine to its fullest extent, so that by the
beginning of the nineteenth century the letting of land to tenants at will,
so integral a part of the old clan system, could be condemned by an agricultural expert as 'one great and general bar to the improvement of the
Highlands and Islands . . . a relic of the feudal system, utterly inconsistent
with the interest of the landlord, the tenants and the state.'[14] And the story
was told of the laird who had seen the error of his ways:

'During my father's lifetime his tenants had no will but his. They saw
with his eyes, and heard with his ears; for they were all tenants at will.
But I thank God I have not one tenant but now feels himself an independent man, and would go to law with me for half a crown.'[15]

Whether or no this was so unmixed a blessing as the age believed, time
was soon to tell.

The second important contribution which Anderson and others made to
the debate about freedom and government intervention was their insistence that government intervention was necessary even although its existing pattern was wrong. They never condemned government activity as
such. Like most men trying to solve an economic problem, their attitude
to bounties was more friendly than their attitude to taxes, but it must at
once be added that their views as to what the government should do to
help the Highlands extended a long way beyond the reduction of taxes
combined with simple subsidies to producers or to would-be producers.
What distinguished their approach and made it valuable was their willingness to see the need both for effort and change on the part of individuals at
all levels and for government action of a possibly rather complex kind. As
Knox expressed it in his evidence before the 1785 Committee,

'To encourage the Fisheries, and to improve these Shores effectually,
something will be necessary to be done by Government, and something
by the Proprietors of Lands; they should co-operate in One efficient
Chain of Measures, suited to the Nature of the Country, the Abilities,
Habits, and Dispositions of the People. . . .'[16]

This is sensible, and no one could call it doctrinaire; but neither could anyone describe it as even the outline of a plan. Such an outline had already
been produced by Knox in 1784, but it seems to have attracted little attention. It was Anderson's achievement to put forward a series of specific

proposals which were set out realistically and in some detail so as to catch
the imagination of the public and carry the debate on the Highlands to a
more advanced stage.

Anderson put forward two sets of proposals. The first was in his *Observations on the Means of Exciting a Spirit of National Industry; chiefly intended to
promote the Agriculture, Commerce, Manufactures, and Fisheries, of Scotland*,
published in 1777 but written, according to the title page, in 1775. (The
particular problems which the book deals with are actually those of the
Highlands.) Eight years after the publication of this book, in evidence submitted to the Committee 'appointed to enquire into the State of the British
Fisheries', Anderson put forward what he called 'the rude Draught of a
Plan' for promoting development in the Highlands. The proposals of 1777
are not identical with those of 1785—it would be disconcerting if they
were. Conditions in the Highlands were changing during these years, in
some respects quite rapidly; and whereas Anderson's book was designed to
attract the attention of the public in general (and perhaps of landowners in
particular) and to cover all aspects of economic development in the Highlands, his later work was addressed to a smaller audience and had a fairly
narrow remit, namely to enquire into the fisheries 'and into the most
effectual means for their improvement and extension'. Nevertheless, the
two sets of proposals have several important features in common, and are
also to some extent complementary.

In his *National Industry* Anderson started from the position that the old
feudal equilibrium in the Highlands had been destroyed, and that a whole
new system of social and economic relations must now be established. The
clansmen were leaderless and disoriented; the affections of tenant and vas-
sal had been 'gradually alienated from one another' so as to produce a situation of social confusion 'which heightens every evil, and makes every
accidental distress come with redoubled vigour'.[17] Moreover, population
was growing and more food was needed. Yet the prospects for agricultural
development were meagre, because 'the country which these poor people
inhabit, is in a great measure incapable of being improved by culture'.[18] It
followed that the region would have to depend on exports derived from
'mines, manufactures, or fishings', if it was to continue to obtain even the
necessaries of life.

Faced with this triad of possibilities, Anderson unhesitatingly, in a few
lines, selected manufacturing as the sector to be developed, apparently on
the ground that it would provide the maximum—or possibly the most
widespread—volume of employment:

'Of these three, the last two are the most universally beneficial to the
people; particularly manufactures, the influence of which might be
easily extended to almost every individual in the country.'[19]

The problem that remained was 'to discover what kind of manufacture could be most easily and quietly established' and to devise the best means of encouragement.

Anderson argued that two criteria had to be satisfied. First, the manufacture must be based upon native supplies of raw materials, and not upon imports. He justified this on several grounds, some of them familiar—imported materials have to bear the cost of transport, dependence upon a foreign supplier entails the risk of political interferences with trade, foreigners might artificially raise the price of their raw materials so as to 'exploit' the native manufacturer. But he gave another reason which is less commonly put forward, and which he placed in the forefront of his argument. He emphasised that any new manufacture would require the learning of new skills, and that this would be particularly difficult in a thinly peopled region where the inhabitants were not 'crouded together, so as to be more immediately under the inspection of those who may be brought to instruct them'.[20] This obstacle to development, he claimed, would be far more serious if the raw materials had to be imported, because 'no master-manufacturer would willingly entrust raw materials, of considerable value, with inexperienced operators at a great distance from himself';[21] small-scale experiments, or learning on a small scale, would therefore be out of the question in this case because

'the expence of carrying away the raw materials, and bringing back the manufactured goods, would become too high for [the entrepreneur] to be able to support.
On this account master-manufacturers are discouraged from settling in these lonely regions; and the inhabitants, even if they were willing to be instructed, are in a great measure deprived of the means of attaining the necessary degree of knowledge in these new arts.'[22]

The second criterion was that the manufacture must not be contrary to the interests of agriculture:

'unstable is the prosperity of that country, which has its chief dependence on the flourishing of its towns independent of its agriculture and peasantry; for a thousand circumstances may totally ruin the one, while the prosperity that results from the other can hardly be affected but by the total destruction of the state itself.'[23]

By what kind of industry is agriculture best supported? Anderson's answer was none too convincing, but it was nevertheless emphatic. Those manufactures are hurtful, he wrote, which require no high degree of skill, and which can be carried on by individuals in their own homes, because in such a case 'the lower ranks of people . . . often . . . young women and children'[24] make an easy income and are attracted out of agriculture, depleting the farmers' labour force; the income which they earn is spent largely on obtaining luxuries from outside the region; the farmers are lured into running down capital in order to compete with the new levels of consumption expenditure; and land becomes subdivided as farmers grow relatively poorer and industrial workers seek security through the purchase of a couple of acres and a cow. Therefore, what is wanted is a concentrated mechanised industry, requiring skilled labour, machinery and extensive buildings, preferably, moreover, one which affords 'a constant and steady demand: for if this demand shall be apt to vary, the poor operators will be often thrown idle'.[25] On this basis Anderson reached the conclusion that the woollen industry—especially 'the plainer and coarser manufactures'[26]— was the best calculated to bring prosperity to the Highlands; a surprising conclusion, for he must have known that the woollen manufacture, which had for so long flourished in England, was still conducted predominantly as a cottage industry.

His next task was to persuade his readers that wool was or could be a raw material economically and efficiently produced in the Highlands. This section of the book—a large part of the whole—is mostly technical, and is to the effect that very fine wool had in the past been produced in Scotland, and that the conditions of climate and soil were such that Scotland, especially the Highlands, was a natural centre for wool growing. The raising of cattle, he argued, had been suitable for the Highlanders 'when robbery was practised as a trade, and . . . no idea of manufactures for foreign export could ever enter into their imagination'.[27] But for those who were now seeking 'the advantages of a civilized life', in which 'industry, and the activity of body and mind, are the qualities that contribute in the highest degree to . . . happiness',[28] sheep were much to be preferred to cattle. This was because sheep-raising, according to Anderson, leads almost necessarily to the manufacture of woollen goods, an occupation 'which would have a powerful tendency to prevent that listless indolence from getting footing among them that must prevail among the other species of grasiers'.[29] Besides this, sheep raising would release the poor grazier from dependence on a distant and unstable market, and from 'the capricious nod' of the drovers who were the middlemen of the trade.[30] Furthermore, sheep were more profitable than cattle, because the weight of meat produced was the same per acre, and presumably of equal value, and sheep yielded wool besides; cattle needed hay for winter feeding, and hay supplies were limited, whereas sheep could largely keep themselves through the winter; and sheep improved the land, 'insomuch that those hills which were continually covered with heath, in a few years assume a pleasant verdure, and carry a much greater quantity of short nourishing grass than formerly. This has lately been experienced in many parts of Perthshire and Argyleshire. . . .'[31] Finally, there was no need to substitute sheep for cattle—many more sheep could be kept without reducing the number of cattle, and indeed the numbers of both could be increased together, for more sheep enrich the pastures and thus indirectly make available larger supplies of hay for more cattle.

It cannot be said that these passages make altogether persuasive reading. In particular, there is no attempt to prove that sheep are in fact more profitable than cattle per acre (which, even if true, would settle nothing); there is no acknowledgement of the fact that different kinds of land are suitable for different purposes; and there is no convincing argument that sheep raising leads almost necessarily to the manufacture of wool in the same region. Also, the idea that sheep improve the soil is at best gravely defective. What happened in the Highlands was that sheep often took over ground which had in effect been prepared for them by the previous presence of trees and cattle. Forestry and cattle raising were complementary over much of the Highlands, but both declined together when the sheep appeared. Sheep and cattle have different food requirements. The grazing-habit of sheep is selective, so that a great deal of pasture that is cropped exclusively by sheep goes rank and decays, or is progressively invaded by coarser grasses. Seedling trees are more readily destroyed by sheep than by cattle. As for heather, it sometimes grows beyond the powers of sheep to control it, and then becomes woody and unfit for grazing; when burned, such heather may generate so much heat as to sterilize the soil, after which only coarse herbage—often bracken—becomes established. The introduction of sheep was bound to upset the balance of plant and animal life in the Highlands, even if over-grazing had not been indulged in. But such ill effects were at first not noticeable. Cut-down woodland soon greened over and sheep throve on it. Some areas, especially in the north-east Highlands, were naturally suitable for sheep. But it was difficult to avoid damage in the long run, and Anderson in the 1770s had little reason for declaring that sheep farming and soil improvement were synonymous.

The main point, however, was broadly correct; provided that there was an injection of skill and capital, sheep raising over large areas of the Highlands could be an economic proposition. And as for the manufacture of wool, into which the inhabitants 'could hardly avoid falling'[32] once they had become sheep farmers, Anderson emphasised two natural advantages which he believed Scotland to possess. Clear running water, he pointed out, was 'indispensably necessary' to woollen manufactures, and Scotland was in this respect very well supplied—'I leave any one who has seen the limpid rapid rivulets in Scotland, to compare them with the dead muddy waters in England, and tell on which side the balance falls'.[33] Anderson went further, and implied that the Highlands could become the rival of the parish of Halifax, a place—here he was quoting Defoe—densely peopled and obtaining its needs from a distance by the export of woollen goods:

'Their corn comes up in great quantities out of Lincoln and Nottingham-shire, and the East Riding; the black cattle from thence, and from Lanca-shire; sheep and mutton from the adjacent counties every way; butter from the North and East Ridings; and cheese out of Warwickshire.

   Thus one trading manufacturing part of the country, in a barren soil, gives and receives support from all the countries round it.'[34]

The inference is plain; the Highlands, not dissimilarly endowed, could develop in much the same way.

   Secondly, Anderson claimed that the Highlands had a great natural ad-vantage in their lochs and rivers, especially the sea lochs which ran inland between the mountains so that 'the only habitable parts of the country may always have the conveniency of a level road to the sea'.[35] Thus goods could be brought in and out 'with the greatest facility'. Especially Loch Ness and Loch Shin, he thought, could be of 'infinite benefit . . . in facili-tating the carriage of weighty goods . . . should extensive manufactures ever chance to be established among them'.[36] Although rather vague about the pattern of communication which natural waterways in the Highlands would actually be able to provide, Anderson laid considerable stress on the Highlands' advantage in this respect:

'. . . the circumstance in which these countries have the most decided advantage over Yorkshire, and perhaps every other part of the world possessing the other advantages they enjoy, is the facility of carriage, not only for their manufactures and provisions, but for their raw materials of every sort; together with the choice of markets that they would enjoy on this account. For, as few of these places are above ten or fifteen miles from some of these arms of the sea on either side, or fresh-water lochs, to which they could always have access by plain and level roads, every article they had to buy or sell in any part of the world, could be trans-ported at an expence scarce perceptible.—And as some of the friths on the east coast run up so far as to be within a few miles of meeting others on the west, the road between the two being carried through a level strath of only eight or ten miles extent, they could have it in their choice to send their goods either to the eastern or western markets; and thus, by an easier and safer navigation than from the Humber, could ship their goods for the Baltic, Germany, or Holland; and with equal facility to Spain, Portugal, Italy, the Levant, or North America; so that they are open to either sea, can take advantage of every wind, and have it in their power to trade to any country on the globe.'[37]

This is certainly a rosy view of the situation, in which the need for at least access roads is barely mentioned. But Anderson was an invincible optimist about the natural advantages of the Highlands. Besides water to wash wool and power machinery, besides cheap transport, besides ideal conditions for

sheep farming, the Highlands stood up well in the comparison with Yorkshire in several other respects:

'Their fewel is in equal abundance, and as easily procured; many of the
hills being covered with inexhaustible [*sic*] stores of fine peat, which
might be easily brought down to their several habitations.

With respect to provisions, the advantage is greatly in favour of Scotland. For there, beef and mutton could at all times be had in prodigious
abundance. . . . Potatoes and garden-stuffs of all sorts could be reared to
the greatest perfection, and in great abundance, at a small expence; the
soil, though steep, being in many places exceedingly fertile, and at present of hardly any value at all.—The neighbouring seas and lochs swarm
with the finest fish of all sorts, which could be caught at all seasons, and
sold to the inhabitants at a price that would be reckoned nothing at all in
almost any part of England. And oat or barley meal, the only kinds of
grain at present used by the inhabitants, could be obtained by sea from the
neighbouring low countries of Scotland or Ireland at a very moderate
price.'[38]

Anderson did not explain how he reconciled this picture of plenty with the
existing poverty in the Highlands, or with his own earlier statement that
there was little scope for agricultural development.

It will be seen that much of Anderson's case for believing in the economic
future of the Highlands rested on his conviction that natural resources
there were plentiful and good. Once this was granted the problem became,
in his view, fairly straightforward. Ordinary men could be relied on to pursue their own interest, and they would be successful, in all probability, provided that they received some education and enjoyed independence. Such
people, Anderson wrote,

'are much more capable than any others of discovering what would most
immediately promote their own interest, and what would be the most
effectual means of prosecuting it.'[39]

It was not for gentlemen, still less for the government, to presume to decide
what should be done, or the best ways of doing it. The task of government,
and of men of property and high rank, was

'to endeavour to discover *bars* that lie in the way of improvements—to
smooth difficulties,—to remove obstructions,—and to prevent im-
positions and frauds of every sort.'[40]

And at this point it was almost inevitable that Anderson should quote—or
perhaps misquote—the well-known words of 'one of the deputies of a
manufacturing town in France to Mr Colbert'—'Leave us to ourselves';
Laissez nous faire.

But if *laisser-faire* is the solution, there is no need for a plan; yet Anderson had one, or at least the outline of one.[41] He wanted the government to

stabilise prices, especially of food and raw materials; to make roads, and other 'channels of communication'; to establish and encourage 'proper markets and marts in convenient parts of the country'; to encourage entrepreneurs to set up business in the Highlands, and support them 'till they shall be thoroughly established in trade'; above all, to encourage fine wool growing by an elaborate system of premiums. He elaborated none of these suggestions except the first and the last. The first he advocated as national policy; the last he tacitly admitted was an exception to *laisser-faire*. Oddly enough, he did not advocate the encouragement or subsidisation of education. But his positive measures he clearly regarded as subsidiary and temporary, effective only in the context of a concentrated effort to develop the woollen manufacture on the basis of native wool, and of the independence of all men.

Such were the proposals of 1777. Anderson became almost overnight an acknowledged expert on the Highlands, and it was natural that when the Committee set up to enquire into the fisheries was preparing its Third Report in 1784 it should invite Anderson to visit the Highlands and report on what he saw and would advise. In the autumn of 1784 Anderson visited the islands and western coasts in a revenue cutter, and in December presented his Report—a document of about 20,000 words plus 15,000 words of notes and further explanations—tending, as he put it, 'to point out the most probable Means of promoting the Fisheries, and the consequent Improvement of those Countries'. This Report appears as Appendix II in the *Third Report of the Committee on the British Fisheries*, published in 1785.

Anderson began by stating—incorrectly—that the total population of the Highlands was about half a million, of whom 240,000 lived on the west coast and another 80,000 in the Hebrides. These people had at their disposal a remarkable array of natural resources.[42] In the Hebrides there were 'extensive Fields of land . . . with an uncommon Degree of Fertility'; the climate was good for corn; there was slate, lead, copper and iron ore; there was 'fine Marble in Tiree . . . only of late discovered . . . superior to the finest Italian Marble yet known'; good coal existed in many places, and there was wool 'not to be equalled by any other wool yet known'. As for fish, they there 'so much abound, as far to exceed the utmost Efforts of Men sensibly to diminish their Numbers'.[43] Yet the people were poor. Anderson did not find this difficult to explain, although his explanation now was rather different from what it had been in 1777. The trouble was, he said, that the natives were too poor to own boats and go fishing, with the result that

'they are obliged to rely upon the Soil . . . Little Possessions (Farms they cannot be called) are sought after by them with an Avidity that is scarcely conceivable, and they cling to these with a Degree of Eagerness

which the Wretchedness of their Enjoyments would not seem to autho-
rize.'[44]

Agricultural improvement was possible, and some indeed had taken place,
notably on Islay and other 'low Arable Islands'. But improvement was at
best gradual, again largely because the people had so little capital at their
disposal. Sheep farming was on the increase, and for this 'a great Proportion of the Highlands of Scotland' was suitable. But sheep farming led to
dispossession and was no cure for the poverty of the people. Graziers
offered high rents, which were not always accepted; many proprietors,
wrote Anderson, 'have rejected very advantageous offers, rather than drive
them [the tenants] away;' but such action, he added, was 'only at best a
Temporary Palliative'.[45]

If this was the problem, what was the cure? First of all, the Salt Laws
had to go. Shortage of capital and other difficulties would in time have
been overcome—'the Highlanders' natural Advantages are such as must
in time have got the better of these Checks'[46]—but the salt laws created
insurmountable problems. The Coal Duties, although less important, also
needed to be removed. This was familiar ground. So also was what
Anderson said about wool, although he said remarkably little: 'The Natives',
he observed, 'scarcely know any thing of its Value in a commercial
light. . . . Those fine-wooled Sheep are suffered to stroll about, neglected,
in small Numbers'.[47] But again it was the law which was mostly to blame:
'if the laws should be so modelled as to admit of a reasonably free Commerce in this Article', instead of imposing absurd restraints on shipment,
especially by sea,[48] the wool trade would expand and the manufacture of
'shauls' and other articles would soon follow.

The case for wool and woollen manufactures was stated on a single page.
However important, these were no longer the answer to the problems of
the Highlands. The crucial requirement, Anderson had now discovered,
was the establishment of markets.

Anderson's general position on this matter was simply stated. The people
in the Highlands, he said,

> 'are hurt chiefly because of the Want of an open Market, to which the
> Commodities they stand in Need of could be sent by Merchants from a
> Distance; and in which the Articles they have to dispose of could be
> freely sold, where a Competition of Merchants could take place.'[49]

Behind this lay some matters of observation. First, he noted that there was
at present no way of disposing of agricultural surpluses and hence no
motive to produce them. If crops failed, the proprietors supported their
tenants, advancing meal at market prices on terms which sometimes appeared onerous but which were seldom adequate to cover the risks involved. If crops were good, everyone had enough to eat, but there was no

way to market what was left, for it was worth no-one's while 'to set out, through tempestuous Seas, in an Open Boat, to find Purchasers of small Quantities among a poor People, along a thinly inhabited Coast'; no better use could be found for good harvests than to increase the distillation of whisky, 'which they are tempted to consume with a hurtful Prodigality'.[50] Secondly, fishermen were sometimes obliged to sell their catch to their landlords at stipulated prices, and it was arguable that these prices were below what would have ruled in a free market. (Certainly native fishermen faced a problem in marketing their catch, and this must have discouraged their industry.) Finally, stores and provisions of all kinds were sometimes supplied by landlords, and this was also felt, rightly or not, to be a means of exploiting the tenantry. What was therefore wanted was an efficient market, one in which prices were ruled by demand and supply, in which buyers and sellers had freedom of choice, and which would simultaneously provide an outlet for and justly reward the enterprise of which the highlanders were capable and which their natural resources could amply support.

How were these markets to be created? Obviously, by bringing buyers and sellers together, in as large numbers as possible. And the best way of doing this was to establish villages and towns—this is the main proposal in Anderson's Report—for towns not only constitute markets but are in their nature the nurseries and guarantors of independence and hence of enterprise. In support of this idea Anderson appealed, in a characteristically eighteenth-century way, to history. History, he declared, showed that slavery to superiors had died away, 'gradually and imperceptibly' because of the rise of towns, in which there was freedom to trade and manufacture:

'By what Means was this Slavery so gradually and imperceptibly abolished in the State, so as to have occasioned no political Convulsions, and even to have excaped the Notice of Annalists and contemporary Historians?

The Answer to this Question is now easy—It was by the establishing of Towns, and granting to the Inhabitants of these, certain Privileges and Immunities that were not at first thought to be of great Moment; but which gradually produced a wonderful Change in our Civil Polity. To these Places of Refuge, People in abject Circumstances, those who were Outcasts from Society, or too cruelly treated by their Lords, fled for Safety and Protection. Without knowing in what Manner to account for it, those who were disposed to be industrious found always abundant Employment there, and were enabled to live at their Ease. Trade crept into these Places, and Manufactures insensibly were established in them— Wealth flowed in upon the People, which enabled them to afford still more and more effectual Protection to the individual Members of their Community—These Places became gradually more and more attractive to those without, and the Fear of driving away their Vassals from their liege Lords mitigated the Severities of Servitude—till at last tyrannic Exertions [*sic*] gradually fell into Oblivion, and we found ourselves in Possession of that Freedom which all surrounding Nations admire.'[51]

This is a significant passage, because it is consciously anti-feudal in tone. Anderson is stating the case for towns but he is also stating the case against the landlords—perhaps more emphatically than he intended. And his argument is a crucial one, because of the importance which he attached to freedom and independence. These, according to his *National Industry*, are fundamental requirements of progress. So towns, it now appears, are the basis of progress, both political and economic.[52]

This latter point Anderson developed with some care. In every way, he argued, men were worst off when living apart. It was only in society that they could develop and make full use of their abilities. In society, 'the Minds of Men, exalted by communicating with others, come to be gradually expanded, till they acquire an Idea of their own united Power and Importance.'[53] But at the same time, economic changes take place. Living together, men 'necessarily create Employment for each other, and thus establish a Market for the Products of their Labour.'[54] At first sight, this market is no greater than it would be if the same number of people lived scattered through the country. But, for several reasons, the mutual demand existing in a large market is more favourable for further development than the sum of market demand in a number of small, scattered communities. For one thing, demand is more stable, because it originates in many sources and not all of these are likely to rise or fall together; a temporary satiation of wants among one group in the community may well be compensated by a rise of demand among others. Also, the production of more than the bare necessities of life is encouraged. In a small village, only one individual may wish to buy fine shoes; but in a town several individuals wishing to do so form a market which it is worth someone's while to satisfy. Thus specialisation and the division of labour are encouraged, the quality of goods rises and the cost falls, partly because of increased efficiency and partly because the competition between traders naturally reduces prices— they are obliged to adopt 'a civil Deportment and a reasonable Charge.'[55] Moreover, such a town generates a large and steady demand for foodstuffs and raw materials. 'Goods of all kinds are constantly poured in upon it from all sides in great Quantities',[56] competition again reducing costs; while the consequent large and steady demand for transport reduces transport costs also—it is cheaper to travel from London to Gravesend than from one Hebridean island to the next simply because the volume of traffic has led to lower unit costs. Finally, the prosperity of the town spreads into the country round about. Agriculture in the neighbourhood becomes 'a

great Business'. The farmers begin to specialise, and efficient trading connections are established with the result that 'the native Products of the Soil
can usually be bought cheaper at the Market of a large Town, than even in
the Places where these are produced.'[57] In all this Anderson is very modern
and very shrewd, arguing the case persuasively for specialisation and the
economies of scale. His view of the market is essentially dynamic, based on
an appreciation of the interconnectedness of supply and demand for each
and every service and commodity, an appreciation which enabled him to
grasp not only that a free market tends to equate private rewards and social
benefits throughout the system, but also that it encourages enterprise and
growth. Thus

   'in whatever light we view the Matter, a large Town seems to be absolutely necessary for giving Scope to the Industry of Man, and for carrying
   Arts and Manufactures to their due Perfection.'[58]

In the Highlands—particularly along the north-west coast and in the
Hebrides—there were no towns and scarcely any large villages and Anderson's proposals to remedy this state of affairs were surprisingly simple.
Villages should be established by proprietors, each 'upon a Spot that should
be approven of by Government, and according to a Plan that should be in
like manner approven of.'[59] Each village was to consist of at least 1,000
feus, each feu one sixteenth of a Scottish statute acre, let at an annual rent
of not more than two shillings and sixpence. If a tenant built a house on his
feu within two years, and occupied it, he would have complete security of
tenure at that rent for all time coming; but if he failed to do so, he would
lose his tenancy. As soon as 1,000 feus were taken, the government would
give the proprietor £1,000 and a charter erecting the new village into a
self-governing corporation. Also, to any six men having taken feus who
promised to become fishermen, the government was to give 'a stout new
Boat, well calculated for carrying on the Fishery in these Seas, with Oars
and other Furniture complete,' provided that the recipients promised also
that the boat would 'never be employed for the Purpose of Smuggling.'[60]
These measures, Anderson reckoned, would quickly result in the establishment of many large villages. But because something else was needed 'to
give a vivacious Stimulus at the Beginning, to put the whole Machine in
Motion', he also proposed the establishment of 'at least One Large Town,
which should serve as a Centre of Trade, as a general Market for all the
adjacent Places. . . .'[61] This was to be a planned Town, with 'Houses of
different Classes', having control over land in the surrounding countryside,
and its own magistracy.[62] Anderson thought that 'perhaps Dunvegan, in
Skye, is the best Situation for such a Town', but added that it might be
sited at Stornoway, Tobermory, Bowmore (on Islay), or on the shores of
Loch Boisdale in South Uist.

These proposals, Anderson calculated, were to the advantage of all parties concerned. The ordinary tenants would obtain 'a fixed Property . . . one of the greatest Blessings of Life. . . . Such a Situation must evidently appear much more desirable to them than emigrating to America.'[63] The fishermen

'would at once obtain Freedom and Independence. The Means of earning their Bread would be put into their Hands, and, as they would be placed together in Numbers, Tradesmen and Artificers would find it their interest soon to come among them.'[64]

The proprietors, Anderson explained at some length, would benefit no less:

'When many Men are settled in One Place, they must not only have Food for themselves, but for Cows and Horses and other Animals, which can only be had in the Neighbourhood. A Market is brought to Hand for all kinds of Vegetables and Grain—Dung is produced, which serves to enrich the neighbouring lands—Barren Plots are quickly converted into Corn Fields—and the Value of his Land around becomes Ten Times greater than it otherwise would have been; so that in a few years a Proprietor who made such an Establishment would find his Revenue bettered by this Alteration, probably Five hundred or a Thousand Pounds a Year . . . (The Reporter has known Cases where the Rent of land has been augmented better than Twenty thousand Pounds a Year, by the increase of a Town in the Neighbourhood). If, therefore, the Proprietor knew his own Interest, he would be a Gainer, should he *pay* the Thousand Pounds to Government instead of *receiving* it. But as Proprietors do not in all Cases see clearly where their Interest lies, and as many of them are apt to grasp at the First Profit as the only One they have to expect, and thus to think of squeezing the Quit Rent as high as it is possible for them to obtain, it is perhaps better for all Parties, that they should thus be bribed to adopt that Mode of Conduct which will tend most effectually to promote their own Interest, while it likewise augments the general Welfare of the Community.'[65]

As for the government, it too stood to gain. The cost per village would be £1,000, plus the cost of boats and fishing gear for as many as chose to apply. At £9 a time, this would amount to £750 if half of the families in the village resolved to be fishers—a total cost to government of £1,750.[66] But to set against this there would be a tax gain. Poor highlanders, Anderson reckoned, paid no taxes. But he calculated that the average tax revenue per head of population in Great Britain was £2, and he assumed that the highlanders, once in the new villages, would pay that amount. Therefore a village of 1,000 families, with five persons per family, would yield a tax revenue of £10,000 per annum in perpetuity, or better. The investment would thus be a good one from the government's point of view, much to be preferred to the existing uses found for public money, such as spending twenty guineas a time 'to raise a single Recruit to the Army.'

It is hard to know at what point to start a criticism of these proposals—they fit together so well, and many of the arguments used in their support are valid and convincing. But, as later critics were to show, what is suggested is full of optimistic assumptions about the availability of skills and resources, and depends heavily on very optimistic cost calculations. Moreover, nothing is said about the passage of time; and the implication seems to be that changes which, if all went well, might have required decades or even generations to accomplish, could be carried through successfully almost at once.

Anderson's proposals for village and town building were the most ambitious as well as the most important part of his plan. But his suggestions for the improvement of transport were also far reaching. He continued to emphasise the natural advantage which the Highlands possessed in lochs and rivers, but he now thought that improvements should be made. First came the Crinan canal, already proposed and advocated by other writers, which could be constructed 'with a Certainty of Indemnification to the Undertakers';[67] no details were given. A road should also be built, 'at no great Distance from the Coast',[68] in order to speed communication between the numerous communities which Anderson expected to see established. Later, as and when the demand for them was created by general economic development, other roads and canals should be constructed. The chief of these was to be in the Great Glen, between Inverness and Fort William, where 'there might with great Ease be formed, with profit to the Undertakers, an extensive Canal'; but this project was to wait awhile, because 'in the present State of the Country as to Finance, the Reporter should be extremely cautious about advising any Undertaking of great public Expense, where it did not appear to be absolutely necessary at the very Moment . . . the Want of it would come to be more felt some time hence, should these Regions be improved.'[69] But although it would be expensive, this canal would be cheap for its size. There should also be a packet boat service along the west coast and between the islands, of which the expense would be 'in a great Measure borne by Government'.

These 'great and radical Works' of town building and transportation were the substance of Anderson's proposals. Once these were accomplished, 'it would be time to think of other lesser subsidiary Aids. . . . In this Class Bounties may be ranked'.[70] Anderson affected to despise bounties; but he devoted a good deal of space to their elaboration. The reason for this was that he proposed a complicated system designed to make bounties available even to small men. There was to be a bounty of 40s per ton per annum for 'all Wherry-rigged Vessels from 15 to 60 tons Burthen' fishing anywhere north of Galloway or Inverness. In addition, there were to be several classes of premiums for the best annual catch relative to size of boat:

'In Consequence of this Arrangement, it must happen that a few poor industrious Men, without Friends or powerful Connections of any Kind, would receive at once the amazing Sum of £240, the Hope of obtaining which would excite a Degree of Vigour and Exertion of which it is difficult to form an Idea.'71

And he pointed out that this arrangement would provide funds to those who had proved themselves best able to use them. The total cost of the premiums was put at £3,500 per annum, and the benefits would be certain and substantial.

Anderson was an enthusiast. To some extent he was blinded by his own enthusiasm. But he possessed the capacity for taking a comprehensive view which enabled him not only to envisage the development of the Highlands along several lines, but also to see this development as something that might fit—indeed, would have to fit, if it was to succeed—into the great pattern of world trade:

'The Prosperity of that Country, were the Measures proposed adopted, the Reporter conceives would be certain and unavoidable. The People being freed from those Restraints that at present tie up their Hands from the Fisheries, would engage in them with Alacrity, and with proportional Success. Being placed within Reach of giving and receiving Mutual Aid in all their Enterprizes, their Exertions would acquire a Vigour with which they are at present entirely unacquainted . . . The quantity of Fish thus prepared for Market would induce Plenty of Merchants to settle in those Towns, who would find a profitable Employment in the Commerce that this would furnish. . . . A ready Market would be provided for fresh Provisions . . . which would give all the Encouragement to Agriculture that ever can be wished for. Ships would be Daily passing to and from Liverpool, and other Ports, with Rock Salt, Corals, and other Articles, wanted for the Daily Use of a numerous, wealthy, and industrious People. In Return for which would be sent . . . Kelp, Slate, Fish, fresh and cured, Oil, Bark, and other Articles. . . . To the West Indies the outward Freight of Fish would enable the Merchants to import Sugar and Rum at a moderate Freight, which would in time give rise to the refining of Sugar. To the neutral islands in the West Indies their Fish would be a most welcome Commodity . . . in Return for which they would procure, by an advantageous Barter, Melasses, which could be there distilled for the African Trade with as great Advantage as in Connecticut. To Spain, to Portugal, the Mediterranean, and the

Levant, their Fish, their Marble, and Manufactures, would afford them
ready Access; and the Articles they would receive from these Countries,
together with Lead, and other native Products and Manufactures, would
lay the Foundation of a Trade to Holland and the Baltic.'[72]

Apart from its boundless optimism, the most notable feature of this con-
cluding passage is the total omission of any reference to wood or woollen
manufactures.

In this and other ways the proposals of 1785 differ from those which
Anderson had put forward in 1777. In the one case, salvation is to be by
manufacturing industry; and little else, except the independence of the
individual, receives much attention. In the other case, however, the impulse
to progress is depicted as coming *via* the creation of villages and towns; as
a result of these, and of improved transport, fishing and other directly productive activities will develop. Certainly the two schemes have common
features; in particular, the villages and towns on which so much stress is
laid in 1785 may properly be regarded as the practical means for achieving
the independence of the individual spoken of so highly, but in general
terms, in *National Industry*. Nevertheless, the emphasis is strikingly different.
Perhaps Anderson had learned more about the Highlands in the ten years
before he wrote his Report. Perhaps he had lost his faith in the possibility
of establishing a prosperous woollen industry in the Highlands. On the
other hand, it is arguable that the Report was written, as it says, 'to point
out the most probable means of promoting the fisheries', and that it applied
strictly to the north-west coast and the Hebrides; whereas *National Industry*
was about development in the Highlands as a whole. In any case, it must
be allowed that Anderson consistently emphasised that the freedom of the
individual from oppressive actions by other individuals was the essential
foundation of all economic progress, while at the same time, and equally
consistently, maintaining that economic development in the Highlands
depended to some extent on public expenditure—both current expenditure for the support and encouragement of private enterprise, and capital
expenditure for the creation of some forms of overhead capital.

Interest in the Highlands intensified in the 1780s. There was continuing
and growing anxiety about emigration, and in 1782–3 this was supplemented by concern over the famine conditions brought about by the
failure of both grain and potato crops due to unusually severe weather.

'I am Minister of this Parish fifty seven years, I have lived to see many
changes, Days of Distress and trying seasons, but nothing comparable to
the years Eighty two and eighty three . . . many families formerly in
easy Circumstances were forced to begg or perish, which last has been
the unhappy fate of several, because their Neighbours had not wherewith to supply the numberless Swarms that stroll from Door to Door . . .

the case calls loud for immediate relief, many many families to my knowledge having been destitute of Salt and Meal to season the green herbs
gathered in the barren fields where Corn was sown but none grows. . . .'[73]
Hundreds were said to have died and emigration was further encouraged.[74]
In 1783, partly as a result of these events, John Knox published the first of a
series of works on the Highlands. Knox was a prosperous London bookseller who had been led, in his own words, 'through curiosity, to view the
rude magnificence of the Highlands of Scotland', but found his attention
'soon attracted by the less pleasing scenes of human misery in all its shapes.'[75]
He first visited the Highlands in 1764, and returned frequently in the
following twenty years. In 1784 there appeared the first edition of his most
important book, *A View of the British Empire, more especially Scotland; with
some Proposals for the Improvement of that Country, the Extension of its
Fisheries, and the Relief of the People.* A second and then a third edition of
this work appeared in 1785, greatly enlarged; followed two years later by
his *Tour through the Highlands of Scotland, and the Hebride Isles.* The essence
of Knox's views is to be found in the 1784 volume, published before
Anderson's *Report*; the later books contain chiefly repetitions of what had
been published in 1784, elaborations, minor modifications and often lengthy
descriptive additions; but also—and this is important—there is a thirty
page postscript to the 1785 *View of the British Empire* which consists of
detailed and pungent comment on Anderson's *Report*.

The basis of Knox's proposals is a political and economic position rather
than—as with Anderson—a philosophical position. Knox emphasised, as
most mercantilists had done, that the world was a scene of widespread war
and perpetual insecurity. The very first words of his book express this view:
'Immoderate ambition, the love of empire, or the thirst of wealth, have
most generally influenced the councils of nations, whether civilized, or
in a state of rude barbarianism. To such ignoble motives, is owing that
endless series of wars, devastations, and robberies, which, instead of
giving stability to the conquering state, hath invariably hastened its fall.
Of this truth, the history of mankind abounds in examples.'[76]
In the middle ages 'the continual drain of money, the waste of blood' produced almost no lasting result; and conditions now, in 1784, are no better:
'though the projects of the middle ages were barbarous in their object,
calamitous in their operation, and delusive in the sequel; yet this nation,
instead of reprobating the destructive measures of their ancestors, hath
considerably improved upon them.'[77]
There are only two certain consequences of war; debt, and accelerated
mortality. At least a million British subjects and allies, Knox estimated.
had been killed in various parts of the globe since the Revolution, besides
about four million 'industrious, inoffensive inhabitants' of Asia, killed or

starved. As regards debt, the national debt had stood at £16 million in
1701, and this had been increased by a series of wars to £136 million in
1775. The most serious of these wars was fought in defence of the American
colonies 'against the encroachments of the French on the back settlements';[78] but the result of an attempt to impose 'a slight taxation' on these
colonies was that they 'flew to arms', causing Great Britain to become
involved 'in a general war with the principal maritime powers of Europe,
of whom we purchased peace, by acknowledging the American independence' and ceding valuable territories to France and Spain—'circumstances extremely humiliating to the dignity of the British name, fatal to
her reputation, and injurious to her commerce'.[79] Worse still, the national
debt rose again, to approximately £272 milllion by the middle of 1784.
In this situation, peace was essential; 'Peace with all the world, and that for
a long continuance, is therefore our only hope.'[80]

But peace, Knox reckoned, would not be easy to maintain. Although
'nature towards this island [hath] been lavish in favours', she had been
hardly less so to France; French population was about three and a half
times that of Great Britain, while the French public revenue was likewise
three or four times as great; France's geographical situation was excellent,
and she possessed valuable colonies. Moreover—and this is significant for
what Knox was to go on to argue—France pursued a policy of internal
improvement by means of government action:

> 'It is well known that Greece and Rome set examples to mankind in
> whatever is beautiful, stupendous, and useful in architecture and science.
> In imitation of those great models, the public works in France are con-
> structed with a spirit, taste, and solidarity, far surpassing the diminutive,
> imperfect undertakings in England; because, in the former country, they
> are the works of government, conducted on the most extensive plans,
> with a view to magnificence as well as general utility. Whereas, in
> England, those works which are of the greatest national importance, as
> highways, canals, and harbours, are entrusted solely to the abilities of a
> few traders, or country gentlemen, whose only views being profit, and
> local conveniency, they are executed upon contracted designs, frequently
> with borrowed money, and consequently subject to such heavy burdens
> as to defeat, in some respects, the ends for which they were undertaken.'[81]

As a result of these differences in natural endowment and in policy there
was reason to fear, Knox argued, that France was more than a rival, that
she might easily become 'a superior, or a controuling power, in every
quarter of the globe'.

It followed from this that Britain could not afford to take life easy, to
hope for the best, and to leave the course of economic development 'to
nature'. A policy of avoiding war was probably no longer possible:

'Our wars, therefore, are in future to be considered, not as wars of choice, but of unavoidable necessity . . . there remains no alternative between a total relinquishment of our transmarine possessions, or a continued, expensive preparation for defensive war.'[82]

And the chief item in these preparations should be a policy of internal improvement. Such a policy had for too long been neglected in favour of vast ideas of extensive empire, and of commercial monopoly, which had resulted in, at best, a precarious, debt-ridden prosperity. But within the country there was still to be found 'the active, invigorating force' which could secure and animate even the most distant branches of a far-flung empire. Britain's weakness was a result of bad policy, of neglecting valuable assets.

'England in 1784, compared with Holland, China, antient Greece, Italy, and Egypt, is yet in a state of nature; still more so, is the northern part of our island. . . .'[83]

And the customary adverse comparison with Holland was extended by arguing that since the Dutch could accommodate over two million people in 9,540 square miles the British should be able to manage at least fifteen million in England, Scotland and Wales.

Having thus set the scene and stated the necessity for internal improvements, Knox turned his attention to 'the northern part of our island'. A good deal of the argument in this section concerns Scotland as a whole—Scotland's importance as England's best customer, the fiscal problems of Scotland, the backwardness, even in the more developed parts of the country, of Scottish agriculture and industry. But from the beginning emphasis is laid on the Scottish fisheries, and on the connection between the fisheries, the supply of seamen, and the maintenance of sea power. The Scottish fisheries, according to Knox, had at one time employed 20,000 men, either 'experienced seamen, or persons who were advancing progressively in the naval profession';[84] and this number could be increased. This was important, because the prosperity of the fisheries and the security of the empire coincided. In the past the Scottish fisheries—'that great nursery of seamen'—had made good the waste both of the merchant service and of the navy, enabling Great Britain 'to carry on the greatest traffic, and to mann the most victorious fleets that the world hath seen';[85] in the future, when 'a powerful, well-appointed fleet, and a proportionate number of men, always in readiness, will ever be necessary, both in peace and war',[86] the possibility of drawing on the Scottish fisheries for additional men would be more important than ever:

'there is not, in the whole system of British politics, an object of greater importance to the defence and prosperity of the kingdoms, than that of increasing the number of hardy, intrepid seamen, by means of the northern fisheries and coasting trade.'[87]

These wide-ranging political considerations occupy Knox for over sixty pages; the following eighty pages are devoted to 'A View of the Highlands Etc.' and contain the essential outline of his proposals. This main part of the book is somewhat scrappy and disjointed. Knox begins by describing the character and distresses of the highlanders; he extolls their virtues and pities their situation. He then concedes that climate and soil 'are greatly against that country',[88] but argues that this is a ground not for abandoning the Highlanders to their fate but for making exceptional efforts on their behalf. Russia, Norway and Sweden have, 'by dint of art', established prosperous cities in latitudes close to or even beyond the sixtieth parallel. Winters there are longer and more severe than in the Highlands; it is therefore due

> 'to the attention of their respective governments, more than [to] the advantages of nature, that so many commercial cities have gradually arisen in the north of Europe, within the space of a few centuries, and that places hitherto obscure are daily increasing in wealth and magnitude.'[89]

The United Provinces likewise, without raw materials, with 'scarcely a sufficiency for home consumption', suffering severe winters, and in extent no larger than the Hebrides, have over two million inhabitants who are 'continually engaged in fabricating an endless variety of articles for sale at home and abroad . . .; such is the influence of an active, vigorous government'.[90]

Having made this point about the importance of government action, Knox turns to the question of natural resources in the Highlands. These, it soon appears, are sufficiently varied and plentiful. Grain could be raised in far larger quantities 'whenever the more fertile parts shall be inhabited by men of property, and knowledge in agriculture', while roots, vegetables and common fruits 'can be raised in any quantity'.[91] There are extensive natural woods—'the sturdy oak and the hardy pine wave their branches over impending precipices, deriving vigour and strength from the boisterous elements of that climate'[92]—and farther afforestation offers 'a progressive, inexhaustible source of wealth':

> 'Few gentlemen in Scotland are unacquainted with the value of that small species of oak, which grows spontaneously upon the hills and rocks. The bark supplies the tanner, the net and sail maker; the wood is consumed in various works of glass and metal. The price is regulated by the demand; and the demand, by the progressive state of arts, manufactures, and commerce, in these kingdoms: consequently the value of this timber is continually advancing, insomuch that a wood, which would bring only £1,000 twenty-five years ago, now sells at £1,500.
>
> This branch therefore, opens a new field of action to all those who have wisdom to avail themselves of it.'[93]

Copper, iron ore 'in many places', lead, slate, marble, limestone and other materials are available. And above all there are fish, in the lochs and the sea.

Knox's proposals for the development of this promising region are brief—some seven thousand words—and they fall under three headings: transport, towns, and the fishery.

As regards transport, two canals should be constructed, one at Crinan and the other through the Great Glen. A canal at Crinan, only five miles long, would shorten the passage between Glasgow and the west Highlands and Hebrides by at least a hundred miles, or a quarter of the whole distance. It would no longer be necessary to beat round the Mull of Kintyre—'a bold undertaking for little open boats' which often resulted in disaster— and the connection between the west Highlands and 'the seats of industry, population and affluence' would be immensely improved. Moreover, the busses sailing from the Clyde for the west coast fishery would be able to reach the fishing grounds far more quickly and more certainly. Glasgow and Loch Fyne would no longer be a world away from Loch Broom, Skye and the Hebrides:

'A voyage, which frequently takes up three weeks, would, by this easy passage, be performed in four or five days, with fewer hands, and in all seasons of the year.'[94]

And the cost would be no more than £17,000.

Of the proposed canal between Fort William and Inverness Knox has little more to say. He enlarges on the beauties of the scenery, observes that 'Lochness appears to have been designed by Nature for population and commerce', and calculates that the line of communication is made up as follows: Lakes, 74 miles; Rivers, 17 miles; and Land, 2 miles; giving a total of 93 miles.

'Thus, by cutting two miles of land [14 feet above the flood mark at Inverness], and deepening seventeen miles of almost navigable rivers, a direct communication may be opened between the two seas; so favourable is Nature, even amidst the wilds of the north Highlands, to provincial improvement, and national unity.'[95]

How the Highlands were to benefit from this communication from sea to sea is by no means made clear. Inverness, it is stated, would benefit— 'Inverness, which is well situated for commerce, would become the emporium of the north, a centrical port between the two seas, giving employment to the industrious'[96]—and the northern counties, especially those bordering the Moray Firth, would benefit by having a faster connection to Glasgow. But it can hardly be said that a case is made out. The cost of the work Knox puts at £50,000, and he states that this is less than the 'accumulated loss' incurred by shipping in a single year in making the passage of the Pentland Firth, arising from 'delays, damages at sea, shipwrecks, captures, extra freight, and insurance.'

The case for building new villages (or towns) and harbours is stated with even greater brevity; indeed, the reader might be excused for not noticing that a case has been stated at all. In a country where soil and climate are unfavourable,

> 'The people should be comfortably lodged, and accommodated with provisions, stores, and firing. This implies the erection of villages at convenient distances. . . .'[97]

That is the extent of the argument. What Knox seems to have had in mind is that economic activity, other than at subsistence levels, needs the support of markets to provide supplies of materials and products needed in the production process and to take off the output of saleable goods. This can be deduced from occasional comments and from his list of the buildings which would be required in each village, which is worth quoting *in extenso*:

> '1. A key or breast, for small craft.
>
> 2. A range of warehouses, for casks, staves, hoops, salt, nets, fish, oil, grain, meal, skins, wool, flax, bark, timber, coals and other bulky articles.
>
> 3. Sheds, for persons employed in gutting, salting, and curing the herrings; with lofts where the people may be sheltered at night, from the inclemency of the weather. Every village should also be furnished with materials for erecting temporary sheds or tents for the conveniency of occasional distant fisheries.
>
> 4. A small market place.
>
> 5. A corn mill.
>
> 6. A church, and house for the minister.
>
> 7. A school house, where reading, writing, the common rules of arithmetic, and practical navigation, may be taught gratis.
>
> 8. A public inn.
>
> There might, possibly, be some difficulty in procuring useful mechanics to settle in these remote parts, previous to the regular establishment of fisheries, and commercial intercourse. Therefore, to encourage adventurers, as coopers, carpenters, net makers, blacksmiths, etc. it would be necessary to build fifteen or twenty dwelling houses, where these persons might live rent free; each house to be accommodated with three small enclosures. 1. For a garden and offices. 2. For potatoes. 3. For the support of a cow.
>
> Such luxuries as these, with variety of fish at no expence, would draw thither useful workmen from every quarter, and give stability to all the valuable purposes proposed by the public.'[98]

This passage makes it clear that the proposed villages are to be a part of the further development of the herring fishery—a fishery concerning which all that Knox has to suggest is that

> 'a small gratuity or bounty to every boat [should] be immediately granted. These boats may be registered, and put under such regulations as the legislature shall judge most expedient for the general benefit of the state.'[99]

Concerning the location of the villages, Knox had done some detailed thinking, and he was able to make a list of the most eligible sites, as follows: Crinan ('the key to the West Highlands'); Oban ('a beginning hath already been made towards forwarding a Town at Oban'); Loch Sunart; Bernera (or Glenelg; 'the usual pass between the continent and the Isle of Sky'); Gairloch; Loch Ewe; Loch Broom ('the chief scene of the western fishery for many ages'); and then, on the inhospitable north coast, at Loch Eriboll, Thurso (already a town), and Wick ('a small but antient borough-town . . . a tide harbour for a few vessels of small burden').[100]

Knox had also considered how these villages were to be paid for. Land would have to be purchased, not only to be built upon, but also to provide an endowment, or territorial revenue, of from two to three hundred pounds for the support of clergyman, school, and other purposes. The expense of land purchase he put at £10,000 per town. Building, he decided, would not be costly. Supplies (including timber!) would be plentiful, and 'the cheapness of workmanship' would also help to hold down costs. All things considered, a village of 'small neat houses' along with the quays, warehouses, etc., as specified, 'might possibly be completed for £10,000'. Total cost per village would thus be £20,000, and, as ten villages were proposed, the grand total would be £200,000. Or, if the transport proposals were included, £267,000.

This fairly ambitious plan, to reconstruct the Highlands for a quarter of a million pounds, when a quarter of a million pounds was a great deal more money, and represented a far larger slice of national resources than today, was put forward in a distinctly sketchy fashion. Money-wise it was a substantial although not a staggering proposal; but Knox's manner of presentation hardly did his ideas justice. The final part of the 1784 volume is a curious mingling of leisurely descriptive passages with practical proposals stated so briefly as to lose most of their impact. And it is perhaps for this reason that Knox republished the book, in greatly expanded form, a year later.

The second edition presents a much more persuasive case, putting flesh and blood on Knox's proposals. It also contains additional comments and revised calculations. As regards the fisheries, for example, there is the specific proposal that the bounty be fixed at 50s a ton with 'every restriction removed', and that this bounty apply to all vessels between 15 and

120 tons; smaller vessels would be registered 'and placed under the same regulations as the busses. . . . Each boat containing five men and a boy might be entitled to a bounty or premium of £10 or £15 annually', and busses would be allowed to buy herring from small boats; thus 'the busses and boats would mutually assist, and be assisting to each other'.[101] This arrangement, according to Knox, would produce a fleet of 500 busses and 4,000 fishing boats, manned by over 25,000 men and 4,000 boys, all seamen.

On the subject of towns the second edition is much more interesting than the first. The inhabitants of towns, it is said at the very start, should be free men,

> 'accommodated with provisions etc. . . . independent of lairds, stewards, or intermediate jobbers. . . . The idea of feudal aristocracy, and of feudal subordination should be utterly extinguished; and every man, of whatever degree or profession, should be master of his own time in all seasons. . . .'[102]

This consciously and determinedly anti-feudal attitude is something new in Knox, something that seems to belong more to Anderson's *National Industry*—although the sentiment is by no means out of place in Knox's work, which is modern and commercial in tone. Knox then goes on, for the first time, to give some details about the planning and appearance of the new towns.

> 'In the first progress of these towns it would be essentially necessary to have a view to conveniency, health, cleanness and neatness. I have often observed and lamented the inattention to these objects in Scotland, where they are made subservient to the interest of individuals, whose influence hath too much weight with magistracy, some of the parties concerned being themselves magistrates, or related by marriage, or consanguinity, to those in office. To this is owing the medley of symmetry and irregularity, of width, and of narrowness, which we often perceive in the same street. To this is also owing that odious deformity, by stairs on the outside of the buildings; and the permitting avaricious persons to counteract the intentions of magistrates, with the view of extorting a price disproportioned to the real value of their property. . . .
>
> When towns are to be erected upon new foundations, the streets should be of considerable width, laid out in straight-lines, crossing each other at right angles. The houses should be built, as nearly as possible, on the same model, and of the same height. A strict uniformity should also be observed in the colour of the stone, lime and slate; in the size and adjustment of the windows. . . .'[103]

In order to secure these results, the committee in charge 'should publish on copper-plate, the plan of each town, and oblige every builder to submit thereto. . . .'[104] Some encouragement to the settlers in these towns was now offered. To every person erecting a house worth £25 'a portion of ground equal to a quarter of an acre should be given in perpetuity, and without a quit rent'; such a prospect, with the freehold

> 'increasing in its value proportional to the increase of trade, and the number of inhabitants, would induce numbers to co-operate with government in raising these towns, and to prosecute the fisheries with unwearied perseverance.'[105]

But those arriving 'in these wilds' after 200 houses had been built, would have 'the benefit of society, and of necessary supplies', and would require no subsidy.

The number of towns to be built falls in the second edition from ten to eight, but the cost per town is calculated as before. Not so, however, with the Crinan or the Caledonian Canal. Knox observes that 'Mr Watts the engineer' has estimated the cost of the Crinan Canal at £48,405; but if the canal were to be twelve feet deep the cost would be near £60,000. How should this money be raised? (a question not asked in 1784). This question is examined with commendable care. A commercial return on the investment, according to Knox, would be $7\frac{1}{2}$ per cent; maintenance costs would be £500 per annum, giving a total annual charge of £5,000. Could this be met by charging the users? If the expected 500 busses became a reality, and all of them used the canal, the necessary income would be produced by a charge of £10 per vessel per annum; but at this rate, half the busses would go round the Mull of Kintyre. To charge such an economic rate would be mistaken, because the canal is to be constructed

> 'chiefly for the benefit of a considerable body of indigent people, who, by means of this canal, and other public assistance, may be brought into the line of action. . . . Any demand beyond 40s per vessel annually upon an average, would be oppressive and detrimental to the main object.'[106]

At this rate, the whole buss fleet might produce a revenue for the canal of £1,000 per annum. As to the small craft, these would be

> 'little Highland boats, passing to and from the Clyde, with cargoes seldom amounting to £20 each trip; and money is of such value with these people, that, to save 5s tonnage, they would risque the voyage by the Mull of Cantire, though, in so doing, many would perish.'[107]

The best policy would therefore be to build the canal at government expense, and operate it as a public service: 'a draft upon the exchequer of Scotland, for £60,000 payable to Mr Smeaton, or Mr Whitworth, engineers, would at once settle the matter.'[108] And as for the Caledonian Canal, (presumably to be financed in the same manner) the cost has crept up from £50,000 to £164,000. The original quarter of a million pound scheme is thus now costed at £384,000, with eight towns in place of ten, and without making any allowance for the cost of the subsidies to the herring fishery.

Knox seems to have written these revisions before Anderson's Report was made public, because his comments on that Report—thirty pages of them—appear as an appendix in the 1785 volume: 'Remarks on sundry Passages in Dr Anderson's Report . . . and his subsequent Evidence before the Committee on the British Fisheries.' Knox did nothing to spare his criticisms and little to moderate his language. He began by accusing Anderson, who 'never saw the West Highlands before August 1784', of having failed during his northern tour to visit many important places and many important proprietors, his conduct in this respect affording 'room to suspect a job, in the fullest sense of the word.' As a result of these failures, he was grossly uninformed, and his Report contained 'little more than gleanings from the late worthy but credulous Dr Campbell' (whom Knox had himself quoted, although only to the extent of two pages, in 1784). His ignorance of the country was shown by his proposal that a profit-making canal could be built so as to provide a passage—described by Anderson as 'nearly open at present'—from Fort William through Loch Shiel to the sea at Loch Moidart. This proposal, wrote Knox, 'could serve only to excite laughter' among those who knew that Lochaber was 'universally allowed to be one of the most barren unimproveable districts in the Highlands.' The doctor knew nothing whatever about Lochaber, or Loch Moidart, or Ardnamurchan, or a great many other places. His proposals were mostly 'ridiculous' showing him to be 'completely qualified for the strait waistcoat'. And when it came to planning new towns, wrote Knox, Dr Anderson 'seems to have given full scope to the flights of his imagination'. Knox's own proposals were for towns on the mainland, with 'back country to the east . . . and . . . the Hebride Isles lying in front'. Towns on the islands as proposed by Anderson—'Utopian Cities'—would mean that 'the greater territory would depend on the lesser', which did not make sense. Anderson's ignorance was again exposed by his choice of Boisdale on South Uist as a good site for a new town, a place well calculated to 'carry on a great trade with the Esquimaux Indians on the coast of Labradore' but not to promote the development of the Highlands. In any case, Anderson's five cities and forty villages would cost five million pounds, not, as he seemed to suggest, about a hundred thousand. Finally, to operate his complex bounty proposals 'would probably require 1,000 additional officers, whose salary at £20 each would amount to a greater sum than hath been paid to the busses, upon an average of years, since the commencement of the bounty'.[109]

There is a great deal of truth in these criticisms. What really angered Knox, presumably, was the fact—and it seems to be a fact—that Anderson had simply adopted, without acknowledgement, the basic proposals made by Knox in 1784—new towns or villages, canals, and a more generous and extensive bounty system. What probably made it still harder for Knox to bear was that to some extent he had himself to blame. His 1784 proposals are presented in such an off-hand manner and such a rudimentary form as to invite underestimation and neglect. Anderson seems to have taken up these outline ideas and to have made an imaginative picture out of a crude sketch. But sometimes his imagination runs away with him. Many of Knox's best-directed criticisms are of Anderson's excesses, in particular of his wildly optimistic notions of finance. Knox lacked—or did not suffer from—Anderson's imaginative power; and he had a much better grasp of practical short-run problems and of costs. Yet it is also significant that Anderson found the pattern and emphasis of Knox's proposals so acceptable. Differing in temperament as much as in their basic approach to the problems of development, both men put forward an almost identical set of solutions for the Highlands. Anderson had at one time advocated industrial development, but he did not do so now, or at least not for the west coast. His plans are grander than Knox's, and far less well costed; but they amount to a larger dose of the same remedies, and in much the same proportions.

With the passage of a little time, inflation of ideas took place. Anderson altered the emphasis in his plans from villages to towns. Villages he declared,

> 'afford scarce any advantages to the inhabitants, above those that are found in solitary hamlets . . . the beneficial progression is, first to establish large towns, and then to allow villages to spring up themselves around them . . . a village planted in any place, instead of rising to a town, unavoidably becomes in a short time a desert.'[110]

And he attributed the failure of the villages established in the 1760s by the Commissioners for the Forfeited Estates to the want of substantial towns in their vicinity. Knox, for his part, greatly enlarged his ideas, possibly in an attempt to keep up with Anderson. Addressing the Fisheries Society in 1786, he complained of the 'pitiful economy' which had characterised previous attempts to develop the west coast fishing, and called for the establishment not of eight but of forty villages 'in the first instance', each to be occupied by 'some men of property . . . with a proportionable number of practical fishers'. Given a sufficient number of settlements, and good houses instead of 'pitiful smoky hovels, possessed by a set of beggars', the Highlands and Islands would soon be as productive as Nova Scotia where, according to Knox, employment had recently increased in a few years from 500 to 10,000.[111] Between Anderson and Knox there was a rivalry which seems to have made each try to outbid the other.

To some extent, by the 1780s, it had become almost entirely a matter of scale and proportion. The ideas which Anderson and Knox advocated were becoming the standard solution to the problems of the Highlands. Back in

1774 David Loch had expressed the view that remoteness from the centres of economic activity, coupled with wretched internal communications, were 'the chief if not the sole causes of the long unpolished and rude state of the inhabitants'.[112] He therefore favoured the building of the Crinan canal, on the model of the Forth and Clyde canal, which, when he wrote, was in the early stages of construction. But he was also, vaguely and perhaps confusedly, in favour of other innovations as well. In Scotland generally he wanted to see an extension of sheep farming and of the woollen manufacture, and in this extension he wanted the Highlands to share:

> 'There is no country I have had occasion to be in, that promises better than our western Highlands for rearing and feeding sheep, that may produce good wool. These numerous hills afford excellent sheep-pasture; and, from their vicinity to the great western ocean, the snow does not lie upon them.'[113]

Anticipating objections, he added that this expansion of sheep-farming could take place 'without incroaching upon a single acre of land, capable of bearing corn, or rearing black cattle. Sheep are pastured to advantage where neither the one nor the other will thrive. . . .'[114] But although an advocate first and foremost of agriculture as 'the source of every nation's strength and wealth, and the mother of all arts and sciences',[115] and in spite of his favourable opinion of the highlanders' opportunities for sheep farming, he managed at the same time to believe that 'the fisheries . . . should be their first care . . . agriculture . . . is not the proper object for this part of the country'.[116] And finally, to complete the confusion, he wrote with enthusiasm of the policy of promoting manufactures, because from these there would arise a brisk circulation of money and thence an increase of incomes, population, and rents.[117] Loch's work is an outstanding example of the futility of putting forward a series of possibly good but uncoordinated and unordered ideas, leaving unresolved the crucial issues of choice and proportion. Most of the ideas put forward by later writers are to be found in Loch, in one form or another; but this is almost as much a criticism as a commendation of what he wrote.

Ten years after the appearance of Knox's expanded proposals Adam Smith published the third edition of *The Wealth of Nations*. Professor Viner has pointed out that it is one of the curiosities of the history of economic literature that Adam Smith took so little part in his published work in the debate about public policy towards the Highlands. The explanation may be that he had never been there. But he did take some part, for in the third edition of the *Wealth of Nations* he made three or four additions to the text, and these include four pages on the herring bounties along with a statistical appendix on the same subject. Predictably, Smith was no friend to the bounty system. He had criticised bounties in general in the first and second editions of his great book, especially bounties on exportation. He now complained that the herring bounty was too large; that it was not paid in proportion to the fish caught; that it should support the small boats, which were best able to operate in the sea-lochs, whereas it supported the busses and thus acted as 'necessarily a discouragement to the boat fishery';[118] that it subsidised exports and thus raised or at any rate maintained home market prices, to the disadvantage of 'a great number . . . whose circumstances are by no means affluent';[119] and finally that its effect was 'to encourage rash undertakers to adventure in a business which they do not understand', to their own and the public loss. The moral was clear: either there should be no herring bounties at all, or they should be paid to the small-boat fishermen. On other topics as they related to the Highlands, Adam Smith remained silent—it is striking, for example, that the only canal to which he refers is neither the Forth-Clyde nor the Crinan, but the canal of Languedoc.

Adam Smith's views, however, were not those of the majority; he may have modified opinion about the Highlands slightly, but he did not change it. There was by 1784 the beginning of a consensus. Almost at the same time that Smith published his third edition, a practical improver like George Dempster, who lived in the Highlands,[120] was able to feel that the lines along which progress could be made were becoming clearer; and it was then, late in 1784, that he wrote one of the few apophthegms about the Highland problem: 'The seas abound with fish, the Highlands with industrious and good people. It will be the business of the legislature to bring these two to meet. . . .'[121] But Dempster, himself a good agriculturalist, did not wish to lose sight of the part that an improved agriculture could play in Highland development, while arguing that state intervention would be best directed towards the fisheries:

'Should . . . the proper encouragement be given to the fisheries, it would produce still more important consequences to the nation, by the improvement the Highlands is [sic] susceptible of in point of agriculture.'[122]

In other words, a policy of developing agriculture and the fisheries simultaneously was preferable to one of developing either alone; the fisheries were to be aided by government, agriculture was presumably to be left to the landowners. To that extent the picture was clear. What was to be done about transport, and how important a town building programme might be, was not so clear. Of the introduction of industry, less and less was being heard; industry was perhaps to be a consequence rather than a cause of economic development. To some extent interventionist planning is always like this. Whatever development is contrived will, if it is successful, draw forward some further development. The problem is to know which projects are most likely to succeed without the support of many others, and which will exert the greatest leverage on the rest of the economy. Crucial policy decisions remained to be made after 1785; events would show whether the course of history was to be determined by these decisions, or whether their effects would be submerged in the general tide, seemingly but not truly resistless, impersonal but not for that reason undirected, of secular change.

5

Fishing and Distilling

The debate about the Highlands had one immediate consequence: it increased knowledge of the area. To those in the south, as Johnson put it,

'the state of the mountains, and the islands, is equally unknown with that of Borneo or Sumatra; of both they have only heard a little, and guess the rest. They are strangers to the language and the manners, to the advantages and wants of the people. . . .'[1]

This could scarcely have been said ten years later. Yet even while information was being gathered, in the later 1770s and early 1780s, the situation was changing. The Commissioners for the Forfeited Estates, hard at work in the 1770s, had concentrated their attention largely on agriculture, communications and trade, and partly because of their efforts trade between Highlands and Lowlands not only continued across the frontier and along the coasts as it had always done, but expanded. And at the same time the fishing industry, with which the Commissioners were not much concerned, spread into the remoter parts of the north-west Highlands, in some ways helped and in many hindered by changing legislation; while a changing pattern of demand raised up the distillation of whisky to a place of importance if not of honour in the highland economy.

Fishing was inevitably a part of Scottish economic activity. 'The whole coast of Scotland,' wrote Knox, 'may be considered as one continual fishery;'[2] and he did not exaggerate. Four kinds of fishing took place. There was the well-organised salmon fishing, the catch going mostly to metropolitan markets. Secondly, for local consumption, there was fishing for haddocks, whiting, and other small fish. Next, concentrated mostly on the coast of Shetland and in the Hebrides, there was fishing for cod and ling, the fish salted and dried in the sun before being sent south. But far surpassing them all in importance, prestige and—men were convinced—potential, was the herring fishery.

Great shoals of herring came down to the Scottish coasts from the northern seas every summer. In the vicinity of the Shetlands the shoals divided, some to pass down the east coast of Scotland and some down the west, these latter again dividing into two streams, one of which passed to

the west—sometimes far to the west—of the Long Island, the other coming
through the Minch and entering, to a greater or lesser extent, the lochs and
narrow waters of the west coast of the mainland. The herring usually
reached Shetland about the beginning of June, and moved steadily southward in the following months. By the 1780s, if not earlier, the first shoals
were followed by others, so that large quantities of fish might be taken
even on the north-west coasts as late as November or December. Prior to
1750, the Scottish herring fishery was centred on Loch Fyne and the Firth
of Clyde, but in the following decade or two both Loch Hourn and Loch
Broom, lying much further north, began to be fished for the vast shoals of
herring along their shores. Visiting Loch Broom in the summer of 1772,
Pennant left the following account:

'[the herring] generally appear here in July: those that turn into this bay
are part of the brigade that detaches itself from the Western column of
that great army that annually deserts the vast depths of the arctic circle,
and come, heaven-directed, to the seats of population ...

The migration of these fish from their Northern retreat is regular;
their visits to the Western isles and coasts, certain; but their attachment
to one particular loch, extremely precarious. All have their turns; that
which swarmed with fish one year, is totally deserted the following; yet
the next loch to it be crowded with the shoals ...

The signs of the arrival of the herrings are flocks of gulls, who catch
up the fish while they skim on the surface; and of gannets, who plunge
and bring them up from considerable depths. Both these birds are closely
attended to by the fishers ... In summer they come into the bays generally with the warmest weather, and with easy gales. During Winter the
hard gales from North-West are supposed to assist in forcing them into
shelter. East winds are very unfavourable to the fishery.'[3]

Herring were caught by two methods. The first of these was known as
small boat fishing. The boats used were open boats of fourteen to sixteen
foot along the keel and six to seven foot beam, with four or five men in
each. These boats, undecked, encumbered with nets, buoys, rope and other
gear, offered no protection and little safety for the crew, who for the most
part sensibly confined their efforts to the lochs and bays along the coast;
even so, loss of boats and men was not infrequent, 'even in the Fishing
Lochs, when shooting or hauling their Nets, without going into a more
dangerous Situation in the open Sea.'[4] The alternative and better publicised
method was the buss fishing. The busses were decked vessels, which might
vary in size from twenty tons to eighty tons or even more. A vessel of
twenty tons needed a crew of six men, and for every five tons above that an
additional hand was required. An eighty ton vessel thus carried eighteen
men, besides three small boats, 20,000 square yards of netting, 144 barrels

11. Loch Hourn, or the Lake of Hell. 'The scenery that surrounds
the whole of this lake has an Alpine wildness and magnificence.' (Pennant)

LOCK JURN.

of salt, 120 casks and stores sufficient for a three month voyage. To build and equip such a vessel was a considerable undertaking; in 1785 it was reckoned that a buss of only about 50 tons cost nearly £500 to build and over £200 to equip. The method of fishing was as follows:

'Every boat takes out from twenty to thirty nets [a net measured 36 feet by 30] and puts them together so as to form a long train: they are sunk at each end of the train by a stone, which weighs it down to the full extent; the top is supported by buoys, made of sheeps-skin, with a hollow stick at the mouth, fastened tight; through this the skin is blown up, and then stopt with a peg, to prevent the escape of the air. Sometimes these buoys are placed at the top of the nets; at other times the nets are suffered to sink deeper, by the lengthening the cords fastened to them, every cord being for that purpose ten or twelve fathoms long. But the best fisheries are generally in more shallow water.

The nets are made at *Greenock*, in *Knapdale, Bute* and *Arran*; but the best are procured from *Ireland*; and, I think, from some part of *Caernarvonshire*.

The fishing is always performed in the night, unless by accident. The busses remain at anchor, and send out their boats a little before sun-set, which continue out, in Winter and Summer, till day-light; often taking up and emptying their nets, which they do ten or twelve times in a night in case of good success. During Winter it is a most dangerous and fatiguing employ, by reason of the greatness and frequency of the gales in these seas, and in such gales are the most successful captures; but by the providence of heaven, the fishers are seldom lost . . .'[5]

This buss fishing was not necessarily confined to coastal waters, but could be carried on many leagues from the shore.

The originators and masters of buss fishing were the Dutch. For almost two hundred years a Dutch fleet made rendezvous at Brassey Sound, in Shetland, towards the end of June. First fishing near Shetland, and later following the shoals along the Scottish coasts, Dutch busses salted and packed the catch on board, then sailed either home to Holland or to the Baltic, and returned (perhaps repeating this more than once in a season), or transferred their catch to accompanying boats called Yawgers or Jaggers whose particular purpose it was to carry the fish to market. There were also two hospital or store ships with additional men and provisions, one of which remained at Brassey Sound, the other sailing with the fleet; and there was sometimes a command ship, which also stationed itself at Brassey Sound. This was 'the fishery', an industry, as Malcolm Gray has put it, 'of majestic vessels and wide-spread markets, [one which] lay deep in the Mercantilist consciousness. Did not the Dutch for two centuries bestride northern Europe with their great fishing fleet and its products?'[6] This was what the British government sought, around 1750, to emulate. To

12. Unapool, with Quinag. 'After six hours rowing about all these solitary creeks, we discovered half a dozen dunghills buried under the lee of a high bank. It was Unapil.' (Macculloch, 1824.)

encourage shipbuilding, provide a training ground for seamen, and gain a valuable trade was the object of policy. That the Dutch—the frugal and persevering Dutch whose interest in the fisheries was already on the decline, although the British did not know it—would be the losers made the prospect all the more attractive. Little notice was taken of the small boat fishing.

Legislation to encourage the fishing industry was already three centuries old, but this did not deter the government from embarking, as soon as the Rebellion was over, on a new and complicated series of supposedly encouraging laws. In 1749 an Act was passed which granted a bounty of 30s per ton to busses employed by a Society to be incorporated as a result of the Statute, the government to pay interest at the rate of 3 per cent per annum on such part of a capital of £500,000 as should be invested in the fishery. Private adventurers were also allowed the bounty of 30s per ton but not the 3 per cent on capital. 'The consequence was, that few individuals took the Benefit of the Law, and little appears to have been done, even by the Society'.[7] In 1757 the bounty was raised to 50s per ton. This had little effect until the war was ending, when progress began to be made, notably in and around the Clyde. But in 1766 regular payment of the bounty suddenly ceased, and as a result several adventurers 'who had launched out extensively into the Fishing Business, on the Faith of Receiving their Bounties regularly'[8] became bankrupt, and were obliged to sell their ships and gear at a loss of—it was alleged—30 per cent. Three years later, when the Society's charter expired and was not renewed, an Act reduced the bounties to 30s per ton, but made them chargeable on the Customs and Excise revenues, thus guaranteeing regular payment.

The progress of the buss fishery during the period was therefore understandably erratic, as the following figures show:

Tonnage of Vessels in the Herring Fishery

1751	148 tons	1759	182 tons	1767	12,556 tons	1775	13,072 tons
1752	300	1760	554	1768	9,554	1776	14,194
1753	518	1761	746	1769	3,868	1777	11,728
1754	404	1762	2,056	1770	862	1778	10,878
1755	78	1763	3,692	1771	1,066	1779	10,192
1756	78	1764	5,132	1772	7,402	1780	8,924
1757	104	1765	7,056	1773	8,340	1781	6,450
1758	182	1766	12,476	1774	11,350	1782	7,056

Source: *Third Report on Fisheries* (1785) Appendix 4

The average size of vessel in the 1770s was about 48 tons. This means that the fleet varied during that decade from about 18 vessels in 1770 to a maximum of 296; and if the ships were manned according to the accepted standard, the employment of seamen was, at the peak, about 3,250.

The government may have regarded such results as reasonably satisfactory; but the legislation was the subject of strong and persistent criticism. It was not only, as Adam Smith complained, that a bounty paid according to the tonnage of the vessel and not according to her success at sea made it 'common for vessels to fit out for the sole purpose of catching, not the fish, but the bounty';[9] there was also the fact that the law imposed many vexatious difficulties and limitations on the very activity which it professed to help. To qualify for the bounty, ships had to rendezvous at Brassey Sound on a date *after* the first appearance of the herring shoals; alternatively, they could rendezvous later in the year at Campbeltown, which was a harbour difficult to get into and even more difficult to get out of; calling here was said to interrupt the busses' voyage to the fishing grounds by 'eight Days upon an Average'.[10] They had to carry a crew along with nets and other equipment exactly as laid down in the Act; all this was checked by customs officers and the slightest mistake disqualified for the bounty. There were also fees, perquisites and bonds to be paid or given, which were said to amount to almost ten pounds sterling on the average. Finally, in order to receive the bounty and sometimes for other purposes as well it was necessary for the captain or owner of the vessel to appear in person at Edinburgh—no easy task in the middle of the eighteenth century if his home was on Islay or Mull or at the Kyle of Lochalsh.

What the Act gave with one hand, therefore, it to some extent took back with the other. It was, indeed, the sort of legislation that made an ideal target for the arrows of Adam Smith's anti-mercantilism. Anderson, who was Adam Smith's apt pupil, put the matter well enough when he wrote:

'The Laws hitherto enacted, however well intended by Government, have failed in Practice, and it was impossible that they should have operated otherwise; they may be considered as the Regulations of Experiment, insufficient and defective, discovering a good Will, and at the same Time counteracting their own Purposes—What one Clause gives in Bounties, other Clauses take away in Duties, Excises, and expensive obligatory Conditions, tending at the same Time to obstruct, instead of promoting that Business.'[11]

But the question is: how did this legislation affect those who lived in the Highlands? At first sight, it might be thought that the most that could be said would be that it did them little good. Obviously, few highlanders could afford to own a buss, or even to take a share in one. Anything from seven hundred to a thousand pounds was needed and 'The Natives upon the Fishing Coasts of Scotland live in general in a State of abject Poverty.'[12] Ownership was centred in the Clyde area, among merchants, farmers or perhaps lesser men 'who join their Purses together to send out a Buss.'[13] (Many were ruined, sooner or later, because of the great variations in the catch; having little capital, few could withstand two bad years in succession.) Moreover, buss fishing required a concentration of time and energy as well as of resources; and few highlanders could give the time and energy, being so much occupied, as an eye-witness put it, 'in providing a miserable Fuel for the Winter, or in managing their own little Farms, or in performing certain personal Services for their Landlord or his Steward, or the principal Tacksmen under whom they hold their precarious Possessions.'[14] Perhaps this overstates the importance of services at any rate as late as 1785; but it was in general true, as was stated by Anderson himself, that 'nothing proves such an Obstruction to the Fisheries as the Operations and the Cares of Agriculture.'[15]

These considerations show only that the bounties were of no benefit to the highlanders. In fact, they injured them. Adam Smith went to the heart of the matter when he wrote:

> 'But the great encouragement which a bounty of thirty shilling the ton gives to the buss fishery, is necessarily a discouragement to the boat fishery; which, having no such bounty, cannot bring its cured fish to market upon the same terms as the buss fishery.'[16]

In short, a bounty to one kind of fishing put the other kind—the highlanders' kind—at a competitive disadvantage. This argument would lose its force if the local fishermen had been allowed to sell their fish to the busses. But they were not. No decked vessel was allowed to purchase herring, under the penalty of forfeiting the bounty. This was because the principal object of the law was to train seamen, not to increase the supply of herring to the public; the busses therefore must stay at sea and catch their own fish. The clause against purchase may have been evaded to some extent,[17] but most of the evidence is against this; it was noted as rather singular, for example, that when the herring were in Loch Fyne, trading boats sailed there in order to purchase their catch from the local fishermen and then to sell it in Clydeside ports such as Glasgow, Ayr and Greenock; and that this had the effect of raising the value of property in the neighbourhood of Loch Fyne. No such good fortune came the way of the native highlanders further north. The best they could do, according to a witness before the 1785 Fisheries Committee, was 'by joining their whole Stock together . . . to fit up an old Net, and purchase a crazy Boat, wherewith they take as many Herrings as they can, some of which they use themselves, and boil up the rest for the Sake of the Oil they afford.'[18] But also, if Pennant is to be believed, there were sometimes opportunities to sell cattle to the busses when their food supplies were running low, and gutting the fish provided employment on shore for some women and children, who were paid 'three-half-pence per barrel for their trouble,'[19] and who occupied little hovels or tents along the edges of the lochs, when the busses were in.

There were other difficulties. It is at least possible that the British busses, which—unlike the Dutch fleet—operated in the lochs and narrow waters round the coast and not out to sea, impeded fishing by the small boats when this was attempted. Even when peacefully managed, a score of busses in Loch Broom may have hindered or intimidated the small boat fishermen; and it was well known that buss fishing was not always peacefully conducted:

'The Crews of Fishing Vessels are in general disposed to be disorderly; they cut and steal one anothers' Nets and Buoys, and some of them have been known to be so much inclined to Mischief, as to fix Nails or Knives to the Blades of their Oars, that by sweeping them over the Buoys, as they rowed through a Train of Nets, they might destroy them with the greater Ease, and let the Nets sink to the Bottom.'[20]

The evidence is scanty, but it may well be that the activities of the buss fishermen from the south sometimes made life difficult for the native fishermen, who were described as 'full of complaints against the buss-men.'[21]

The role of the landlords is also unclear. Anderson, who was inclined to overstate the wrongs suffered by the tenants and other poor folk in the Highlands, asserted that on the west coast north of the island of Barra, as far as fishing for other than local demand was concerned, the landlords rack-rented their tenants and then compelled them to take up fishing on terms which could be profitable only to the landlords themselves. Superiors, he declared,

'furnish to their immediate Dependents Boats, and the necessary Apparatus for fishing, for which they charge whatever Rates they think proper to impose; they also lay in Meal, and other Necessaries, which they give out to their Dependents in small Portions, as it is wanted, at what Prices they please to exact. To obtain Payment for these Articles, these People become bound to go out a-fishing, as often as possible, and agree, even upon Oath in some Cases, not to sell any Fish they shall catch, but to bring the Whole to their Superior, who agrees to take them all at certain Stipulated Prices of his own making also. By these Means some of these Superiors have contrived to squeeze the poor People to the utmost Degree they can possibly bear and usually arrange Matters so as to get them into his [*sic*] Debt. They are then unable to find the Means of emigrating to other Countries, and are afraid to propose to alter their Situation, lest they might be stript of their All. They therefore live in a State of abject Indigence and Slavery.'[22]

This account of the rôle played by landlords is not supported by other observers. But there may be something in it, for there is ample evidence that in Shetland, at any rate, tenants were indeed compelled to fish for the rent on the landlords' terms; they depended on the landlords for boats, lines and hooks (they were engaged in white fishing), and the landlords took a share of the catch if there was one.[23] This was a system very much like share-cropping in the American South, fifty to a hundred years later, where shortage of credit made necessary the pledging of cotton crops to merchants against seed and future supplies.[24] The disadvantage of such a system is not so much the costliness of credit—even critics admitted that the landlords in Shetland charged no interest on their advances—as the chronic indebted-ness which it tends to generate, along with excessive resistance towards new practices or methods of production. This conservatism—the result of a man's anxiety in a situation of impoverishment and debt that at least a mini-mum income shall be secured and unusual risk of loss avoided—was noted in Shetland, where, even when the fishing failed, the same system was still pursued in the hope that more successful fishings in succeeding years would extinguish the balance owing by the tenant.[25] In an economy where nothing was more needed than new enterprise and technical innovation, it was disastrous that landlord and tenant alike should be in the grip of a sys-tem which all but precluded change.

Further and related difficulties arose on account of the Salt Laws. Trade in salt used for fish curing was governed by Acts passed in 1719 and 1735. These Acts exempted from payment of the Excise Duty of 10s per bushel all foreign and home salt used to cure fish which were exported. But to pre-vent salt being exempted unless actually used for this purpose was difficult; and it became, as the 1785 *Report* put it, 'a Case of some Intricacy to devise Plans for preventing Frauds in that Respect'. The arrangement hit upon was that all importers had to land their salt at a Custom House, where it was carefully weighed by the customs officers; then had to give their oath that the salt was to be used only to cure fish for export; and then, with two sufficient sureties, had to give bond for the whole value of the excise duties; after which, and only after which, the salt could be removed. The bond could be recovered only when the importer produced at the custom house such quantities of cured fish, ready for export, as would account for the quantity of salt imported by him, or a document from the officers of the Salt Duty certifying that such an amount of fish had been or was about to be exported. Any deficiency had to be produced in actual salt, or else the curer had to pay for a Custom House officer to travel to the curer's port, and for the expenses of his being there while he inspected the salt store. If in any of these respects the law was not complied with by the 5th of April after the importation, the Commissioners of the Salt Duties commenced an action for recovery of the penalty in the bonds. And there were many fur-ther complications:

'If any of the Salt remains unused, a new Bond in the same Terms must be granted for it, however small the Quantity; nor can it be moved from the Place where it is lodged, without an express Order from the Custom House; nor can it be shifted from one Vessel into another, did these Vessels even belong to the same Person, without an Order from the Custom House; nor can a Bushel of that Salt, in any Circumstances, be sold to any Person, without getting a new Bond at the Custom House for that Quantity'[26] etc., etc.

Also, fish landed at one port could not be shipped to another until the quantity had been checked by customs officers and an order authorising the voyage had been received. Infringement of any part of the law carried heavy penalties.

It is hard to believe that all this complicated and restrictive legislation can have done anything but depress the herring fishery which it was designed to help. Curers were relieved of the 10s per bushel excise duty, but the expenses of bonding, weighing surpluses, and settling the Salt Account could easily exceed the amount of the duty. Delays to trade were inevitable and must often have been costly. The Board of Customs may have acted, as was alleged, as reasonably as possible,[27] but the fact remains that 'the least mistake' laid a curer open to heavy penalties. And again it was the highlander who was the worst affected. Anyone living in the Western Isles and wanting to take part in the herring fishery had to have salt delivered to a customs house which might be a hundred miles away (the only Custom House on the west coast north of Oban was at Loch Broom), appear there in person and then have the salt weighed, re-loaded and sent on to his home port. Working on a small scale was uneconomic, because a bond for the minimum quantity of salt cost 10s 6d 'besides the Fees of Office.' A man of small capital might also have understandable difficulty in finding friends who could take the risk of standing surety for him to the required amount; and he knew, besides, that if anything went wrong and proceedings were begun against him, he must, if new evidence appeared which established his innocence, pay to have the prosecution set aside. Little wonder that the salt laws were described as 'a confused impolitic Mixture,'[28] or that Gaelic-speaking highlanders, poor as well as illiterate, took only a very small part in the herring fishing.

Nor was fishing the only aspect of life in the Highlands which government legislation adversely affected. There was also the fuel problem. The issue here was the existence and impact of the Coal Tax. This tax was even older than the Salt Duties. In 1710, when the temporary law imposing a duty on all coals carried coastwise to any port in England, from the ports of Newcastle and Sunderland, expired, a new Act was passed, which imposed a duty of 3s 8d per ton upon all coals carried coastwise from these or any other ports in Great Britain, to any part of the country whatever. There was thus imposed upon Scotland, for the first time, taxation of a kind with which England was already familiar. But the economic circumstances of the two countries were different in important respects. Coal was mined in England in a number of widely separated areas, and river and canal navigation, although in its infancy, was developing rapidly. As a result, many parts of England were not dependent for coal supplies upon the coastwise trade from Newcastle and Sunderland, and were thus unaffected by the tax. But in Scotland coal mining was almost wholly confined to Lanarkshire and the shores of the Firth of Forth. Many parts of Scotland were out of reach of these lowland coal-fields, except by sea; and this was particularly true of the Highlands, where there was no local supply. Hence coal was available in the Highlands only after payment of the 3s 8d tax per ton, whereas it was available free of tax in many parts of the lowlands and of England. This placed the Highlands at a serious disadvantage. It meant that tax plus transport costs frequently amounted to more than the price of coal at the pit head, and this meant both that the development of industry was retarded and that the labour force was wastefully employed in digging peat.

The first of these points must not be exaggerated. 'No one circumstance,' declared Anderson, 'has contrived more effectually to repress the industry of the people, and to prevent the establishment of manufactures among them, than the want of coal.'[29] But coal was not widely used as an industrial fuel before 1800, except in a few iron-making and coal-mining localities. Industry still depended largely on water power, and the availability of this in the Highlands was not affected by the Coal Tax. It was a stronger argument that the coal tax hindered the burning of lime for use in agriculture, directly depressed the highlanders' standard of living and diverted resources from their best uses. The highlanders had to depend on peat, and winning the peat absorbed many man-hours which could, in some cases at least, have been better spent in modernising agriculture or developing the herring fishery. Complaints on this head were frequent:

'The principal disadvantage under which this parish labours, is the scarcity of fuel.—The few heritors, and the better sort of farmers, now burn coal. But it is of the greatest disadvantage to the parish to want fuel, or not to get coal at an easy rate; for it costs generally 2/2 the barrel, and the farmers and cottagers spend all the summer, and part of the harvest, in procuring some bad turf.'[30]

Throughout the eighteenth century the situation was growing worse. The nearest peat mosses were becoming exhausted, and men (and women and children) had to go progressively farther afield for fuel: 'Peat moss is . . . becoming scarce;'[31] 'the common tenants and cottagers depend chiefly upon turf, the peat mosses being almost exhausted.'[32] There is no denying that the Coal Tax was inequitable, bore heavily on the poor, and led to maldistribution of resources; and these defects were in no wise compensated by its importance as a source of revenue, for the net proceeds over the whole of Scotland in the 1780s did not exceed £3,000 per annum.

There was one industry in the Highlands, however, which there was no need to encourage: the distilling of whisky. Nowadays we think of whisky as the traditional highland drink, but prior to the last few decades of the eighteenth century its use in the Highlands was not especially widespread or conspicuous. Until 1700, or perhaps as late as 1750, the common beverage of the highlanders was ale—'strong frothing ale from the cask'[33]— and it is said that most of the whisky then drunk in the Highlands came from the south. Highland gentlemen preferred to drink claret, which until about 1780 was exempt from duty, and rum and brandy which were landed on the west coast and thence conveyed all over the country. But from about 1770 ale began to be replaced by spirits, and the distilling of whisky to absorb an increasing amount of highland barley, time and ingenuity. Some proprietors sought to put down distillation—Pennant found that the Duke of Argyle 'takes great pains in discouraging the pernicious practice'[34] —but their efforts had little effect, and in many parishes distilling soon became the principal method of converting produce into cash for the payment of rents. In the 1790s it was said in Wester Ross that 'whisky may, in fact, be called our staple commodity',[35] and the same was probably true in Islay, Kintyre and several other districts.

Whisky was made either from malted barley or from an inferior grain called bear or bigg. The malt, having been dried over a peat fire, was mashed in a quantity of hot water, causing the starch in the grain to change into sugar, after which yeast was added. This liquid, called 'wash', was then subjected to a process of double distillation. The apparatus in common use was exceedingly simple. It consisted of a 'pot' still, which resembled a large copper bell, from the head of which there was a connection to a coil of copper pipe, narrowing along its length, and surrounded by water in order to cool it. The 'wash' was poured into the still, and brought to the boil. Steam escaped into the worm, cooling took place, and a liquor called low wines, or spirits of the first extraction, was thus obtained. These low wines, on being distilled a second time, were sold for consumption.

Whisky was distilled throughout Scotland, which from 1786 until 1815 was divided for tax purposes into Highlands and Lowlands, along with a small but not unimportant intermediate district. The Highland line, as far as whisky was concerned, was traced along the north shores of Loch Fyne, down to Tarbet, across to Callander, then up through Dunkeld to Fettercairn, north to Fochabers, and round through Elgin and Forres to the Moray Firth. It thus enclosed almost all the usual highland areas (except the Mull of Kintyre) and included also substantial parts of Angus, Aberdeenshire and Moray. The output of whisky in Scotland was divided about equally between the Highland and Lowland districts, with the advantage being usually in favour of the Lowlands; such, at any rate, was the situation in the late 1780s, when figures are available. The amount of employment directly provided by the industry was not great. To work a forty gallon still—the standard size—required two men, or at most three.[36] Around 1790 there were about 350 legal stills in the Highlands, which would have provided employment for not many more than 1,000 men. But a good deal of secondary employment was generated by the industry. It demanded grain, which the law required should be obtained within the distiller's own district, although highland distillers were known sometimes to obtain their supplies from the lowlands. Peat was needed for malting the barley; coal was wanted, if it could be bought at a reasonable price (4s the ton was a fair pit-head price in the 1780s), for heating the contents of the still; or alternatively peat could be used. It was sometimes believed that peat was not suitable, but this depended on the construction of the still. High temperatures were not necessary—indeed, it was essential not to allow the liquor to boil:

'Heat a Still too much, instead of distilling it throws off boiling liquor, and the operation is thereby totally destroyed; hence arises the prodigious difference in the operation of the Lowland and Highland Stills; the former, by means of its capacious and elevated head, is capable of bearing a great degree of heat without the risk of boiling over, or, as the distiller's phrase is, running foul; a proportional quantity of steam is generated, and it has sufficient room to form a distinct separation with the liquor in the Still the Highland Still; has no such scope, and consequent advantage; an equal degree of heat, by making it run foul, would destroy the operation; it is therefore necessary to apply only a low degree of heat, and the quantity of steam produced must be proportionally small.'[37]

Finally, a good deal of transportation was required, both of the raw materials to the distillery, and of the finished product to consumers. Thus further employment was provided.

All this was very much complicated by government taxation, which affected the industry in a number of ways. Until towards the end of 1785, tax was levied on the (supposed) quantities of wash, low wines and spirits made by the distiller. This system 'gave great opportunities to the distiller to elude the vigilance or purchase the connivance of the Excise officer',[38] and the revenue which resulted was notoriously below what should have been, besides being obtained only from those who proved unlucky enough, or unskilful enough, not to be able to evade payment.[39] Moreover, the regulations obliged every distiller to work on a scale which could be contemplated scarcely anywhere in the Highlands, either because of local scarcity of grain or scarcity of customers.[40] As a result, many gentlemen and reputable farmers distilled whisky for their own use—which the law allowed them to do—either in their own houses, or more commonly by employing poor people to distil for them; and at the same time, 'obscure and indigent persons, in places of concealment'[41] operated small illegal stills and sold whisky; some of the poorest of these people, around 1780, were selling a coarse spirit made chiefly from potatoes.

Not all highland whisky was consumed locally. From time to time, in order to obtain provisions from the Lowlands, a string of little ponies tied head to tail, sometimes as many as one hundred, would set off from a distilling district carrying small kegs of whisky to use as barter, and would return in two or three weeks, each loaded with a boll of meal, or some cloth or metalware. Although important to the highlanders the trade was small, partly because Dutch gin was available throughout Scotland, smuggled, at 35s per anker of nine gallons, housed on shore. But at the end of 1785 an Act was passed which charged duty according to the quantity of spirits that a still was supposed capable of producing, according to size; and this Act did not penalise operation on a fairly small scale. This enabled the highlanders to engage fairly in the business of distilling, which suited the proprietors, who had a new legal market for their grain, as well as a more reliable supply of whisky. For a time, 'all ranks concurred in supporting the law, and the office of an informer became even reputable'.[42] (In the years that followed, the rates of duty were from time to time altered, and in 1815 both the still licence system and the distinction between Highland and Lowland were removed.[43] Not until 1822 and 1823, however, were Acts passed which radically changed the law in a way calculated to encourage legitimate distillation.)

The new system, established by the Act of 1785, led to a great deal of trouble in two ways. First, the rate of tax was calculated on an assessment of the productive capacity of a still of any given size. But productive capacity depended not only on the dimensions of the still but also on its design and on the speed of working—the number of times, that is, that it could be filled and emptied in twenty-four hours. The distillers therefore set out to re-design their equipment so that the conventional measurement of size would understate the productive capacity of the still, and to speed up their working. In both directions their efforts were successful, with the result that the duty per gallon came to depend very much on the size and shape of the still, on the quality of the equipment, and on the number and skill of the workmen. This would not have mattered so much had it not been the case that the lowland distillers were more resourceful and energetic than their highland counterparts in modernising their equipment and so reducing the effective rate of duty.[44] But—and this was the second source of complaint—taxation per unit of (supposed) capacity was set at a

lower level in the Highlands than in the Lowlands, on the grounds that
grain in the Highlands was of an inferior quality, that the harvest was more
precarious, and that the highland distillers were less well supplied in terms
of both skill and capital than those in the Lowlands. In case the system
worked unfairly, a few complicating restrictions were added, and it was
forbidden to sell highland whisky in the Lowlands.

The government could hardly have done more to create sources of friction, and encourage smuggling; their measures, it was correctly remarked,
'serving only to torment the manufacturer without securing the duty'.[45]
Each district complained that it was overtaxed by comparison with the
other. All distillers complained that taxation diverted demand to illicit
stills, and this became increasingly true as rates of duty were raised. Towards the end of the century the effective rate of duty seems to have varied
from as little as fourpence a gallon (which would have been paid only by
the most efficient—or dishonest—distillers) to as much as one shilling per
gallon and even more. Retail prices varied a good deal, partly because of
good and bad harvests, partly because of great differences in the quality of
spirits offered for sale. In 1794 and 1795 spirits were astonishingly cheap,
good whisky selling for as little as 3s per gallon—'the lower orders purchased a half gill . . . for a half-penny. The unavoidable consequences of
such prices were a great consumption of Spirits, and constant scenes of in-
toxication'.[46] More usually, malt whisky ten over proof was retailed in the
1780s at about 5s 6d per gallon and in the 1790s at about 6s 6d.

These, however, were the prices of legally produced spirits; and as the
rates of duty rose in the 1790s so the inclination to evade the law became
stronger. (An Act of 1795 which prohibited all distillation, in order to
conserve grain, and which remained in force until 1797, was a further
encouragement to illegal working.)[47] If the effective rate of duty was between sixpence and a shilling per gallon, and the usual price was around 6s,
then spirits on which no duty had been paid might sell at 5s to 5s 6d per
gallon; and if they were weaker, or of inferior quality, at a good deal less.
A difference of about 10 per cent or 15 per cent on the retail price was a
substantial consideration, and apparently it was enough. Illicit distilling
flourished, particularly in the Highlands. The 1798 Committee referred to
the problem in plaintive terms:

> 'notwithstanding all the care and provisions of the legislature to pro-
> hibit the private making of Spirit, and our most unremitting attention
> and strictest injunctions to our officers to carry the same into execution,
> it is an unquestionable truth, that throughout Scotland, and particularly
> in the remote Highlands and northern counties, a great deal of Spirits
> are distilled both for sale and for private use. The injury the revenue
> thereby sustains is considerable . . .'[48]

Just how much illicit distilling took place will of course never be known, but the following official figures provide some indication:

Account of illegal Stills seized and condemned in Scotland

LOWLANDS : HIGHLANDS			LOWLANDS : HIGHLANDS		
1778	2		1788	149	434
1780	169	253	1789	192	402
1781	927	767	1790	162	296
1782	819	1,121	1791	79	259
1783	857	667	1792	91	158
1784	127	524	1793	62	193
1785	779	992	1794	33	175
1786	566	479	1795	25	168
1787	560	725	1796	464	799
			1797	58	859

Source: *Report on Distilleries* (1798) Appendix 36

Well over a thousand illicit stills seized in the Highlands alone in 1782! Over six thousand seized in the course of the 1780s! These staggering figures indicate defiance of the law on an altogether exceptional scale. Their considerable annual fluctuations reflect changes in the law and, no doubt, in the assiduity, resourcefulness and determination of the customs officers.[49] But they leave it beyond doubt that illicit distilling was an important industry in the Highlands in these years. The number of illicit stills discovered—never mind the number actually in operation—seems, in the 1780s, to have been never less than the number legally operated, and sometimes two or even three times as great. What happened in some parts of the country was hidden—perhaps mercifully—in obscurity:

'Kintyre . . . is the best Grain country in Argyleshire. People from England settle there as farmers. It is supposed there are unlicensed Stills, tho' none have been as yet detected; but it was said the officers there durst not do their duty. Knapdale is a Grain country, and exports Barley and Malt to the islands. Mr Ross senior customs officer for the Highland District thinks it very probable, that there are distilleries in this country, tho' for the reason assigned concerning Kintyre, he has not been able to acquire any knowledge of them.

With regard to the island of Harris and Lewis, I could get no information . . .'[50]

Islay, on the other hand, was better known. It was fertile country, and much grain was grown there. Distilling was carried on, and some revenue was collected. When the 1795 Act was passed which prohibited distilling in Great Britain, the farmer of the excise on Islay 'took up' about ninety stills, some of them with a capacity of over eighty gallons. This display of conformity with the law, having a decisive effect on the islanders' incomes, produced an equally decisive response:

'After these Stills were taken up by Mr Campbell, from the distillers, and lodged in his own house, the distillers got over from Ireland tinkers, who fitted up for them cauldrons and boilers as Stills; between 90 and 100 of which, some of then upwards of 100 gallons, were seized by the Excise officers during the prohibition. After the prohibition was removed, Mr Campbell's lease of the Excise revenue of Islay was not renewed; and the people of the island, finding they were not to get licences[51] for a trifling sum, as before, were much displeased, and resolved not to take out licences, but they made no resolution not to distil. Mr Ross says, they are distilling perhaps to a greater extent than ever, sending their Spirits to Argyleshire, Inverness-shire, Mull, and even to Lewis, to Galloway, and Ireland, but there has not been a licence taken out for distilling Spirits, nor has a shilling of Excise revenue been paid in Islay since the prohibition.'[52]

It would perhaps be charitable to say that occasional conformity with the law was the most that was achieved in these years, or even expected.

There are two ways of regarding all this enterprise devoted to 'supplying the inhabitants with an article which they cannot want, and must have in one way or another'.[53] It has to be admitted that it promoted trade; and the extension of production for exchange, and thence of regional specialisation, was very desirable. Islay, as noted above, was exporting whisky to a number of markets in the 1790s, and received in return barley, malt and other commodities. Farther north there was a good deal of inter-regional trade between districts where barley grew well and areas of poorer soil and a wetter climate. And there was also trade, albeit illegal after 1786, between the Highland and the non-Highland divisions, much of it *via* Callander and Stirling. But there were heavy costs. Barley, not yet harvested, was sometimes sold to distillers at a low price by poor farmers who were in a temporary difficulty; when the crop ripened, the sellers might find themselves without food for the winter, and the money spent. In this way, even legal distilling could have a bad effect. Cheating the excise was a gamble of a different kind, and many a family experienced sudden rises and falls of fortune which, in the long run, must have been demoralising and have disinclined men to steady work. Enterprise and ingenuity, which might have been more productively employed, were spent on outwitting the customs officers.[54] Moreover, many Highlanders were unable to understand why the produce of the soil should be taxed. They reckoned that without illicit distilling they would be unable to pay their rents, and it seemed particularly outrageous that it was the landlords themselves, acting as magistrates, who imposed fines on those unlucky enough to be caught. The fines were seldom more than a few pounds and were often as little as five or ten shillings;[55] what was much more important was the sense of injustice and, as illegal distilling spread in the 1790s and later, 'the progress of chicanery, perjury, hatred and mutual recrimination, with a constant dread and suspicion of informers—men not being sure of, nor confident in their next neighbour'.[56] Illicit distilling was indeed, as eighteenth-century writers complained, a moral evil. Too much was being founded on defiance of the law and on hopes of growing rich quickly without working. What made matters a great deal worse, this pattern of behaviour was not confined to illicit distilling; illicit distilling was only part of a larger scheme of things. Scots whisky competed with Dutch gin, smuggled into the country and sold in the 1790s at about £2 5s per anker of nine gallons, delivered ashore; and Dutch gin was only an item in every smuggler's stock in trade.

Smuggling was an important form of enterprise in the eighteenth century. The vessels used were of all sizes up to about three hundred tons, many were armed, and the crews numbered from half a dozen to a hundred men. Cargoes consisted chiefly of spirits, tea, tobacco, snuff, East India goods, wine, drugs, lace, cambrics and silks. Because duties on many items were so high, smuggled goods enjoyed a tremendous competitive advantage and therefore a ready sale. The duties of Custom and Excise payable on the cheapest kind of tea, for example, were over 100 per cent of the price at the point of export, and on the better kinds of tea about 75 per cent. The duty on brandy in the 1780s was 9s per gallon, but it was generally sold on the coast, by the smugglers, at 3s to 4s per gallon; as a result, upwards of four million gallons of brandy and other spirits were landed in Britain illegally every year in the early 1780s.[57] Several hundred vessels were employed in the trade—'a mixed system of war and trade' as it was described[58]—and the revenue cutters and the customs officers were both outnumbered and outgunned. Revenue cruisers were sometimes fired on and even sunk, and it occasionally happened that customs officers were made prisoner and kept aboard the smugglers' ships while the cargo was landed.

Perhaps the principal concentration of the trade was on returning East Indiamen:

'It is well known that when ships are expected from the East Indies, smuggling vessels, and boats of various sizes and descriptions, and from every part of the coast, cruize for them in the British channel, and carry on a constant traffic with them, from the entrance of the Channel to their arrival in the Thames. As soon as the laden ships arrive at their moorings, the places near which they lie become the resort of smugglers, and resemble a public fair; and the River is crowded with boats, watching hourly opportunities to convey goods out of every part of the ship . . . the smuggling is managed with little risk, through the collusion and corrupt practices of the lower class of revenue officers, who receive ascertained and known prices for their assistance. . . .'[59]

Ships returning from the West Indies were similarly welcomed. The consequences for the regular sale of tea, silks and similar items were of course extremely unfavourable. In Scotland smuggling was principally carried on by smaller vessels than in the south, from twenty to fifty tons, carrying spirits and tea from the Continent, and by small boats bringing tea, soap and salt from Ireland.[60]

It is sometimes supposed that smuggling in the eighteenth century was a business with which the highlanders were more concerned than other men; but this is not the case. No doubt smuggling increased in the Highlands in the second half of the eighteenth century just as many other kinds of enterprise expanded there because money incomes were rising and because transport across the country was becoming easier and safer. But, understandably, not a great deal is known about the trade. In the 1770s small and unarmed sloops, usually manned by Scots crews, operated along the coasts, aiming to slip past the revenue cruisers in the hours of darkness, land their goods at some loch or headland, and immediately afterwards stand out to sea; if intercepted, such vessels either attempted to escape, or their crews submitted to capture and then tried to convince the customs officers of the innocence and legality of their proceedings. But after 1782—partly as a result of the ending of the American war—things grew much worse. The south-west coast of Scotland, from Southerness Point to the Cumbraes, continued to be the great scene of smuggling, but the trade was now organised in a different manner. Besides a number of luggers and wherries, and of large rowing boats (some with 12 or even 16 oars), which brought over tea, spirits and tobacco from Redbay and the north-east coast of Ireland, as well as from the Isle of Man, larger vessels from 60 to 300 tons were now employed, carrying from 10 to 24 guns, specially built and fitted out for the trade in Dover, Folkestone and other ports in the south of England. Manned by 'numerous crews of outlawed, or foreign stout and desperate persons,' these vessels took on their cargoes at Flushing, Ostend, Gothenburg or Copenhagen, and sailed for Scotland. The Commissioners of Excise described their activities as follows:

> 'Armed in the strongest manner with carriage and swivel guns, and small arms . . . they come openly, in the daytime, often in pairs, upon the coast of Scotland, with a determined resolution of running their cargoes under force of arms, or of resisting, to blood and death, every attempt by His Majesty's officers, to prevent them. On one bottom they thus sometimes bring eight hundred chests of Tea, and a thousand ankers of foreign Spirits, all which are quickly dispersed. . . .'[61]

Cargo was sometimes landed under cover of the ships' guns, and was escorted considerable distances through the country, strings of fifty or a hundred horses being accompanied by one or two score of armed men.

This was an exceptionally well-organised trade, most of the goods being brought over on commission, and imported under the direction, of 'one or other of three sets of smuggling merchants and farmers' whose head-quarters were in Galloway and Ayrshire. These persons occupied exten-sive farms, for which they paid unusually high rents, and they kept large numbers of men and horses, ready to assist in getting cargoes ashore and in distributing them through the country. Smuggling on the east coast was on a smaller scale, and engagements between smugglers and the revenue cruisers were less frequent.[62] In the Highlands, operations were on a still smaller scale. Smuggling vessels cleared out from Bergen, Ostend or even France, usually carrying salt, tea and spirits, and made in the first instance for North Faroe, which was a Danish possession. North Faroe was an entrepôt for the trade, where local smugglers might find a constant supply of prohibited goods, and from where it was only about thirty-six hours sailing to the mainland, Skye or the Long Island. What was not landed in the north-west was carried on to Kintyre. From the smugglers' point of view the Highlands offered two or three advantages. Once ashore, con-cealment was easy on account of the rugged and deserted nature of the country. Small highland horses could be obtained, for a moderate hire, to carry smuggled goods along unfrequented tracks to the centres of popula-tion. Above all, the only employment which a great many highlanders could find 'after they had finished their little labouring of the ground',[63] was subsistence fishing and helping the smugglers to convey, by boat or on horseback, their goods from the point of landing towards the final con-sumers: 'Their Wages for this Service was ordinarily paid in Spirits.'[64] It is true that by comparison with what went on in the south-west, smuggling in the Highlands was not important. On the other hand, the trade pro-bably employed a larger proportion of the inhabitants, who were 'seduced into smuggling by the great apparent Gains in that Trade',[65] and whose energies therefore were not available for other purposes. Indeed, it is symp-tomatic of the highland economy that smuggling appeared to be both so profitable and so important. The structure of comparative costs appeared to leave little scope for engaging in any trade which faced lowland competi-tion and which depended on legitimate long-term gains.

But this was the sort of view that Knox and Anderson had set out to challenge, and in the 1780s many facts seemed to support them. The cattle trade was doing increasingly well; sheep farmers now ran their flocks in almost every highland county; the herring fishing was ready for expansion, apparently held back only by inept legislation. Given a few legislative changes and a reasonable amount of well-directed enterprise, it was not difficult to believe that a new and more prosperous chapter in highland history was about to open.

6

Steps Forward and Back

A policy of Highland improvement commanded widespread support by 1785. Much had been published on the subject; after the war of American Independence, the highlanders, who had displayed their first class fighting qualities in North America, were regarded as valuable allies rather than potential rebels; the development of the Highlands was beginning to be seen as a substitute for the now lost opportunity of developing the American colonies; and when Pitt came to power in 1783, his friendship with Dundas made it easier to secure a sympathetic hearing for Scottish problems.

The easiest changes to bring about were—as they often are—legislative changes. In the summer of 1785 a Bill was passed which removed some of the obstacles previously placed by Parliament in the way of the bounty-aided herring busses. The Bill contained three important provisions. First, it advanced the date of the start of the herring fishing season by two weeks. This had the effect of allowing British busses to commence fishing at the same time as the Dutch and not, as previously, a fortnight later. Secondly, it abolished the rendezvous arrangement, which had required vessels, in some cases, to sail hundreds of unnecessary miles to Bressay or Campbeltown before they could even begin to fish, and which had brought the whole fleet together even though the shoals of herring might be widely separated. Finally, the Bill permitted the busses, but only after they had been at sea for three months, to buy fish from the small boat owners. All these provisions had been advocated by numerous writers in the preceding five or ten years, and by the last it was hoped, no doubt, to rescue the local boat fishermen, at any rate to some extent, from the unequal competition to which the bounty system condemned them.

This Bill, however, was only the first part of the legislative reforms. It was followed in 1786 by another which resolved the argument about the relative merits of a tonnage bounty and a bounty paid on the amount of fish actually caught (a barrel bounty) by providing for the payment of both. Busses would in future receive a reduced tonnage bounty of 20s per ton only, but would also receive 4s per barrel of herring. Given reasonable luck at sea, this meant increased encouragement for the busses. The small boatmen, however, were not forgotten, and were now subsidised for the first time; those landing fish from non-bounty vessels were to receive 1s per barrel. A few crumbs thus fell from the rich men's table, but it could hardly be said that this piece of legislation transformed the native Highlanders' opportunities.

There remained the entanglement of the salt laws. Few believed that the government could afford to abolish the duty on salt, and even its reduction was not seriously discussed. But how to facilitate the use of salt for curing herrings without thereby facilitating tax evasions and swindles of one kind or another was not easy. For many years no change was made in the law, in spite of its serious and indeed ludicrous defects. Some relief was given by the building of a new custom-house at Tobermory and by enabling the existing custom-house at Isle Martin, a few miles north of Ullapool, to deal with salt. These changes meant that the number of effective custom-houses on the west coast was increased from one to three—the third was at Stornoway—so that fishermen did not in general have so far to travel in order to collect and register salt.

This must have improved the situation, although perhaps only marginally. A few years after these changes were made, it was observed with respect to Barra that 'the severity of the salt laws hinders the poor people here from using any other than what is got from the custom-house, which lies at the distance of 20 leagues',[1] while on the mainland, at Eddrachillis, the salt laws were said to be still a cause of 'immense loss'[2] to the inhabitants. Such instances could be multiplied. Gradually, further improvements were made. In 1795, the Treasury began to permit the delivery of salt to curers who had no warehouse. An Act of 1798 relaxed the severity of official action against uncancelled salt bonds, abolished the stamp duty on bonds, and permitted the transfer of salt from one curer to another without payment of duty. These changes reduced the number of vexatious difficulties put in the way of the herring fishing industry, and according to the Earl of Kinnoul in 1798, 'no complaints on the subject [of salt] have lately been made'.[3] It is doubtful whether this should be taken to mean that the situation was satisfactory. In 1801 there was talk of abolishing the salt duties altogether, but the resumption of war put tax reductions out of the question and it was not until 1825 that all duties on imported salt were abolished. But by that time, at any rate as far as the north-west Highlands were concerned, most of the harm had been done.

Not all of the above changes were effected by the government. The custom-house at Tobermory was built by the British Fisheries Society; and it was this organisation of private individuals which did most in the twenty or thirty years after 1785 to realise some of the more ambitious proposals of

Knox and Anderson for the development of the herring fishing industry.[4]

The British Fisheries Society—its full title was the British Society for extending the Fisheries and improving the Sea Coasts of this Kingdom—was incorporated in the summer of 1786, a semi-philanthropic organisation of a kind not uncommon in the eighteenth century, empowered to collect capital, to buy land for lease to fishermen and curers, and to build houses and sheds for their use, but forbidden from issuing money or from 'engaging as a Corporation in any trade'. On the basis of this programme, it held out to subscribers the hope of modest dividends. As a money-making proposition the Society can never have ranked high; but it was a patriotic venture which commanded widespread support in Scotland and furth of Scotland. It was authorised by Act of Parliament to collect subscriptions to a total of £150,000, each member being required to hold at least part of one share of £50 and none being allowed to hold more than ten shares. Even before the Society was established subscriptions had been received 'at the Shakespeare [Coffee House, London], to the amount of £7,000 or thereabouts';[5] and by the spring of 1789 almost £25,000 had been subscribed. Ten years later the sum was almost £40,000. Of this total more that £6,000 was subscribed by Scotsmen resident in India, and besides the private members—many of them landowners or merchants in London or the Scottish ports—five corporations held shares in the Society, namely the cities of Edinburgh, Glasgow and Perth, the Highland Society of Scotland (begun in 1778)[6] and the Company of Fishmongers in London. In 1819 fourteen persons held the maximum of ten shares, but the usual number held was from one to three.

The affairs of the Society were managed by a Governor and a Deputy Governor—the Duke of Argyll and the Earl of Breadalbane were the first to hold these offices—and by thirteen Directors, who included at the start William Wilberforce, the Earl of Moray, Sir Adam Fergusson and George Dempster, as well as other influential people. The Directors met—often once a week in the early part of the year—in London, until 1806 at Waghorn's Coffee House, Old Palace Yard, Westminster. A great variety of business came before them. Not only were questions of general policy considered,

> 'but they were even consulted on such trivial matters as to how the chimneys of the inn at Ullapool could be prevented from smoking, how the church there was to be heated, and whether the shed on the Island of Ristol should have iron bars over the windows.'[7]

There was also a permanent secretary in London. But many of the Directors frequently visited the Highlands, at least in the early years, and they conducted their business to a large extent through local, specially appointed agents.

The principal object of the Society was from the start to establish fishing villages in the Highlands—it had virtually come into unofficial existence when Knox gave to a special committee of the Highland Society a lecture entitled 'A Discourse on the expediency of established fishing stations or small towns in the Highlands of Scotland and the Hebride Isles'. Nor did the directors waste any time in setting about this business. In the spring of 1787 they solicited advice from highland landowners and others as to the most promising sites for villages, and a few months later a group of directors set out for the west coast in order to see and perhaps to decide for themselves. Within a few weeks they had settled on Tobermory as a suitable site, and shortly afterwards on Ullapool and Lochbay in Skye. The land at Tobermory was owned by the Duke of Argyll and another proprietor, both of whom offered advantageous terms for the sale of several hundred acres, and the transaction was soon completed. At Ullapool the Society purchased from Lord Macleod, in 1788, thirteen hundred acres of farm land as well as the island of Ristol, a few miles away north of Achiltibuie. Later in the same year the Society acquired land at Lochbay.

Ullapool may be regarded as a test case for the policy of establishing fishing villages. Tobermory became a success, but partly from causes which had nothing to do with fishing, or which could not be expected to operate at other places on the west coast; Lochbay was a failure, partly for adventitious reasons; but the development of Ullapool was neither promoted nor hindered by exceptional circumstances or events.

Pennant visited Loch Broom in 1772 and left the following description: '[Loch Broom], narrow, of a vast depth, and running many miles up the country. At its head receives a river frequented by salmon in April.

This parish is one of the largest on the mainland of Scotland. . . . It has in it seven places of worship, three catechists, and about two thousand examinable persons: but is destitute of a parochial school. None of the people except the gentry understand English. . . .

It is a land of mountains, a mixture of rock and heath, with a few flats between them producing bear and black oats, but never sufficient to supply the wants of the inhabitants.

Cattle are the great support of the country, and are sold, to graziers who come for them even as far as Craven in Yorkshire, at the rate of thirty shillings to three pounds a head. A great deal of butter and cheese is sold to the busses. . . . The common servants have thirty shillings per annum, house, garden, six bolls of meal and shoes. The dairy maids thirteen shillings and four pence and shoes: the common drudges six and eight pence and shoes.'[8]

Loch Broom was already well known for the large number of herrings which entered it in the season, and the farm of Ullapool, on the north east shore about mid-way between the sea and the head of the loch, offered a first class site for a village. There were about a hundred and fifty acres of flat ground, excellent for building on, slightly elevated and yet adjacent to the beach; supplies of peat and limestone were available; and the hills rising from the shores of the loch, some wooded, others 'craggy and desolate, the resort of eagles',[9] protected the site and made this natural deep water harbour 'so secure, that no vessel within it has ever been known to drive from her anchorages'.[10] Communications to the eastward were poor —a track led towards Dingwall and Inverness—but nature could hardly have done more to help, in the general context of the West Highlands. Ullapool was, and is, an advantageous and a beautiful situation.

Its merits had not been unnoticed. In the 1750s the Board of Manufacturers had set up a 'station' at the head of the loch for the spinning and knitting of stockings, but the scheme was a failure; in 1787 the buildings were 'a perfect ruin' and it was thought that they had probably never even been completed—'public money . . . appears to have been all jobbed away.'[11] In the 1760s, as already noticed, the Commissioners for the Forfeited Estates had settled a handful of soldiers and sailors, returned from the Seven Years, War, in rent-free houses at Ullapool, with some land to cultivate, but the results were meagre, and by 1773 this scheme too was abandoned. But a private individual, John Woodhouse of Liverpool, who had 'played a large part in setting up the fishing industry in the Isle of Man and organising trade from there with the Mediterranean,'[12] was more successful. In 1775 he was granted a forty-one year lease of Isle Martin, where he built a herring fishing station and three years later was able, according to David Loch, to cure 1,000 barrels of herring at a time 'on the Yarmouth method'. The fish were bought from local boatmen, and were shipped to London, Hull and Liverpool as well as abroad. On the island of Tanera, also in the loch, another fishing station was begun by private venture in 1783. This comprised warehouses for salt, barrels, nets and so on, five smoking houses, a pier, and a house for the manager, a man 'of extensive mercantile talents',[13] who came from Stornoway. Between fifteen and twenty acres of land were under cultivation by 1787, and the enterprise owned six decked vessels and about thirty boats. Salt, meal, casks and nets came mostly from Liverpool, Greenock and Leith, and the practice here too was to purchase herring from the native fishermen, or to employ them directly.

Thus the Society did not find Loch Broom an utter desolation when it commenced to lay out its new village in 1788. The plan of the village seems to have been the work of David Aitken, a surveyor from Tain who accompanied one of the directors on a visit in 1787. Aitken's was a simple rectilinear plan, with five main parallel streets cut by others at right angles, and the street fronting the loch reserved for storehouses and public buildings.

The main streets were set sufficiently wide apart to allow for gardens behind each row of houses, but the communicating roads had no houses on them and ran along the sides of the settlers' gardens. This arrangement of houses and gardens adds greatly to the spaciousness and charm of Ullapool. In one respect Aitken's plan was departed from, to the advantage of the village. Aitken intended that the front street, along the loch shore, should run parallel to the other main streets and not follow the curve of the bay. But from the start buildings on this street followed the line of the shore, and when Telford was advising the Society in 1790 he gave the opinion that this should continue. Telford also wanted a circus at the junction of what are now Quay Street and Argyll Street to house a market with arcades and 'shops or parlours', but although the Directors approved this idea nothing was done.

The building of the original village of Ullapool was mostly carried out in 1788 and 1789. There were two contractors, one of whom sailed from Dunbar with a cargo of bricks and tiles, timber, twenty cartloads of lime, household furniture, two pairs of cart wheels, a cart and a plough; he also took with him masons, joiners, a slater and other skilled men. The contract was for the building of a pier, a warehouse and an inn, for a total cost of £1,063;[14] and for eleven houses (most of them for £20 each), three sheds (including a smoking house) and a storehouse for salt and casks, all for £850. The Society was to lease the buildings to one of the contractors at an annual rent of $7\frac{1}{2}$ per cent of their cost, on condition that he kept them in repair and himself became a settler at Ullapool.

Progress was rapid, and although the standard of building was not what it might have been and there was trouble with the pier, by 1792 the Society had provided all the public buildings which it considered necessary.[15] The point of the operation, however, was to attract settlers; or, as the secretary to the Society put it, 'The great object being . . . to accommodate the lower class.'[16] The problem of how to lease the land was settled as follows:

'The land was classified into three types at different values. The first comprised the whole of the town as planned by David Aitken. This was divided into small lots just large enough for a house and a kail yard or garden, and could be leased for 99 years, those nearest the harbour at the rate of £5 per acre and those in other streets at £2 2s per acre. Secondly, every settler with one of these town lots was entitled to half an acre of arable land. This was ground that had been cultivated by the farm of Ullapool and lay near the new town ready to be planted with potatoes, bear and oats. The tenants might lease this for five years only (in case it should later be needed for building) at a rate of ten shillings an acre. Thirdly, each tenant might lease for ten years up to five acres of uncultivated land at the rate of one shilling an acre, with an undertaking by the Society to repay at the

end of the ten years the expense of certain enclosures or improvements.
Thus each settler had enough land to produce a part but not the whole of
his food.'[17]

In addition, every settler was given the right to dig for peat, stone, limestone and shell sand, and, for a small fee, to pasture two cows in summer-
time on the adjacent moorland. Houses were to be built according to the
Society's regulations (it was laid down, for example, that along the street
'no Stable Byre or Outhouse or Peatstack shall be erected'), and a settler
might obtain half the value of his house as a loan from the Society after the
house was built. Such loans were repayable within ten years, and a number
of settlers took advantage of them.

With this guidance and assistance—the total cost to the Society by 1796
was £7,778—Ullapool grew into a small village, and in 1794 it was described as follows:

> 'In this village there are now about 72 houses, of which 35 are slated, the
> rest are thatched with turf, fern roots, and heather . . . There is a red
> herring house, where they cured last year 500 barrels fine red herring.'[18]

The population at this date must have been between four and five or six
hundred.

This seems at any rate a promising start. Ullapool was, of course, only
one village, and Knox and Anderson had proposed from eight to twenty.
But other villages were developing on the west coast in the 1790s. The
Society had purchased 2,000 acres of land at Tobermory at almost the same
time as they had acquired the farm of Ullapool, and the two villages were
developed simultaneously. Tobermory possessed an exceptionally fine harbour, but it was distant from the fishing grounds and the soil round about
was poor. The village was planned along the same lines as at Ullapool, except that it had to be divided into two parts owing to the steepness of the
ground, and leases were granted on the same terms. The Society built
storehouses, sheds, a couple of workshops and an inn, and settlers were
attracted. Agriculture apparently made little progress—most of the land
seems to have remained under grazing—and the introduction of manufacturing, in the form of spinning woollen yarn, seems to have been only
moderately successful. Small boat fishing was almost out of the question,
because the lochs which the herring frequented lay across the open sea.
Nevertheless, Tobermory possessed the natural advantage of a good harbour, and, especially after the Society had persuaded the government to
establish a custom house and a post office there, it attracted a good deal
of coastal and some Atlantic trade, as well as the busses. In 1792 exports
'consisted of kelp and salt, a little wool and a few cargoes of herring and
cod, while the inward entries included corn, coal, wine and spirits'.[19] A
year or two later Tobermory was described as follows:

13. Ullapool, Ordnance Survey, 1968. A tiny example of formal
eighteenth-century town planning, still preserved amid the mountains.

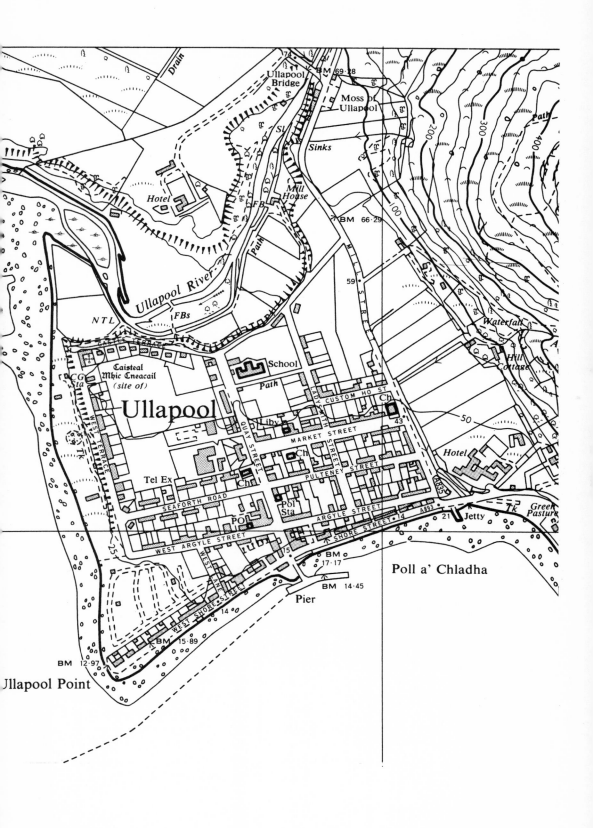

Drain

Ullapool Bridge

BM 69·28

74

Moss of Ullapool

Sl

Sinks

Mill House

Hotel

FB

BM 66·29

Path

59

100

200

300

400

Path

Ullapool River

FBs

N T L

Waterfall

Hill Cottage

CG Sta

Caisteal Mhic Cneacail (site of)

School

Path

Ullapool

50

Liby

LADY H ST

CUSTOM HO ST

Ch

43

WEST TERRACE

Tk

Ch

MARKET STREET

CHURCH STREET

Hotel

Tel Ex

Ch

PULTENEY STREET

SEAFORTH ROAD

Pol Sta

ARGYLE STREET

Hotel

A 835

Pol

SHORE STREET

14

A 893

21

Jetty

Tk

Green Pasture

WEST ARGYLE STREET

WEST LANE

15

BM 17·17

Poll a' Chladha

BM 14·45

Pier

WEST SHORE STREET

14

BM 15·89

Ullapool Point

BM 12·97

A. Grant del.

Heath sculpt.

ORAN BAY in ARGYLESHIRE

'The village now consists of 15 houses, built with stone and lime, 2 stories in height, with slated roofs, and between 20 and 30 thatched houses, 1 story high. The population is about 300 souls. In this village are a few people, who follow the mercantile line, and serve the settlers and neighbouring districts in goods imported from the Low Country. A boat-builder also, and a cooper, have settled there, and find pretty constant employment in the building of boats, and making of barrels for the fishing: And there is a considerable store of salt kept there, for supplying the buss and boat fishers, in the fishing season. In the year 1792, there were 47 vessels and boats cleared from this customhouse, for the herring-fishery; and as they were successful last year, there is cause to hope, that the number will be greater this season. There are, of other crafts, 1 smith, 1 wright, 2 tailors, 2 shoemakers, and 3 or 4 small inn-keepers; also a corn-mill with a sufficiency of water to work machinery, to a considerable extent, in all seasons.'[20]

This development was achieved for less expenditure than at Ullapool, because there was no need to build a pier and the freight charges to Tobermory from the more developed parts of Scotland were not a serious burden.

This last could not be said of the venture at Lochbay, on the west coast of Skye. A thousand acres of land were purchased late in 1790, but progress was slow. Freight charges and travelling expenses to so remote a spot were very heavy, there were difficulties in using the local stone, and the absence of a custom house created problems even in importing materials. Nevertheless, a storehouse, a schoolhouse and an inn were built by 1795, planned by Telford, and there were probably about 150 settlers living in a village laid out similarly to Ullapool and Tobermory, and renting their land on the same terms as the Society's other tenants. Fishing was for cod and ling rather than for herring, and fish were plentiful; but the soil was good, and the settlers preferred to farm rather than to fish, living as far as possible 'by their crofts alone.'

There were a few other places along the coast where developers and tenants struggled to improve their situation. Oban, where the first house had been built about 1715, was rather more prosperous than Lochbay. A custom-house had been established in 1765, and a number of busses frequented the harbour. About 1778 'the spirit of building arose in this village, and has been gradually increasing',[21] encouraged by the Duke of Argyll and Mr Campbell of Dunstaffnage, who jointly owned the land. By the 1790s there was a school, 'built by the Duke of Argyll, and the inhabitants', with about forty to fifty pupils, and in spite of the absence of a quay there were about a score of sloops employed in the fishing and coasting trade. There was also a tannery and a brewery, and the population may have been as large as 500 or 600. Inveraray, near the head of Loch Fyne,

14. Oban is often referred to as the gateway to the Western Isles. Dunollie Castle, shown here, was once a stronghold of the lords of Lorne.

was the creation of the Duke of Argyll; 'the houses . . . commodious and well built . . . not one thatched house in the whole of it'.[22] This beautiful little town was as much an appendage to the castle as a commercial venture, but there was a spinning school, and at Clunary, seven miles away, the Duke had established a factory for the production of cloth and carpets in 1776.

Much the largest village on the west coast was Stornoway, which had been 'going forward upon a regular plan' well before the Fisheries Society was founded. From its excellent harbour some three dozen or so busses sailed every year for the fishing grounds, manned by local crews. There was a custom-house, a post office, a spinning school—'many poor girls have been rescued from habits of idleness and vice'[23]—and, after 1788, a regular packet service to the mainland. By the 1790s this was a weekly service, subsidised by the government and the Earl of Seaforth, in almost equal proportions. There were by the mid-1790s sixty-seven slated houses, 'built at a considerable cost, because all the materials are imported, the stores not excepted'[24], and the population was put at 760. There were also two schools with over 150 pupils.[25] This was clearly a well-founded and thriving community, and not, like almost all the others, in some sense experimental.

Excepting Campbeltown, which was old-established, and which had connections as much with the south of Scotland and with Ireland as with the Highlands, these were the only villages of any size on the west coast, a total of six, three of them founded around 1790. Villages now well known did not then exist. At Portree there were '30 families about the place without land'[26] and they carried on a little fishing and ferrying; but in 1786 Knox could find no more than 'an appearance of a village.' Bowmore, in Islay, was similar. At Gairloch there was nothing, and it was the same at Mallaig. Poolewe was a landing place for cattle from the islands—'The beasts were thrown overboard in Loch Ewe and made to swim ashore'[27]—and by 1803 there was an inn at Kinlochewe for the convenience of travellers; but there was no real village. The Duke of Argyll had endeavoured in the 1780s to establish fishing villages at Creich and Bunessan, on the island of Mull, and at Scarinish on Tiree, but seemingly with little success. On the south shore of Loch Torridon the local proprietor, around 1785, erected a little fishing station, principally for cod and ling, consisting of a covered landing stage, a salt house, a curing house about eighty or ninety feet long, and a granary; there was no village, but there were probably some huts attached, for this development is spoken of by one or two contemporaries with respect. At Lochinver there was the fishing station of Culag, and there, 'when the herring fishing offers successfully, may be seen occasionally two, three, or four score, and sometimes a greater number of ships'[28]; but there was no native settlement. The highlanders did not live on the coast, because they were not fishermen; they lived in the glens, with their cattle, or in the little

15. Stornoway, Island of Lewis; 'with equal commodiousness and elegance laid out in regular buildings and streets.' (Buchanan)

View of Buildings erected on LOCH TORRIDON

fertile spaces among the hills, mostly in farm towns, or 'tenant-steads', small collections of often temporary huts inhabited, as a rule, by from two to as many as a dozen families.

Even from their foundation many of the west coast villages were struggling for survival. Two difficulties in particular beset them. The first was the highlander's reluctance to abandon the land. This was, in Selkirk's words, 'the greatest of all impediments to the progress of the fisheries on the Western coast and Isles',[29] and it was, according to Dr Dunlop, 'to be the undoing of the [Fisheries] Society'.[30] As early as 1787 the problem had been stated by Maclean of Coll in a letter to the Society. This letter, by a laird who knew the highlanders well and who was not prejudiced against them, is worth quoting at length.

'I am one of those who entertain the opinion that the erecting of wharfes, houses etc. as proposed by the Act of Incorporation, will not alone be sufficient encouragement for the extension of the Fisheries and forwarding of other views of the Society, my reasons for entertaining this opinion chiefly proceed from the difficulty I apprehend that will be found in inducing the people to inhabit the proposed towns and villages, for it is to be considered that there is not at present in this country any distinct body of men who live solely by the Fishing, that and indeed any branch of business or trade is carried on by people possessed of lands and who only make the fishing etc. a very temporary object or casualty. . . . If the inhabitants of those countries can procure the bare necessaries of life by their labour from the grounds they possess their ambition leads them to no further effort, nor do they in general desire to meliorate their condition by any other exertion of industry. . . . This is so much the case that tradesmen of all descriptions are not to be got without procuring farms for them and no sooner is this procured than they become farmers solely.'[31]

A great deal of evidence supports this view. The Society's policy was to encourage agricultural improvement and to introduce industry where possible. At Ullapool, for example, the tenants were helped to use lime and shell sand, turnips began to be grown, and uncultivated land was drained and sown to corn and grass. In both Ullapool and Tobermory attempts were made to establish some branch of the woollen manufacture, as the Duke of Argyll was doing further south at Inveraray. But the villagers' principal response to this diversification of employment seems to have been a refusal to specialise in any occupation in particular, and especially to cling to agricultural employment—perhaps because they believed, as Selkirk suggested they did, that it was 'impossible by fishing alone to earn a livelihood'.[32] The consequence was that at Ullapool, 'when the shoals of herrings come to the neighbourhood, the whole inhabitants of the village may be considered as fishermen and fish curers; for they are all then more

16. Fishing station, Loch Torridon. The long building is the curing-house, the small shed attached is the salt-house.

or less concerned in that business;'[33] and at Lochbay in 1807 'there were only two boats in the village and no trade or manufacture of any kind. The settlers remained indolent and scraped a living from their crofts until the harvest failures of 1808 and 1809 robbed them even of that.'[34]

On the north coast fishing was better attended to, although here again the same problem arose. Thurso, 'at the top of a spacious and beautiful bay'[35] was a little town with lively plans for expansion. It boasted two schools, two 'very good inns',[36] a custom house, a post office and a bank. In 1798 the population seems to have been about 1,500. There was a variety of employment, and this included work for skilled men; besides weavers, shoemakers, boat builders and the like, Sinclair lists three watch and clock makers and even a barber. There was a cart and plough manu-factory, a tannery and a bleachfield. Flax was spun and woven, and coarse woollens and plaidings were made. Thurso was the commercial centre of Caithness, and its success was founded on a fertile hinterland and on a good although unimproved harbour. By the mid 1790s Thurso's coastal trade had been increasing for twenty years. The main exports were grain and herring. Between 1770 and 1800 the number of barrels of herrings cured at Thurso increased over eight fold, most of them being sent coastwise to London. Yet even here fishing was a secondary occupation. There were a number of decked vessels, and a large number of small open boats with about half a dozen men in each. Sinclair reckoned that there were about 780 fishermen 'along the coast' but that of these only

> 'about 40 men (and these reside at Thurso), are constantly employed in fishing; the rest are farmers, tradesmen, or day-labourers, as well as occasional fishers; and, unless in the summer, during the herring-fishing season, fishing to them is but a secondary object.'[37]

Thurso at this time was undoubtedly one of the most thriving towns in the Highlands—if Caithness is to be regarded as a part of the Highlands. In importance it came a long way after Inverness, but it compared with places like Stornoway and Campbeltown. South of Duncansby Head, on the east coast, lay the little port of Wick. Wick was smaller than Thurso—the population was about 1,000—but here too in the 1790s were often to be found a score or more vessels 'on the bounty'. The harbour was as nature had made it and the facilities were poor, but there was no scarcity of fish, and by the 1790s Wick exported more barrels of herring than Thurso; well over 12,000. Most of the herring were caught by small boats, 'and it is an agreeable sight, in a fine evening, to see upwards of 200 of them at once under sail, the crews in high spirits, setting out for the fishing.'[38] These boats, however, would only go to sea 'in very promising weather' because of the open and dangerous nature of the coast, and the crews, once again, were only part-time fishermen:

'There are hardly any real fishermen . . . those alone excepted who resort to Wick from different parts of the kingdom, during the season of herring fishing only. Such, however, is the desire of gain that pervades all sorts of tradesmen here, that they betake themselves to the herring fishing when they think it likely to turn to better account than their own particular business. Weavers, tailors, shoemakers, house and boat carpenters, blacksmiths, masons etc. in this and the neighbouring parishes, having made a little previous preparation, repair to the fishing boats, go to sea in the night, the only time for catching herrings, and spend all the day in sleep, by which their customers are sure to be ill served. Husbandmen, and even small farmers, hire themselves out, during the fishing season, for 8d, 1od, or 1s—per night; and during the course of about three months, masters are at a considerable loss for servants to carry on the business of their farms.'[39]

Wick was a prosperous place, and it was believed with justice that 'the fisheries of Wick are as yet in their infancy.'[40]

The second difficulty which the west coast villages encountered was one of those unpredictable changes in the movement of the herring shoals which occasionally took place. The herring, as a contemporary put it,[41] was 'a shifting ambulatory fish,' and from about the middle of the 1790s there were some fifteen years—fifteen crucial years—when the fishing in the Minch was poor. At Stornoway, for example, the principal fishing port of the north west, catches declined from a peak in 1793,[42] and Oban reported fewer fishing vessels from about the same time, a result of 'the decrease of that trade on the north west coast.'[43] Uncertainty was always a drawback of the herring fishing; the risk of a poor season's catch made men without capital reluctant to cut themselves off altogether from the land. These years, from 1793 or so to 1805 or even 1810, confirmed their doubts; and even when the fishing recovered it was no more than moderate for only seven or eight years and then again relapsed. Also, in the 1790s the war began. Even in the Minch fishing vessels risked capture by enemy cruisers, and besides the enemy cruisers the press gangs were at work. Fishing can hardly have seemed an attractive proposition. After Trafalgar there was less risk at sea, but a new difficulty arose for the west-coast fishery: the decline of the West Indian market. From a national point of view this was offset by the appearance of new markets in Europe, resulting from the gradual liberation of the continent and the failure of the Dutch to maintain their predominance in the herring trade. But a European market was not convenient for the west coast, and the decline continued.

Thus after only a few years of existence the projects of the Fisheries Society were in difficulties, and the difficulties continued and deepened. Lochbay was a failure, the tenants at Ullapool—some of whom may have exhausted their little capital in house building—were mostly unable to pay their rents, and although Tobermory was more prosperous it depended on the coastal and trans-Atlantic trade rather than on the herring fishery. Tobermory was different because it enjoyed good communications and proximity to markets; especially after the opening of the Crinan Canal trade with the Clyde and Loch Fyne was within its scope. These advantages could not be enjoyed at Ullapool or Lochbay. But the Society decided to make one further effort, and in the midst of its troubles in 1803 purchased several hundred acres of land at Wick.

This was a venture of quite a different kind from the others. Lochbay and Ullapool, and to a lesser extent Tobermory, were settlements in the wilderness, a casting of bread upon the waters. But at Wick the Society sought to build upon success. Its plan was threefold: to build a bridge over the Wick river, to build a harbour, and to build an extension to the town. The bridge, designed by Telford, was the smallest item and was completed in 1808 at a cost of £2,000, half of which was subscribed by local landowners. The harbour was a much more costly affair. There was not even a pier in existence; boats off-loaded and stacked their catch on the beach. Fortunately, an Act of 1806 authorised the distribution, for the purposes of further economic development in Scotland, of money obtained from working the Forfeited Estates, and £7,500 was given to the Fisheries Society to help build the harbour at Wick. Telford produced a plan, a local architect-contractor named Burn went to work and in 1811, for a total cost of £14,000, the harbour was completed. Meanwhile the new town, Pulteneytown, was rising on the south side of the river. Like the Society's other towns, Pulteneytown was planned by Telford, and as at Tobermory the plan was rectilinear with the dwelling houses on the higher ground and storehouses and curing grounds below. Building lots were about 50 feet by 100, and were let on a 99 year lease at a rental of from 20s to 25s, according to situation. Houses had to be completed within two years, the superior houses 'to be two stories high and covered with slates, the [others] one story and covered with slate or tiles; and both agreeable to Mr Telford's elevations'.

The arrangements which governed the letting of agricultural land, however, were significantly different from those at the Society's other settlements. The land was divided into lots of about five acres and let for 21 years, the rent rising over the period from 2s 6d to 20s per annum. Moreover, a settler might hold more than one five-acre lot, and the Society appears to have encouraged settlers willing to grow food for sale to acquire more land and thus concentrate landownership into fewer, larger units. On the other hand, 'a very strict rule'[44] stated that no fisherman or cooper might own agricultural land. This rule was intended to facilitate the emergence of professional fishermen and coopers, who were encouraged to settle by being given town lots free of rent for the first three years. In effect, this meant that settlers could choose to come as farmers or fishermen, but could not conveniently, if at all, plan to be both. This policy was made possible both by the already developed state of the fishery and by the superior soil and climatic conditions of Caithness, which made commercial grain growing a far more attractive proposition than in the west.

The Society's efforts were successful from the start. The first application for a lot in the new town was received in 1803 (from a venturer already working in the fishery) and by 1812 about 60 lots had been taken, mostly by folk living in the vicinity. The local quarry was reported to be 'like a rabbit warren, all alive.'[45] By 1813 the population of the new town was 300, and by 1819 almost 1,200. In the latter year a custom-house was set up. The foundation of prosperity remained the herring. Boats from the Firth of Forth appeared in Wick as early as 1806, and in 1809 the Deputy Governor of the Society reported:

'From the great resort of persons employed in the Fishery, a Guinea and a Guinea and a half per month was paid for a mere lodging room at old Wick and even at that unexampled price a lodging was difficult to be procured.'[46]

By 1814 fishing vessels came to Wick from Wales, the Isle of Man and Shetland, and 4,000 strangers were reported to be in Pulteneytown for the fishing, which continued 'exceptional' and 'good beyond all experience.' By 1830 the resident population had risen to over 2,000, and during the fishing season another 7,000 were to be found in the neighbourhood, including crews from Norway, Holland, France, Cornwall and Ireland. In the twenty years from the building of the harbour the herring catch at Wick rose from 10,000 to nearly 200,000 barrels per annum. In the town there was a rope and sail manufactory, several shipyards, a brewery and the inevitable distillery. Rents were paid, and the harbour dues were sufficient to finance the building of a new outer harbour begun in 1823.

The success of Wick had no parallel elsewhere. Tobermory was a trading port, large enough to have a regular steam-boat service to the Clyde after 1826, and there were a few minor manufacturing establishments in the town, but that was all. In Ullapool, 'as the numbers increased the situation grew worse;'[47] most of the population in the early 1830s were 'cottars in possession of lots of land in the suburbs'[48]—inhabitants, that is to say, of a shanty town of dilapidated black huts. When the writer on the parish of Loch Broom in the *New Statistical Account* wrote his entry in 1844, he found Ullapool scarcely worth a mention, noting merely that the harbour was 'in tolerable repair.'[49] As for Lochbay, it was an acknowledged failure long before then. At least some of this must be blamed on the partial disappearance of the herring. The west-coast fishery was never so good again as it had been in the early 1790s, and it was always unreliable. There were shoals in the Minch in the 1820s and the 1830s, but not such prodigious shoals as once there had been, and the lochs, creeks and bays were in some years almost deserted; 'the ever memorable destitution of the years 1836 and 1837'[50] was partly the result of the decline of the herring fishery. Out of a total population in the Highlands of around 300,000, these three villages attracted in forty years about 3,000 people. Only Wick, based on good natural resources, with manufacturing activities arising naturally from its staple employment, became a dynamic, self-supporting centre of activity.

The failure of the new villages—not a complete failure but a substantial one—might have been avoided had it proved possible to establish manufacturing activities as Anderson had hoped. But beyond a little spinning and carding at Tobermory nothing was achieved. There was, however in, these years a great expansion in the Highlands, almost all of it in the west, of manufacturing activity of a peculiar kind, the manufacture of kelp.

Kelp is both a collective name for a variety of seaweeds, and a word used to describe the calcined ashes of these seaweeds. Such ashes contain low grade vegetable alkali, and they were industrially valuable in the eighteenth century as an intermediate product used in the manufacture of soap, alum, glass and other items. As a rule, Britain depended on alkali imported as crude weed-ash or wood-ash, or as refined pot-ash or pearl-ash; on barilla from the Mediterranean or on wood-ash from North America or the Baltic. Kelping, the production of alkali by the incineration of seaweed, was the home source of supply; one of the foundations of the British chemical industry, it was being carried on in Scotland as early as 1694. But this home industry was not very competitive with imports, and it was in any case not at first established in the Highlands.

During the eighteenth century, however, the industry gradually expanded, encouraged by duties on competitive imports. About 1735 it seems to have been started on North Uist, and after about 1750 was to be found at several places along the west coast and in the Hebrides. The production process was simple. The raw material consisted of a variety of seaweeds—tangle or red ware, prickly tang, black tang, bell-wrack—which grew on the rocks between the low and the high water marks, in the case of some species seldom out of the sea even at the lowest spring tides. The kelpers worked along the shore or went out in boats, cutting the weed from the rocks, and then carrying it up the beach, in creels or barrows, and spreading it out to dry. The seaweed was then reduced to ashes in the following way:

'The kilns that are made use of for this purpose, are either erected with stones on the sand, or dug in the beach, of a circular form, and about

17. Gribune Head in Mull. The smoke is caused by burning kelp on the shore.

twelve inches deep, and about four feet broad. In these [the kelpers] make holes for the free circulation of the air . . . [when] they imagine they have about one third of a ton of kelp, they begin to stir it strongly, or to rake it with a clumsy instrument of iron formed for the purpose. Much of the excellence of the kelp depends on the perfection of this operation. Great care must be taken to keep it free of sand, of stones, and of every sort of extraneous matter. The contents of the kiln must be made perfectly liquid, and somewhat resembling the metal in a furnace; and in this state it is sometimes very difficult to preserve it of the requisite purity. The liquid requires to be left in the pit to cool, which it generally does in about two days, when it congeals and hardens into a solid pon-derous mass, which is broken and piled up on the shore, till an occasion occurs to ship it for the market.'[51]

The kelping season was limited, extending from late spring to early autumn, and the weed was sometimes given a year to recover before being cut again. The geographical distribution of the industry was also limited. There were pockets of activity along the west coast, mostly from the Kyle of Lochalsh north to Assynt; but the great centres were the islands, expecially the Long Island; Lewis, Harris, North and South Uist, Barra—these were the great names in the kelp trade, followed by Skye, Mull, Muck and many others.

And great names they were when the trade suddenly expanded, as a result of the high cost of imports and the difficulty of obtaining imports at all, caused by the outbreak of the Napoleonic War. Kelp prices were no-toriously volatile: 'The price of no commodity in the country varies so much as that of kelp.'[52] These words were written about 1795, before kelp prices climbed steeply upwards. Two distinct price series, unfortunately separated by a number of years, give some idea of what happened:

Kelp prices per ton on the island of Mull[53]		*and on one Highland Estate*[54]	
1770–79	£4 3s	1815	£10 10s
1780–89	£5	1816	£9
1790	£5 15s	1817	—
1791	£4 15s	1818	—
1792	£3 15s	1819	£10 10s
1793	£3 10s	1820	£9 15s
1794	£4 10s	1821	£8 15s
1795	£6 6s	1822	£6 15s
1796	£8 4s	1823	£7 10s
1797	£8 8s	1824	£7
		1825	£7
		1826	£6
		1827	£5 10s
		1828	£4 15s
		1829	£4 17s
		1830–36	£4

18. Tanera More, the largest of the Summer Isles, lying off the entrance to Loch Broom; the mountains of Assynt beyond.

In the years between these two series kelp prices reached their highest levels. £20 a ton, even £22 a ton is mentioned; no doubt for kelp of the highest quality, perhaps from Lewis, or Barra. Buoyant from the last years of the eighteenth century, the industry enjoyed its greatest days of prosperity from about 1806 or 1807 to the end of the war.

A commodity which thus in a few years reached double or treble the price at which it had stood for the preceding twenty-five years was not to be neglected. Prices of most goods and services were high during the war, but not as high as this. Much money was to be made in kelp—by someone. At first, landlords were on occasion willing to allow others to organise the making of kelp, and to market it, on payment of a moderate rent. But as the eighteenth century drew to a close such arrangements became more and more uncommon. It became the practice, enforceable at law, for land-lords to reserve the kelp to themselves. This insistence upon the rights of property, still combined with the old practice of leasing, was plaintively explained by the parish minister at Eddrachillis, writing in the *Old Statistical Account* in the 1790s:

> 'Upon the shore of the glebe, which extends about $\frac{3}{4}$ of a mile, grows a profusion of sea-weed, of the sort fittest for kelp: to this the present incumbent thought he had a right; and that he might convert this sea-weed to his own benefit, as a small addition to his small stipend; but in this he unexpectedly found himself opposed by the family of Reay, who thought fit to dispose of this very sea-weed, as well as the rest on their estate, by lease to a Peterhead company; and upon his giving interruption to them, he was obliged to defend himself in a process for damages before the Court of Session, who, after considerable expence and trouble to the incumbent, thought fit to decide the affair against him. He is thus deprived of the benefit of the whole sea weed growing on his glebe, which was useful to him for other purposes, as manure to his land, and pasture to his cattle in the cold season of the year.'[55]

But leasing was only a phase; what endured, and dominated the industry, was the landlord's determination to have his kelp and to market it himself. Tacksmen were increasingly forbidden to cut the kelp on their farms, and it became the custom to let land with kelp shores only to small tenants, who could then be employed by the landlord to process and deliver the product to himself.

The kelp industry thus created opportunities for paid employment, and on a considerable scale. The high kelp prices, it was said with excusable exaggeration, 'set every person making kelp;'[56] and certainly in some parishes the entire labour force was so employed in the summer months. The rate of payment to the kelpers in the 1790s, working up to fifteen hours a day in dry weather at what was described as 'a very warm and troublesome task,'[57] seems to have been between 25s and 35s per ton. It is not easy to see just how this rate of payment was arrived at, for the bargain was struck between a monopsonist employer on the one hand and a labour force with very limited alternative opportunities of employment on the other; and it is significant that when kelp prices rose to very high levels, the rate of payment to kelpers did not go beyond two to three pounds per ton. Because the season was short and kelp could not be made in wet weather, it was the landlord's interest to employ as many people as possible. The shores were therefore portioned out in small lots, and it became difficult for a family to produce more than three or four tons in a season; in Harris in the 1790s it was said that 'the man who gets more than a ton for his lot may think himself lucky.'[58] These payments were sometimes supplemented by small payments in kind. The only other costs incurred by the employers were for freight and insurance, which usually worked out between one pound and thirty five shillings per ton.

These arrangements ensured for the landlords a golden harvest. With a largely captive labour force and costs of production and marketing set at £4 per ton or less, the pure profit at £10 per ton was £6 and at £20 per ton was £16. And some of the great landlords in the north-west were very large producers:

'In 1809 the gross returns to Clanranald from sales of kelp amounted to £13,277, less than a quarter of which went in expenses of manufacture, leaving a net income of £10,047: and this on an estate with a land rental—itself swollen by the general rise in rent as well as by the special kelp increment—currently of no more than £7,500, and earlier in the eighteenth century of less than £1,000.'[59]

Clanranald enjoyed an income of this order from 1808 to 1810. In 1811 his income was about £11,000, and this fell gradually in the following six years to about £8,000. Lord Macdonald, with large holdings in Skye and North Uist, received similar amounts. Lord Seaforth and Macneill of Barra benefitted to a far smaller but still substantial extent, and there were many others who received more in these years from the kelp than from their regular rents. The returns should not be exaggerated. The amounts received by Clanranald and Lord Macdonald were perhaps six or seven times greater than those which accrued to the second order of producers; and what was received annually in the peak years from 1808 to 1810 was almost double what was received annually in other 'good' years between 1800 and 1817. Nevertheless, although the returns to individual proprietors were typically far less than in the extreme cases often quoted, it remains true that very large additional sums came into the hands of highland landowners in these years. One agent alone estimated that from 1807 to 1817 he 'paid the different proprietors within a trifle of £240,000.'[60]

Yet it is doubtful, and perhaps more than doubtful, whether these great gains to a few landowners were of any permanent benefit to the Highlands. They provided the means for agricultural and other improvements; how far they were used for this purpose will be considered later. But a large part of the trouble was that the landlords' gains were not complemented by gains, financial or other, for the rest of the population. Money wage rates for preparing and delivering kelp were very low. Moreover, it was commonly the case that less money than this changed hands, or even no money at all, because the kelp wages were set off against the non-payment of rent. Tenants were often in arrears with their rent—even a single bad season, or a fall in cattle prices, might make payment impossible. Arrears accumulated. There is also evidence that on some estates—North Uist for example— rents soon became adjusted so as to draw back from the tenant some of his kelp earnings.[61] On Tiree the system worked in the following way:

> 'The kelp was sent to Liverpool. The product of the kelp went back to Edinburgh to the Duke of Argyll's agents there. They drew the full amount, and after retaining the entire rental of the island of Tyree in their own hands, they *occasionally* [my italics] sent back to the factor £500, £600, and I believe one year £800 sterling, to Tyree, to be paid to the kelp manufacturers. . . .'[62]

Thus whole parishes, and whole estates, became entirely dependent on kelp. This situation existed as early as the 1790s, and in the following decades grew commoner and more acute. Payment of the rent entitled the tenant to live on the estate, and put him in the way of 'paid' employment. But the payment was illusory; the factor for Harris and North Uist put the matter very frankly when he said that the tenants 'certainly made a great deal of money by manufacturing kelp; they paid their rents entirely by it.'[63] In some cases the receipt of wages must have meant that the agricultural produce of the tenant's holding was more largely available for the tenant's own use than it otherwise would have been. But this was not always nor continually the case.

Thus the extent to which the kelp manufacture was allowed to introduce a money economy into the Highlands was minimal. And in other ways, too, it failed to bring lasting benefits. During the summer, the tenants' attention was fixed on kelp-making, with the result that 'their crofts and lots are neglected, potato fields are overrun with weeds. . . . The kelping system is a great obstacle to agricultural improvement.'[64] Their ability to save was increased only to a trifling extent, or not at all. They learned no useful skill. Equally important, supporting activities and skills were not required. Whereas the herring fishery promoted coopering, boat-building, net-making, sail-making, the construction of smoking sheds and so on, the kelp manufacture flourished without linkages of this kind; it was simpler than the simplest extractive industry. Almost all that it needed was manpower; and of this, unhappily, it encouraged the production and the retention. To some extent, in all probability, there was a simple Malthusian response; the means of subsistence were for a while a little more plentiful, either directly or through an increase in money income, and population rose accordingly. This process seems to have been assisted by the landowners, however, who for a few decades found it to their interest to have a sizeable labour force on their estates, and who helped to make this possible by arranging for the subdivision of holdings:

'. . . if an honest Highlander . . . happened to have a son, he did not object to his son marrying and settling in life early, and giving him a part of his holding, where young Donald settled with his wife, and soon had a family; and if he, the original crofter, had a daughter, she married, and there was a further partition of the original croft; and this practice was continued till most of the crofts, originally intended for one family, had on them two or three, and sometimes four families. The proprietors . . . did not put a stop to this practice; they found they had full employment for all who settled on their estates, in consequence of the kelp trade and the herring fishery.'[65]

This was the process of crofting out the farms, a process especially widespread on coastal estates. Tenants' holdings became first smaller and then diminutive. The resulting arrangement of land-holding, rents and seasonal non-agricultural employment was a precarious balance of people, obligations, and resources. When the herring fishery failed, as it did intermittantly on the west coast, hunger increased and rents went unpaid; when the kelp industry collapsed, the coastal economy of large parts of the west Highlands was in ruins.

Tarriff protection and war were the essential supports of the kelp manufacture. The war ended in 1815. The salt duty was reduced in 1817, stimulating the manufacture of alkali from salt; in 1822 and 1823 the salt duty was further reduced, and large reductions were made in the duties on barilla, pot-ash and pearl-ash. These measures caused consternation in the west Highlands. Petitions were presented to Parliament, the *Inverness Courier* complained that 'a thriving population must be destroyed to gratify a few individuals,'[66] and the proprietor of Harris wrote to the Secretary of State about 'the ruin of the landed proprietors in the Hebrides and on the west coast, and . . . the destitution of a population of more than 50,000 souls.'[67] But all was in vain. The manufacture of alkali from kelp, even at subsistence wages, was a high-cost process. The future lay with imports, and the salt mines of Cheshire. The kelp estates changed hands at ever falling prices, and the increased population now faced chronic under-employment as well as periodic starvation.

Another industry of which much was at one time expected was the manufacture of linen. During the eighteenth century linen was the most widely distributed of all Scottish industries, with concentrations particularly in south-east Perthshire and Forfarshire, and during the second half of the century it was growing rapidly. Many improvers believed that the industry could be as successful in the Highlands as in the Lowlands. It was, after all, a native highland industry, one of the original components of the traditional subsistence economy of the clans. The Commissioners for the Forfeited Estates spent a good deal on its encouragement in the 1750s and 1760s, and also in the 1750s the Duke of Argyll, in the pursuit of industrial development, was requiring his tenants in Tiree and elsewhere to grow flax and to pay a portion of their rents in spun yarn,[68] which was then sent to a linen factory at Dunoon.

By the 1790s the industry was scattered across the eastern, central and south-western Highlands, but in the great majority of places it was a cottage industry employing only women—'the women here are always employed in spinning linen, excepting a few weeks during harvest'[69]—and for the most part it depended on imported raw materials. Occasionally the yarn was woven locally, but more often it was what was called 'factory yarn', spun only to be exported to the manufacturing centres further south. It was this commercial branch of the industry, in which the Highlands served only as a supplementary source of supply of the intermediate product, that grew in the eighteenth century. The Highlanders were thus involved in only a part of the process—'travelling merchants gather our yarn, and bring home our flax seed.'[70] At Cromarty, for example, in the 1790s, there was 'a great quantity of lint sent from Aberdeen and Inverness, to be given out by agents among the women in this district and the surrounding countryside, for spinning, by which they can earn from 3d to 4d per day.'[71] Wages were certainly low—at Tain the spinners earned 'with difficulty' $2\frac{1}{2}$d per day[72]—but sometimes earnings were valuable as a source of ready money with which to pay the rent. In one or two places the manufacture of linen cloth from locally grown flax persisted as a complete process until the end of the century, usually a part of the dwindling subsistence economy. At Avoch, for example, linen making was the principal manufacturing activity, the cloth being 'made entirely of flax raised by the tenants themselves, spun in their houses, and woven within the parish,'[73] and at Blair Atholl 'almost everyone had a share in that business.'[74] But as a rule, by the end of the century, linen workers were employees, working to supply mills beyond the highland frontiers. In a few places the industry reached a position of importance, round Brora, for example, and in the neighbourhood of Blairgowrie; but this was unusual, and occurred mostly in districts which are not easily regarded as belonging to the Highlands proper.

Then, after 1800, the industry began to withdraw from the Highlands, to concentrate increasingly in and around the industrial centres further south. This was an example of a process which was soon to become familiar. One cottage industry after another succumbed to the competitive power of factory production. The merchants could do nothing to reduce costs in cottage industry once wages and their own earnings were at a minimum; but in the factories technology was reducing costs all the time. In a decade or two, water-driven spinning mills took over almost all commercial production, and very few of these, if any, were in the Highlands. Along the Highland frontier, in the south-east, there were a few centres. There were spinning mills at Blairgowrie, sending their yarn mostly to Dundee, or Alyth, or Coupar Angus, and in the country round about there was some handloom weaving of Osnaburgs and coarse sheetings; near Scone there were large spinning mills, and at Perth there was one of the largest bleaching fields in Scotland. But these places are on the edge of the Highlands, belonging more to the fertile straths and coastal lands than to the hills and glens further inland. Among these remoter places, the merchants no longer travelled with lint and yarn. No doubt for a time they struggled to secure an output of reliable quantity, delivered when required, or at least without too much irregularity and uncertainty. But these were always the weaknesses of the cottage industry, added to the expense of transporting raw materials and finished goods among hundreds or even thousands of cottage producers. And in the Highlands, where concentrations of population were conspicuous by their absence, this task of transportation must have been particularly slow and costly.

Indeed, the problems of time and distance lie, as many contemporaries realised, at the heart of the Highland problem. Transport spells accessibility. Without it, markets are limited, the division of labour has little scope, and poverty results. Both Anderson and Knox, particularly the latter, had urged the importance of improving communications, both within the Highlands and between the Highlands and other parts of the country; and this line of policy received general support, especially as regards water transport, in which great improvements were being made in England in the 1770s and 1780s. The idea that a canal should be built through the Great Glen was put forward by several writers in the 1780s; but it is something of a surprise to find that as early as 1773 James Watt was instructed by the Lords Commissioners of Police to report on this project. His report, dated March 1774, appears as Appendix 22 to the Third Report of the Fisheries Committee, 1785. It does not seem to have been published before that date.

Watt's Report is the first—and as it was to turn out, it remains the best—statement of the case for embarking on the grandest of all projects for improvement in the Highlands. It is of moderate length, some twenty-eight pages including ten pages of tables of cost estimates, and is divided into five sections, as follows: General Answers to the Instructions; Description of the Country; Concerning the Size of the Canals; The Advantages of the New Communication; Particular Description of the Tracts of the Canals. Of these, the fourth and the fifth together comprise about sixty per cent of the text.

Watt's instructions were to estimate for a canal nine feet deep from sea to sea, and to report on its feasibility and desirability. He recommended and calculated for a canal ten feet deep, putting its cost at £48,405; and from an engineering point of view he gave detailed reasons for believing that the project would not be unduly difficult to execute.

When it came to economic argument and justification, however, Watt was very cautious—admirably so: 'To point out the Advantages such a Communication would be attended with, is rather distinct from the Business of an Engineer. . . . There is no Part of the Whole Subject for which I find myself so little qualified.'[75] He began by calculating that the mean distance that would be saved by using the canal instead of going round the north coast was 157 miles. 'But the Passages, by the Canal and by the Sea, are of different Kinds, and cannot be compared by Distance. The Nature of Sea Voyages is such, that no determinate Number of Miles can be affixed to a Day's sailing—We can only reason upon Probability.'[76] He posed two questions: what was the average time needed for the northern passage? and how many ships per annum used it? Figures were not available to answer these questions, but Watt 'conjectured that the Average Difference of Time of the whole Passage from Buchanness to Mull, by the Orkneys, and by the Canal, would be about Six Days;'[77] but upon this saving of time he felt unable to put a value. There was also the question of insurance:

'In the Winter Season, there would be a considerable Saving upon the Article of Insurance. I am told it would be about £2 per cent by Canal, £3 per cent by the Orkneys. This would amount to about 4s upon a Ton of Tobacco, and to about 2s upon a Ton of Oatmeal—In the Summer Season these Savings would vanish, as at that Time Premiums round the Orkneys are only about 30s per Cent, and would not be remarkably less by the Canal.'[78]

Such were Watt's attempts 'to prove', as he put it, 'the Quantity, and more especially the Value' of the identifiable items of immediate saving.

He then proceeded to consider the more remote benefits which the canal might bring. Of these he noted four:

1. Clyde busses would be able to pass through the canal to the east coast to fish for herrings when the shoals were on that coast, and the east coast fishers would be taught how to catch herring and would in their turn be able to visit the west coast. Thus 'the migratory State of the Herring Fish-

ing' would be matched by the mobility of vessels. This, Watt felt, might be an important advantage, for the movements of the shoals were never certain:

'About a Century ago there was a very plentiful Herring Fishing upon the Coasts of Fife, and in general upon all the East Coasts of Scotland; many Fortunes were made by it, and Towns built or enlarged in Consequence of it. The fishing exists no longer, and the Towns are mostly in Ruins—Such a Fate may some Time attend the present plentiful Fishing upon the West Coast; and though it should return to the East Coast . . . the Country will not immediately receive the same Advantage from it, as the People must have Time to acquire the necessary Experience and Stock in Trade.'[79]

2. The shipment of grain from the east of Scotland to the West Highlands would be facilitated. Upon such shipment the people in the west largely depended, for the western districts 'produce but a small Part of the Corn necessary to maintain their Inhabitants, even in the penurious Manner they live at present.' Watt reckoned that 1,500 tons of oatmeal were shipped from the eastern counties to the west coast annually. This trade could not be sensibly reduced, because the advantage of the western districts lay in the production of hay and black cattle; and if the herring fishing were to boom, the need for foodstuffs would increase.

3. The canal would help to improve the trade in timber. Highland forests were in some places good, but the highlanders

'are so indolent, and inexpert in the manufacturing and Management of Timber, and the floating it down the rapid Rivers which lead to the Sea has been found so troublesome and expensive, that Foreign Timber is sold at the Mouths of these Rivers nearly as cheap, and better manufactured, than our own Produce.

If Care were taken that a proper Quantity was suffered to stand until it were fit for Ship building, I submit [that] the planting with Oak and Fir the Mountains of this Tract for at least Two Miles upon each side the Canals and Lakes, would be a great advantage to the Nation. In the present State of the Country such a Forest would be almost useless, but if the Canals were to be executed, they would furnish an easy Means of transporting the Wood and Bark; the Country would probably become more populous; and people acquainted with the maintaining of Timber would flock to a Place where they were likely to find so much Employment.'[80]

4. At Easdale and Ballachulish were produced 'the best slates for covering houses.' Better transport would make effective a large demand for these slates on the east coast of Scotland, 'no part of which naturally produces that Commodity.'[81]

Based apparently on a single short visit to the Highlands, this Report is a model of its kind. Watt does what few do in such situations—he asks the right questions, treating the problem as one of uncertainty in a world of limited knowledge. The result is an admirable example of what would nowadays be called cost-benefit analysis. First the costs are calculated; then Watt calculates the direct benefits, noting the lack of data concerning the number of ships on the north passage and giving advice on how to collect this information for future use; he then surveys, although he does not attempt to quantify, the indirect benefits. This approach makes the Report remarkably modern in tone, although it is in any case clearly the product of penetrating observation, and of an acute intelligence. The general impression given is that the canal should probably be built; but Watt was careful to stress the provisional nature of his conclusions:

> 'The principal Disadvantages are the great Expence, and the Length of the Navigation within Lands. . . . Although the Advantages are very apparent, yet I have not been able to ascertain either the Time that would be saved, or the Tolls that could be afforded to be paid by Vessels using this Passage. I have endeavoured to point out the Means by which these may be known, and have thrown all the Light upon the Subject my present Knowledge permits.'[82]

Nothing so careful and judicious was ever again attempted.

Until the end of the century the Caledonian Canal remained a dream. Then, in 1801, the government commissioned Telford, who for the preceding ten years had been surveyor to the British Fisheries Society, to report on the transport problems of the Highlands. According to his Report, dated April 1803, his enquiries related to five aspects of Highland development:

> 'I. What regards rendering the Intercourse of the Country more perfect, by means of Bridges and Roads.
>
> II. Ascertaining various Circumstances relative to the Caledonian Canal . . .
>
> III. The Means of promoting the Fisheries on the East and West Coasts.
>
> IV. The Causes of Emigration and the Means of preventing it.
>
> V. Improving the Means of Intercourse between Great Britain and the Northern Parts of Ireland. . . .'[83]

Most of this report deals with roads and bridges. Telford had already surveyed the route of the canal in 1801, but the survey was a purely engineering one, and he seems not to have offered advice about the desirability or otherwise of the project, which he costed at £350,000. Nevertheless, there can be no doubt on which side Telford's influence was felt. He already knew the Highlands, which was an advantage, and he was an enthusiast for

19. Inverness. Said by Newte to be 'Tolerably built, but the streets narrow and dirty.'

N Grant pinx.

J Phillips sculp.

INVERNESS

Highland development—which was another matter: 'If they will only grant me £1 million to improve Scotland [i.e. the Highlands],' he wrote to a friend in 1802, 'or rather promote the general prosperity and welfare of the Empire, all will be quite well and I will condescend to approve of their measures.'[84] Telford was sure that the canal should be built. This was also the view of the Highland Society of Scotland, whose advice Telford sought and incorporated in his Report. According to the Society, the canal would provide benefits 'incalculably great'; somewhat more specifically, it would be the means

'of improving the Habits of the Country by Teaching Lessons of systematic Industry, and of affording at once the Excitement to undertake, and the Intelligence as well as (to a certain moderate Extent) the Means required for instituting those Fishing and Manufacturing Establishments, on which the future Prosperity of the Highlands must be founded.'[85]

The decision, however, depended neither on the Society nor on Telford but on the government, advised by the Parliamentary Committee on Highland Roads and Bridges; and in June 1803 the Committee gave its opinion.

The Committee reviewed at some length the disadvantages of the northern passage, and evidence about this was taken from a number of witnesses. That it was difficult and dangerous everyone agreed. The time required varied from five days to two months, and the average was reckoned at 'above a fortnight.' By comparison, the canal, it was thought, would normally be traversed in five days. The north passage was clearly dangerous, but 'some difference of opinion prevails as to the Extent of that Danger.' An effort was made to estimate the number of vessels going by the Orkneys, and the losses incurred. It was reckoned that the average number of vessels was 800 per annum, that their average tonnage was 150 tons, and that all these ships and their cargo were to be valued at about four million pounds. It was also reckoned that the losses from shipwreck, total and partial, for the three years 1800 to 1802 amounted to £320,000. These calculations—if such they can be called—cannot be taken seriously. The number of vessels was deduced from the number of losses, and these were obtained by reading the shipping reports in several Edinburgh newspapers. The average tonnage per vessel was simply a guess, the total value of ships and cargo was another guess, and what significance was in any case to be attached to the notion of total value was not and is not clear. To be fair, the Committee does not seem to have attached importance to these unhelpful figures. The considerations which carried weight are summarised in a crucial paragraph of this brief Report:

'Your Committee are therefore deeply impressed with the immediate Necessity of employing the People of the Country in the Execution of

20. Kilchurn Castle on Loch Awe, a stronghold of the Campbells; garrisoned by them against the rebels in 1745.

that great National Work; which will excite a Spirit, and introduce Habits of Industry; and will most probably check the present Rage for Emigration, and prevent its future Progress.'[86]

To encourage industry and to prevent emigration—these are the grounds on which the decision was reached. Clearly, the Committee was swayed by the general arguments relating to the need for improved transport put forward in Telford's Survey and Report of April 1803, in which much was made of preventing emigration by the provision of employment, and of the importance of supporting the fishing industry by means of improved communications. But these were only general, impressionistic arguments. What was lacking, and what the Committee failed to produce, even although it had before it cost estimates for the canal by other engineers which went as high as £600,000 or £700,000, was any serious attempt to balance the probable expenditure against the foreseeable gains.

The Committee's Report was published in June 1803. Before the end of July a Commission had been set up with instructions to superintend the building of the Caledonian Canal. This Commission included eminent and influential people such as Sir William Pulteney and Nicholas Vansittart, Chancellor of the Exchequer. Telford was the engineer, and the government undertook to find the money. Work went ahead on the basis of the estimate of £350,000, and on the assumption, presumably, that Telford was correct in supposing that construction could be completed in seven years.[87]

A start was made immediately, in 1803. The line of the canal was marked out, surveys were made for harbours and docks, and negotiations were begun for the purchase of land. Construction work was at first concentrated at the two ends of the canal and on the great basin for shipping at Clachnaharry, near Inverness. As the years passed, short sections of the canal along the line of the lochs were also excavated at irregular intervals. The scale of the work rapidly accelerated: £20,000 were expended in 1803–4, and in 1804–5 expenditure reached £50,000, at which figure it remained for many years. Conducting operations in the Highlands on such a scale immediately created problems. 'We can hardly get anything for money'[88] complained one of Telford's lieutenants whose work was centred on Fort William. Sufficient food for the labour force was never easily available, neither oatmeal nor potatoes, and the organisers of building were constantly on the search for supplies, which they usually sold to their workpeople at prime cost. It was also necessary to erect huts and sheds for the workers, and at Corpach there was built

'a small Brewery . . . that the Workmen may be induced to relinquish the pernicious habit of drinking Whiskey [*sic*]; and Cows are kept at the same place to sell them Milk on reasonable Terms.'[89]

At this time the labour force reached a maximum of about 900 in the summer months.

Other needs were likewise met as far as possible from local sources. Stone was quarried along the shores of Loch Ness, and granite at Ballachulish. Limestone came from Sheep Island, near Lismore. The chief requirement, however, was for timber. Bargains were struck for supplies of fir, ash and birch to be brought from the forests belonging to Lochiel and Glengarry; much of it was floated down the rivers into Loch Lochy and Loch Oich. It was cheap, at least to begin with; from ten pence to fourteen pence per cubic foot. But the oak that was needed for lock gates had to come from the Baltic; and later, oak being so dear, the lock gates were made of iron transported all the way from Derbyshire and Denbighshire. Not all iron had to be imported—some items came from the Inverness Foundry; but iron rails and wheels, iron castings, and equipment for a saw mill came from Glasgow and Liverpool, while pumping machinery was supplied by 'Messrs, Boulton, Watt and Co.' of Birmingham.

The volume of employment that was provided by building the canal varied a good deal according to the stage that construction had reached and according to the season of the year. At first it was quite modest—only about 150 men were employed on average in 1804. But this figure rapidly increased, and in the years around 1810 to 1812 the average employment was little short of 1,000; in the following ten years, however, it was only about half this figure. Work was very largely concentrated in the months from April to October; but even in this period the supply of labour was unreliable due to the demands of sowing, reaping, potato-lifting, peat-cutting and fishing—not to mention the opportunity, in a good season, to 'have a glorious spell at the whisky making.'[90] Men came and went as it suited them, much to the exasperation of supervisors and engineers. Occasionally, supply exceeded demand. This was sometimes a consequence of work coming to an end on the roads, and on at least one occasion it resulted in a petition, unfortunately undated but probably relating to 1812, presented to the Canal Commissioners 'from those between the East end of Loch Lochy and the West end of Loch Ness':

'That the formation of Highland Roads and Bridges in the North of Scotland, and the Caledonian Canal, held up to the Memorialists a Source of Industry, which would put an end to the apparent necessity of Emigration among the lower classes of Society in the district of Country where the Memorialists reside; as well as in many other districts to the North and South of this line.

This hope, so Sanguinely entertained was realised by the Memorialists in the commencement of the Glengarry line of Road from the Military Road at Aberchalder towards Loch Urn—In forming this beneficial

Road many of the Memorialists derived very considerable benefit and no person could work but had it in his power to do so, near his Own home and a variety of articles of consumpt in the Country received a ready Market from the Influx of Many Occasioned by the public Undertaking.

This Road being now completed . . . the Numerous Inhabitants in and About the foresaid Great Glen . . . are laid idle.

In this very severe Year the Memorialists feel much the Want of public Employ and Many of them may be Obliged to seek for Subsistence at a distance, and thereby induced to desert their Native Country.

As one Object which the Nation had in View in these Publick employs was to find labour for the lower Classes of the Community which is amply supplied in the east and West end of the Canal, as well as the improvement of the Country at large, it would afford the greatest relief to your Memorialists if the centrical district of the Canal was commenced so as to find Labour for them and share in its contiguity—; For having already reaped the benefit of public employ they feel the want thereof (particularly in so severe a season as this present) more than if they had Never tasted of its Sweets. . . .'[91]

There then follow the names of about 350 who describe themselves as crofters, of 70 tenants and of 30 tacksmen. Also about this time, in 1812, there appeared another surplus of labour 'owing to a Temporary Depression of Trade at Glasgow, which had thrown 700 Masons and Workmen out of Employment there'.[92]

This raises the question how far the employment which was provided was in fact taken by highlanders. It was often alleged, in Parliament and elsewhere, that the work was being mostly done by lowlanders and Irishmen. Certainly skilled men—masons, bricklayers, wheelwrights, carpenters, men to split timber or slate roofs—had to be found from beyond the Highlands; if they had not, the highland problem would not have been what it was. But the evidence is emphatically that the canal was built by Scotsmen and that most of them were highlanders. 'I expect', wrote one of Telford's superintendents of works in 1805, 'that men will be dropping in fast from different quarters if the weather continues open. I expect a considerable quantity from Lissmore . . . and about the same quantity from Skye.'[93] Telford's own estimate in 1805 was that the majority of those working at the west end of the canal came from Kintyre, Lismore, Appin, Skye, Arisaig and Morar, and those at the east end mostly from Caithness, Ross-shire, Moray and Aberdeenshire—the last two, admittedly, not Highland counties. Later, in the early 1820s, a table was prepared purporting to show the number of 'natives' (i.e. Scots) and 'Strangers' who had been employed over the years in the north east or Inverness district. According to this table, a typical distribution was three Englishmen, one

21. Basin of the Caledonian Canal at Muirtoun, near Inverness.

E. Pugh del.

J. Greig sculp.

Basin of the Caledonian Canal at: Muirtown, near Inverness.

Welshman, one Irishman, and at least three or four hundred Scots. This seems a little hard to believe; also, one is bound to wonder just how the provenance of all these men was satisfactorily discovered. But the fact remains that most of the employees seem certainly to have been Scotsmen, and probably a majority of them were highlanders.

Building began in 1804, the canal was opened excluding the Fort Augustus section in 1819, and vessels were finally able to pass through from Fort William to Inverness in 1822. What had been proposed to be done in seven years thus took eighteen. And as the time lengthened the cost rose. Telford's first cost estimate of £350,000 was raised in 1804, just before building began, to £474,000 plus an amount for land put at approximately £15,000. Six years later, at the end of 1809, 'The Caledonian Canal was deemed to be Half finished . . . when £276,000 had been expended; and at that time a progressive Estimate made with the greatest care amounted to £289,000'[94] —plus £10,000 for 'Land and Payment for Damages;' a total of £575,000. By the 1 May 1813, £469,000 had been spent, and Telford now calculated that £235,000 more would be needed, plus an approximate £18,000 for 'land and management'; a total of £722,000. Three years later the figure was revised upwards by £42,000, mostly an allowance for 'contingencies'. Two years after that, in 1818, £746,000 had been spent and £164,000 more was said to be needed. When the canal, although admittedly not complete, was opened in 1822, £905,000 had been spent. Expenditure thereafter slowed down; but when the Commissioners surveyed their labours in 1839 the figure for spending totalled over £1,000,000, and the canal was still not finished.

It was often said at the time, and has been repeated since, that the rise in cost which thus took place is to be accounted for by the general rise in prices due to the war. This is only partially true. Certainly prices rose during the war; they had already risen a good deal between 1795 and 1800, before the estimates of cost were submitted. Between 1804 and 1812 the wages of an ordinary workman on the canal rose from about 1s 6d to about 2s 6d per day. Lochiel's timber, which cost around a shilling per cubic foot in 1804 cost three times as much by 1812, and

> 'as the needs of the Canal cut deeper and deeper into the woodlands on the Lochiel and Glengarry estates and in Glenmoriston, the supply of suitable wood dwindled, and more and more had to be imported at greatly increased rates.'[95]

But, as is well known, timber prices probably rose faster than any others during the war; the Commissionres' expenditure on timber was a small part of their total expenditure; and from 1812, when the canal was not very much more than half finished, prices were tending downwards, back to their 1804 levels and even to the lower levels which had existed before

22. Loch Oich, with Invergarry Castle; towing through the Canal.

1804. A good deal has also been made of the cost of acquiring land. When the canal scheme was first launched on a wave of public enthusiasm, some offers of land were made, or at least spoken of, which were distinctly generous, and the figure for land purchase was put at £15,000. Lairds, however, had second thoughts about the terms on which they should part with their property, and by 1822 something like £50,000 had been paid for land, including £10,000 to Glengarry whose claim for almost double that amount was described by a contemporary as 'a conspiracy formed against the public purse.'[96] The increase from £15,000 to £50,000 is a large one in terms of percentage; but it cannot go far to account for the increase of total cost in these years from £500,000 to over £900,000.

The fact is that Telford underestimated and seriously underestimated the difficulties of the project. There were continual problems and complications caused by unsuitable soils and inadequate foundations, especially round Fort Augustus and at the outlets to Loch Lochy; there were floods which swept away half-completed work and made necessary costly repairs; some of the locks, especially the sea lock at Clachnaharry, proved very difficult to build; Loch Oich had to be deepened, and this proved extraordinarily troublesome, due to the large number of big trees, or at least the remains of big trees, embedded in the bottom on the loch. Even so, whereas the final plan provided for a minimum depth of twenty feet, the canal as opened in 1822, 'when only partially completed and fit only for very limited use'[97], had a minimum depth of a mere twelve feet.

The promoters of the canal thus underestimated the costs; what benefits arose from the expenditure of a million pounds? The incontestable benefit was the provision of employment. Sampling the accounts suggests that over the years when the Canal was being built between 60 per cent and 70 per cent of the Commissioners' expenditure was on wages; and this made a direct contribution to employment and money income in the Highlands. Roughly speaking, there was an addition of £30,000 a year, perhaps more, to the money income of the region which cannot initially have exceeded £200,000 per annum. This must have done a great deal to extend the money economy, and to make some saving possible, although at the same time it must have helped to drive up local prices. What did not go on wages went mostly on other kinds of local expenditure, and therefore also into highland pockets. Most of this money was presumably spent in the Highlands, at least initially, and thus would create further income and employment in the region; but some of it went to landlords under the headings of 'Quarries' or 'Timber,' and this may have leaked away on the purchase of imported goods from the south. Not more than 5 per cent or 10 per cent of total expenditure seems to have been on imported supplies or freight. Generally speaking, the canal was built with spade and stone, and it boosted money income and expenditure principally in its own vicinity, including the north-eastern fringe of the central Highlands.

The employment created was mostly for unskilled men, and there is not much evidence that important skills were learned. To this extent, the benefit was rather limited. What is more surprising is the very small volume of permanent employment which the canal offered. In 1826 the establishment along the whole length of the canal was 50 persons, who were mostly paid about £3 per month. There was thus secured the employment of 50 people with a total annual income, between them, of about £1,800 per annum, as a result of a capital expenditure of close on a million pounds! The provision of permanent employment had never, admittedly, been one of the avowed aims of the promoters; but with so little direct permanent employment created, the profitability of the enterprise, closely related to its success in facilitating and stimulating trade, becomes a crucial issue. Here again the evidence is clear. When costs were continually rising and the date of completion was continually receding in the years after 1812, the Commissioners kept up their spirits with the expectation of an annual income of the order of £40,000; but at no time before 1839 did the tolls reach ten per cent of this figure. As a rule, gross income was between £2,000 and £3,000 per annum; running costs were about the same.

For a few years after 1822 hope was still possible. Canals, it was argued, 'came slowly into use.'[98] Herring began to be shipped through the canal from Wick to Glasgow and to Ireland, and supplies of birch wood for barrel staves and brushwood for kippering began to pass in the reverse direction from Glengarry and Glenmoriston. The trade of Inverness expanded a little, and optimists reminded one another that the canal was, after all, shallower than had been intended — deepening it to fifteen or even twenty feet would solve the problem. But the situation did not improve. Deepening was carried out, but the cost was substantial and the return imperceptible. Charges were raised in 1825 from $\frac{1}{4}$d per mile to $\frac{1}{2}$d per mile per ton, but business seems to have been worse afterwards than before. Because of the uncompleted nature of the canal, accidents were frequent and even whole stretches of water were from time to time unusable. In 1827 there was a serious shortage of water in Loch Oich, and this, coupled with trade depression, made matters worse — 'many Ship Masters have been known to recur to the circuitous passage of the Pentland Firth rather than pay 2s 7d per ton for passing through the Canal.'[99] When the Select Committee on the Caledonian and Crinan Canals reported in 1839 it did not mince its words. The Caledonian Canal was dangerous, because Loch Lochy was held back at Gairlochy Lock 'by only one pair of gates;' if these gave way there would be widespread flooding and devastation. This was far from impossible, because 'very extensive failures in some of the lock-walls have recently occurred. From the imperfect original construction of many portions of the Canal itself, the leakage thro the banks is so great as to render it impossible to maintain uniformly such a depth of water as would render it at all times navigable for vessels of a moderate size. The whole works appear to be in a dilapidated and insecure state, and their condition is daily becoming more alarming.'[100]

Even if enough water were made available the winds were often contrary and unsteady, so that vessels were frequently delayed 'for days, and even weeks.' Towing paths could not everywhere be built because of the nature and steepness of the hillsides, and the only answer was to introduce expensive steam tugs.

The Caledonian Canal was a failure, one of these conspicuous white elephants conceived by ambitious and ingenious engineers and enthusiastically brought to birth by misguided politicians. The cost greatly exceeded expectations, and the benefit fell vastly short of them. The promoters were a little unlucky: war raised many costs, the west-coast fishing declined and failed to revive. But the main difficulties could have been foreseen; some serious attempt could have been made, along the lines pioneered by Watt, to collect data and calculate the probable return on so large and uncertain an investment. No comparable effort on behalf of the Highlands was ever again made, nor could it perhaps have been expected; this made the failure of the Caledonian Canal all the more crucial. Nor was it a defence to say, as was often said, that the canal was never intended to be a commercial proposition, that its purposes were to stop emigration, provide employment, and teach the highlanders how to work. The employment of a fluctuating labour force of a few hundred men, chiefly on unskilled work, was no great achievement. Of itself, it led and could lead to nothing. What was wanted was profitable employment, employment which paid for itself and which generated more employment. Innovations in transport depend for their success on cost reductions which are crucial in the sense of making profitable many activities which were before unprofitable: new ventures are begun, and thrive. This happened with the Monkland Canal in Lanarkshire, and with the Forth–Clyde Canal. But along the banks of the Caledonian Canal no new enterprises sprang up, because there was no foundation for them—no minerals, little timber, poor crops—nor did the canal bring into profitable connection commercial centres the scope for whose energies might thus be increased. The Caledonian Canal was an expensive highway connecting nowhere with nowhere, a vehicle for trade where there was no production. Its building brought money to the Highlands. Some of this money must have gone to buying goods from the south, thus developing Highland–Lowland trade and connections. In the absence of continuing employment in the High-lands this, along with the increased possibility of saving, no doubt did some-thing to facilitate and encourage that emigration which it was the objec-tive of the canal's promoters to reduce.

The Caledonian Canal was by far the most costly attempt to improve communications in Scotland in these years. By comparison, the Crinan Canal was a small affair, costed by Rennie at a mere £63,000 in 1793, when an Act was obtained on the initiative of the Duke of Argyll. The building of this canal had been widely advocated in the 1780s, and private indivi-duals were found willing to take shares in the enterprise, the profitability of which Anderson had confidently prognosticated.[101] The canal was opened 'in an incomplete state' in 1801 after the expenditure of over £100,000, and in order to complete it the government then advanced £25,000, the canal being transferred on mortgage to the Barons of Exchequer in Scotland. Expenditure continued until 1816, by which date over £180,000 had been spent and the canal had fallen into 'a very dilapidated state'. Government then supplied another £19,000 in order 'to repair and com-pletely finish the Whole in a secure manner.' The revenues thereafter ob-tained were on average scarcely sufficient to cover running expenses and repairs, 'and no dividend or interest has ever been paid, either to the origi-nal proprietors, or to the Government.'[102] The canal was used only by small coasting and fishing vessels and by steamboats plying between the Clyde, Fort William and Inverness. The scarcity of users was due partly to insufficient depth of water ('often not more than 7 feet'), partly to prob-lems of navigation and the dilapidated state of the works, but largely, no doubt, to the collapse of the west-coast fishing trade, on the success of which so many hopes had been founded.

If the canals were a failure, what of the roads—those roads which, ac-cording to Sir James Steuart, were to lower prices at market, increase the profits of carriers, and raise the landowners' rents? In a few districts there were some miles of tolerable road even before 1800. The military roads constructed by General Wade and his successors from 1725 to the end of the century had done something to facilitate travel. Between 1725 and 1736 Wade built about 250 miles of road as well as a few dozen bridges in-cluding those over the Garry, the Tummel, the Spean and the Tay at Aber-feldy. His successors in the eighteenth century increased this to a mileage of about 1,000, with many more bridges. The trouble was that these roads were often neither well nor conveniently built, and large parts of them were quite inadequately maintained. Thus the road from Dunkeld to Fort Augustus, at least at its southern end, was 'just sufficiently broad, but not conveniently formed for a horse to travel. There were no bridges. The Duke of Atholl, in going from Dunkeld to Blair in the 1740s was carried in a sedan chair . . .'[103]; and according to the Commanding Officer in Scotland in 1785, 'These roads have in many places been very ill-constructed and, excepting a few stages, are at present in very bad repair.'[104] At this date less than 700 miles of road were being maintained, and the usable mileage was shrinking. The main routes were along the south side of the Great Glen from Inverness to Fort William; from Fort William south to Callander or to Loch Lomond; from Fort Augustus south to Dunkeld or Crieff: and from Dalwhinnie along the Spey Valley to Grantown, then south over the hills to Braemar, and on through Glenshee to Blairgowrie and Perth. North of the Great Glen there was almost nothing: a road from Contin to Poolewe, and another from Fort Augustus to Bernera 'at the back of Skye.' The layout of this road seems to have left a good deal to be desired, and may not have been untypical:

> 'The bridges were first erected by contractors, who made choice of these points over the waters where materials could be had at the cheapest rate; by this means the roads were unavoidably lengthened, and carried over steep and high precipices, up and down hill. . . . From its present situation it is impossible to ride it.'[105]

These roads, and extensions of them, were the best; they satisfied, in places at least, the cardinal requirement, 'passable in winter.' In a few of the more progressive localities there seems to have been the beginning of a network of roads—in Mull, for example, and in the Black Isle. But in more remote areas such as Kintail, attitudes as well as roads might be different:

> 'There are no statute or military roads within the parish. Some remains of a military road are to be found along the shore of Lettercoil. . . . Till of late, the people of Kintail, as well as other Highlanders, had a strong aversion to roads. The more inaccessible, the more secure, was their maxim.'[106]

As the end of the century approached, however, such a point of view was becoming less common. Contemporaries wanted roads, and were probably not difficult to please in the matter; any track along which a horse could be ridden in reasonable safety was regarded as a road, and if it could be used by wheeled vehicles or remained open in winter it was a good road. Yet as late as 1790 in scores of highland parishes there were few roads even in the restricted sense of the word. Of Dingwall it was said, 'The roads in this parish are exceedingly deep in winter;'[107] of Bracadale, 'There are no turnpike roads nor bridges in this parish . . . the roads are still, for the most part, in a wretched state;'[108] of Kilfinichen, 'There are no bridges and no roads;'[109] and in Assynt, as might be expected, conditions were primitive in the extreme—'There are no bridges between Assint and Dornoch, nor one between Assint and Tain . . .;' and between Assynt and Brae of Strath Oykell there were, it was reported, 'no houses; none of accommodation;

the whole tract to Assint, is a perfect wilderness. . . .'[110] The situation was improving, but only gradually. When the Duke of Atholl travelled from Dunkeld to Blair in the 1790s he no longer went in a sedan chair, but in a carriage drawn by six horses; the distance is about twenty miles, and the time required was twelve hours.

In April 1803, Telford submitted his report to the Treasury on highland roads and bridges. South of the Great Glen his principal recommendation was the building of three large bridges to replace ferries at Dunkeld, Fochabers and Beauly, with another at Dingwall. The bridge at Dunkeld —'of the first importance to the central Highlands'—he estimated would cost £15,000; but the Duke of Atholl, who owned both ferries at Dunkeld, was willing to pay half the cost, provided that he could recover his outlay by a toll. At Fochabers work had already begun, led by the Duke of Gordon; this bridge would cost at least £12,000, but the Duke and others had promised to meet half the cost. The other two bridges were smaller, and Telford estimated them at £5,000 each; these two, he wrote,

'are greatly wanted in order to facilitate the Communications with Ross-shire, Sutherland, and Caithness; they are equally so for the North West Coast of the Main Land and the Northern Parts of the Hebrides; they are the Roots from which a great Number of Branches of Roads are to proceed, which are necessary for the Improvement of the Country, and the Extension of the Fisheries.'[111]

Farther north he recommended a number of projects. Thus the road from Fort William along the north shore of Loch Eil was to be improved, and then carried westward to the sea at Loch Ailort and on to Arisaig and Morar:

'This would open a very direct Communication from the Clyde to the Fishing Lochs at the Back of Skye, to Skye itself, and to the Islands. . . . This would prove of great importance to the Fisheries, on Account of facilitating Intelligence, which is one of the most necessary Steps to promote the Success of this Business.'[112]

Other roads were required from the Great Glen to 'Skye and the Fishing Lochs which lye at the Back of it.' These were partly to help the fisheries; but they were required also because 'there are many fertile vallies which hitherto have remained nearly inaccessible; it is incalculable the Loss which the Public has sustained, and are about to suffer, from the want of Roads in this Country.' There would be benefits, Telford maintained—again in-calculable—to landowners as well as to fishermen; the public revenue would be increased; and emigration would be checked. The cost, 1,000 miles of road for £150,000. This expenditure Telford proposed should be spread over six years, the bridges to be built in the first three years. This meant an annual expenditure on roads and bridges of £37,333 for three years, followed by £25,000 per annum for the succeeding three years: a total of £187,000. As much of the benefit would accrue to landowners, Telford thought it only reasonable that the cost should be shared equally between them and the government.

The essence of all these proposals, if not the details, seems to have been accepted without debate, and in June 1803, the Commissioners for Highland Roads and Bridges were appointed. Offers and enquiries concerning new roads soon came from individuals or from groups of landowners, and after a time the counties began to impose uniform assessments on all landowners. The number of parties, besides the Commissioners, involved in each scheme made organisation very troublesome—'You can hardly form an idea of the difficulty in getting even two or three proprietors to come forward together or the *pushing* it requires'[113]—and there were also severe and persistent difficulties in finding competent contractors. Nevertheless, roads were soon being built. One of the first was the road from the Great Glen through Glenmoriston and Glenshiel to Kyle of Lochalsh; this was expected to facilitate the droving traffic from Skye as well as the coastal fishing trade. Another road was pushed up Glengarry to the top of Loch Hourn—wild country, but, Telford claimed, the road was 'of the utmost importance as a drove road from a very extensive tract of country.' Roads were built in Skye, and with much difficulty and after many years a road was completed from Loch Carron on the west coast by way of Achnasheen to Dingwall on the east. Further north a road was built from Dingwall to Bonar Bridge and on to Wick and Thurso, and another from Bonar Bridge to Tongue. The greatest difficulties were encountered in what was almost the most southerly of all the Commissioners' roads: the Laggan Road. This road, from Spean Bridge past Loch Laggan to Kingussie was designed to replace Wade's road from Fort Augustus over the Corrieyairack Pass and along the upper reaches of the Spey to Laggan Bridge, a road blocked by snow almost every winter, and now abandoned. Although only 42 miles in length this road took thirteen years to build, at a cost of almost £550 per mile.

The road-building and the bridge-building programmes were complementary. The bridges which Telford had recommended in his Report should be built at Dunkeld, Fochabers, Beauly and Dingwall (Conon Bridge) were duly completed, the first two before 1810, and at least seven other substantial bridges were built.[114] Another major work was the construction of an earthen mound almost 1000 yards long, at the head of Loch Fleet, with flood-gates to control tidal water and the fresh water flowing down the River Fleet. This, along with Bonar Bridge, which like so many others replaced a dangerous ferry, was to facilitate the droving traffic on its way south to the great tryst at Muir of Ord near Beauly. By 1821, when

23. Bridge of Brora, Sutherland.

Mess Griffith del.

P. C. Canot sculp.

INVERARAY CASTLE.

the Commissioners for Highland Roads and Bridges ceased to be responsible for new work, they had built over 1,100 bridges.[115]

The pattern of communications which was thus created between 1804 and 1821 was fairly complex. It is hard to say whether or not it should have been planned differently. To some extent, the very question is misleading because there was, in a sense, no overall plan — the Commissioners could only co-operate with landowners where the latter put forward practicable and reasonable schemes. Moreover, judgment is difficult because lines of communication which are to promote economic development should not so much cater for existing needs for transport as encourage the appearance of new needs; and as far as the appearance of new needs goes, it is all too easy to be wise after the event. Looking at what was done, perhaps the most striking feature is that most of the roads which were built run east and west, joining various places on the Atlantic coast to the Great Glen. This was evidently done in order to encourage the fishing and the cattle trade, although it is not obvious that much business flowed or was ever likely to flow between Loch Moidart and Ballachulish, or on the long route from Dingwall through Achnasheen to Loch Carron. More easy to justify is the improvement of communications in the Great Glen itself and in the Spey Valley. Another obviously constructive step was the building of the road from Inverness to Wick and Thurso, for by 1810 these were two of the fastest growing and most prosperous towns in the Highlands — although it should be added that coastal vessels provided, in good weather, alternative transport from both of them to Inverness and other ports further south. As for the road from Bonar Bridge to Tongue, it bisected the county of Sutherland and could be said to open up a large area of previously inaccessible country.

What was achieved was very much along the lines which Telford had proposed in 1803. But the cost, and the time taken, were very different. Six years, Telford had thought, would suffice; seventeen years were required. The cost of the road building program did not work out, as originally suggested, at an average of £150 per mile, but at about £400, and the cost of the bridges also exceeded expectations — Bonar Bridge cost £14,000 instead of £5,000, and the bridge at Craigellachie, not separately mentioned in the original proposals, cost over £8,000. The total estimate in 1803 was £187,000, but by 1821 just over £470,000 had been expended, of which approximately £270,000 was public money, the remainder having been contributed by landowners large and small in the Highlands.[116] The response by landowners had exceeded expectations; but so had the costs. To some extent, this was because of the general rise in prices and wages during the war; but, as with the Caledonian Canal, this can explain only a small part of the total. Once again the difficulties had been under-

24. Inveraray Castle, building from about 1750 to the end of the century. 'The space between the front and the water is disgraced with the old Town.' (Pennant)

estimated. The great enemy of highland roads—and bridges—is water; and Telford soon realised that only by the most careful attention to the line of the road, to foundations, embankments, culverts, and surfaces could he hope to prevent whole stretches of road from being soon undermined or even washed away altogether. He protected his roads with great skill:

> 'Toward the hill there is a low stone line. If the hill be cut away, it is walled a few feet up, then sloped, and the slope turfed; if there be no slope, a shelf must be left, so that no rubbish may come down upon the road. The inclination is toward the hill. The water-courses are always under the road, and on the hillside back drains are cut, which are conducted safely into the water-courses by walled descents, like those upon the Mount Cenis road, but of course upon a smaller scale.'[117]

This was road building to an altogether new standard. Telford's roads were to the old ones what a Georgian mansion is to a bothy. Yet even Telford underestimated the damage that could be done by highland weather, and hardly had the road system been well begun before the problems of maintenance and repair arose in a serious form, to cause the Commissioners both anxiety and expense.

Contemporaries were vastly impressed by the improved roads—not all of which incidentally, were built by the Commissioners—and criticisms were few. That mail was now delivered two or three times a week in most villages of any size seemed particularly marvellous—'one of the greatest improvements imaginable.'[118] Small towns began to be connected to the outside world by coach services, at least south and east of Inverness and up the east coast to Wick. From Dingwall, for example, by the 1840s there were 'roads in all directions . . . along which coaches and carriers are continually passing.'[119] As early as 1808 the first stage coach began to run regularly between Inverness and Perth, and by 1821 there was a regular service between Inveraray and Oban. Such examples could be multiplied, and through the 1820s and 1830s the situation continued to improve. Thus, after finishing the great bridge at Dunkeld, the Duke of Atholl

> 'subsequently widened, embanked and cut miles of turnpike road and opened up the Athol districts. Before 1809, the traffic was mostly all conducted on horseback. There was a post runner to Dunkeld, but there was no post beyond it, except his Grace's runner to Blair. Now [1843] there are nearly twenty carriers that pass Dunkeld weekly to the Highland districts. There is the daily mail to Inverness through Athol, and a stage coach to Perth thrice a week. In the summer months there are daily stage coaches from Dunkeld to Inverness, Dundee, Lochlomond, Perth, etc.'[120]

Communications in some parts of the Highlands remained primitive. In the district of Fortingall they were 'but indifferent' in the early 1840s; Loch

Broom, at the same period, had no turnpike road or public carriages, and still relied on 'a foot-runner, who carries the post letters twice a week from Dingwall to Ullapool.'[121] Many roads were poorly maintained or for considerable periods were not maintained at all. But it is beyond doubt that between 1810 or so and 1820 the greater part of the Highlands was 'opened up to the public' and made accessible.

The question is, however, what effects this had on the life and economy of the region. Who used the roads? The drovers, no doubt, continued to bring their cattle from all over the Highlands to the great cattle markets at Crieff and Falkirk; this was the trade which Telford had especially wanted to encourage; although it should be added that steam vessels on the west coast were taking some animals to market by the 1830s. Woolmen and commercial travellers penetrated into new districts, some of them, by the later 1820s, coming no longer on horseback but driving in gigs; and along with them 'a variety of vagrants such as gypsies, ragmen, vendors of crockery, tinsmiths, egg dealers and old clothes men.'[122] Such people had for many years wandered through the Highlands, bringing a little trade, and a little news, to the glens and villages. Now there was even the beginning of a tourist trade. Visitors began to come, moderately adventurous men of letters, sometimes, like Southey, who when he reached Strome Ferry was impressed that 'ours was the first carriage that had ever reached the ferry,'[123] and who noted that at Kenmore 'the children have the vile habit of begging, to the disgrace of the parents who suffer and most likely encourage it. . . .'[124] In order to supply the needs of travellers, inns were established and inn-keeping became a trade—although it was often combined with some other occupation, such as farming, or possibly smuggling. Value for money does not seem to have been a feature of the business:

> '. . . in these Highland inns, whether you have anything to eat or nothing, attendance or none, you must pay as much for the want of everything as you do for the enjoyment of everything at Ferrybridge or Barnybymoor.'[125]

In some places such as North Uist, the conspicuous change which took place was the increased use of carts; in others, such as the neighbourhood of Dingwall, and in Caithness, better roads must have encouraged the process of bringing into cultivation remoter areas of waste land. Thus the Highlands became more unified, more known, more commercial. But did these changes which the roads brought with them (after an expenditure of half a million pounds, not to mention what was spent on the Caledonian Canal) amount to real economic development, to an appreciable raising of the standard of living? After all, however greatly highland communications had been transformed, much else remained the same. There were still no manufactured goods to transport; no great centres of population had appeared; much trade continued to go by sea, where by the 1830s steam packet services were bringing great improvements. The Highlands remained a somewhat backward agricultural economy—with a good road system. Did this make sense? Visitors sometimes found it a little paradoxical: 'to find such roads in the wild western Highlands,' wrote Southey, 'is so surprising, everything else being in so rude a state. . . .'[126] Even Telford, in a possibly incautious moment, remarked that 'The Highland Roads are a luxury in travelling,' and compared them with the 'execrable roads' in the Lowlands.[127] Yet in the Lowlands there was much manufacturing, and some of the most modern farming in the world. Clearly, the economic justification for the highland roads was the use which highland agriculture made of them; or perhaps it would be more accurate to say, their effectiveness in contributing to the development of highland agriculture. There was also, of course, the social impact of the roads, and this may be thought to have been distinct. But as the lives of almost all highlanders were still bound up with agriculture, it was through agricultural change that the first impulses towards new ways of life were usually felt. Men, crops and animals—these were still the elements of the problem. How agriculture developed was not directly decided by public policy but by the landowners and the people themselves. It is to their efforts in the field of agriculture that we must now turn.

7

More People, Less Land

The population of the Highlands in the second half of the eighteenth century cannot be accurately known. The first British census was taken in 1801, and its results are thought to be somewhat less than absolutely reliable. Approximately fifty years earlier, Alexander Webster had carried out an enumeration of the population of Scotland, parish by parish; and although his results are open to more serious doubt, Webster's methods and authority encourage one to believe that although his figures may be wrong they cannot be far wrong. An intermediate check is provided by the figures gathered between 1791 and 1798 for publication in the *Old Statistical Account*, but these figures are clearly questionable as regards Caithness, Inverness-shire and Perthshire, and this must throw serious doubt on the remainder. Subsequent British censuses, however, give population figures which can be accepted without reserve. The figures thus available are as follows:

County	Webster c. 1750	OSA 1790s	1801	1811	1821	1831	1841
Argyll	66,286	76,101	81,277	86,541	97,316	100,973	97,371
Caithness	22,215	24,802	22,609	23,149	29,181	34,529	36,343
Inverness-shire	59,563	73,979	72,672	77,671	89,861	94,797	97,799
Perthshire	120,116	133,274	125,583	134,390	138,247	142,166	137,457
Ross and Cromarty	48,084	50,146	56,318	60,853	68,762	74,820	78,685
Sutherland	20,774	22,961	23,117	23,629	23,840	25,518	24,782
Total	337,038	381,263	381,576	406,233	447,307	472,803	472,487

Three points deserve comment. First, population growth levels off between 1821 and 1841. Only three counties—Caithness, Inverness-shire, Ross and Cromarty—have larger populations in 1841 than in 1831, and in each of these cases the growth of population is less in the 1830s than in the 1820s. Population growth never recovered. There were thus more people living in the Highlands in the 1830s and the 1840s than there ever had been before, and more than there ever have been since. The steady decline of population from those days is one of the best known facts of highland history.

Secondly, and equally important, there was a good deal of population growth—if Webster is to be believed—between the middle of the eighteenth century and 1801. By modern standards the overall growth was not rapid, a mere 13 per cent or so in fifty years, or about one quarter of one per cent per annum. But it is almost certain that if we could have the figures for the first half of the eighteenth century they would show a rate of population growth very much less than this; the probability is, indeed, that population hardly grew at all in the first half of the century, and that the growth in the second half was unprecedentedly rapid. Moreover, it is also probable that most if not all of the 13 per cent growth was concentrated in the last two or three decades of the century. There are no figures to support this statement. But it is in line with a number of remarks scattered through the *Old Statistical Account* to the effect that 'population must have increased considerably within these last 20 years,'[1] or 'in the opinion of the oldest people in the parish population is more than a third what it was 30 years ago,'[2] or 'the population of this parish had, of late years, considerably increased;'[3] and the factors which would explain more rapid population growth—to be examined shortly—for the most part come into operation after about 1770.

The third point deserving comment is not observable in the figures already given. This is that the population of the Hebrides, and to a lesser extent that along the west coast of the mainland, increased a good deal faster than population in the Highlands as a whole. The islands of Lewis, Harris, South Uist, North Uist, Barra and Skye contained, according to Webster, just under 19,000 people about 1750, but they contained over 33,000 in 1811, an increase not of 13 per cent but of over 75 per cent. Webster's figures may be wrong, but there is no reason to suppose that he wildly underestimated the Hebridean population as compared with population in other highland parishes. In the mainland coastal parishes between Campbeltown and Assynt over the same interval the population increase was less, but still it was of the order of 60 per cent. Compared with the rest of the Highlands this is a remarkable differential, and one which was almost certainly present before 1800. The picture is therefore one of population growth which was very rapid in some districts, and which at the beginning of the nineteenth century had already been under way for two or three decades.[4]

The old stability of highland population gave way to rapid growth for a complex of reasons. One of these was possibly the practice of inoculation against smallpox. Although regarded by some as 'a provocation to Divine Providence,'[5] inoculation spread into many districts in the later 1780s and the 1790s and was said to have saved many lives. It has to be added that modern expert opinion does not take the view that inoculation had much effect in reducing the death rate in the country as a whole, so its effects in the Highlands may not have been as great as contemporaries believed. This is almost certainly a minor point. What mattered fundamentally was not medicine, but land and food. Nearly all the evidence supports the view that the increase of highland population between 1770 and 1830 was essentially founded upon an increase in the means of subsistence. It is not dificult to argue this convincingly in a general way. Contemporaries appealed to the practice of early marriage: 'The Highland girls of this parish for the most part marry at the age of betwixt 16 and 21 years; the lads at that of betwixt 20 and 25;'[6] 'Early marriages, which have become habitual for ages back, increase the population in a ratio almost incredible.'[7] But this simply drives us back to the question: why did people marry so young? And the answer must be the classic one: because they could afford it. Opportunities to make a living were on the increase. Until the 1790s the herring fishing was an expanding business on the west coast. The boat fishermen played a part in it, young men up and down the coast found employment with the busses during the season, and the busses brought a little trade into the lochs and bays between Campbeltown and Lochinver. After 1800 there was expansion at Wick and Thurso. In the south-west the growing commercial prosperity of Glasgow was an important influence. Kelp was even more important. A growing industry from the 1770s, it was a booming one from about 1795 to 1820—and it was particularly important in the Hebrides, where population grew fastest. Proprietors of kelp estates were glad to have a large population available for the tasks of manufacture, and they were known to encourage the multiplication of their tenants by the sub-division of holdings. But this brings us to the problems of land-holding, and to the verge of the problems of agriculture—and this is the heart of the matter. Subsistence in the Highlands was for nearly everyone a question of agricultural production, and of agricultural production in which they themselves were almost always directly involved. Trading was not of great importance; neither, except for a minority, was fishing; even kelp, although it mattered a great deal to a substantial proportion of the people for a few decades, was subsidiary. What really mattered, what affected everyone indirectly and almost everyone directly was agriculture and the changes which took place in it—the introduction of new technology, the altered attitudes of landowners, the extension of farming, changes in land use and in the terms of land holding.

The principal crops grown in the Highlands were oats, barley or bear, pease and potatoes. The emphasis varied from district to district, according to climate and soil. In Assynt the only grain crop was oats; in Dingwall, with a better climate and a better soil, some wheat was grown and there were even some sown grasses for hay. Turnips were grown in a few places, but in the 1790s they were still a rarity.

The yields obtained from the grain crops were almost uniformly poor, especially in the west. Sinclair stated the average quantity yielded by oats in lowland Scotland as from 10 to 16 pecks per boll, whereas in the northern districts of Argyll, in the west of Inverness-shire and Ross, and in most of the islands the return was reckoned between 4 and 6 pecks or about three to one; according to another writer, 'over the Highlands and Islands, in general, the increase of this grain cannot be estimated so high as four to one. . . . Nowhere in Britain, nor perhaps in Europe, is there so much labour exerted, to procure such an inconsiderable crop.'[8] Rye did rather better, but exhausted the soil more quickly, and bear, at least in the islands, did better still. But, except in a few favoured places, the yields were very low. There were several reasons for this. The growing season was short, and the tenants were apt to shorten it further by late sowing; the weather could not be relied upon, and in some places such as North Uist drought could be as harmful as too much rain—'A dry summer scorches the sandy soil, and a wet stormy autumn destroys everything the ground produces;'[9] little attention was paid to the quality of the seed sown; and the rotation of crops could not be practised because turnips, sown grasses and clover were only beginning to be introduced at the start of the nineteenth century.

There was, however, one great innovation; the planting of potatoes. Introduced to South Uist in 1743,[10] potatoes were grown extensively in that island, in Skye and in Arisaig by the mid 1760s, and between the 1760s and the 1790s there was scarcely a parish in the Highlands into which potato growing did not spread. Within thirty years of its acceptance in South Uist and Skye, the potato had become a staple and essential article of almost every highlander's diet. In the neighbourhood of Loch Ness, it was reported in the 1790s, 'within the last 30 years, the tenantry in general have run much upon potatoes . . . this article of late years constitutes the principal part of their crop;'[11] round Tarbat, on the shores of the Cromarty Firth, potatoes 'are used in every family, and constitute the principal support of some of them, during nine months of the year;'[12] in Kintail, potatoes were said to provide 'more than one-half year's subsistence with the fish and herring Lochduich furnishes in the months of August and September;'[13] while in the far north, near Loch Laxford, potatoes were 'a considerable part of the food of the inhabitants' in the 1790s although 'scarcely known'[14] thirty years before. Thus in a few decades the Highlands became, as far as subsistence was concerned, almost a potato economy. And as in Ireland, the multiplication of the inhabitants was, in part at least, a consequence of this sudden, substantial, easy but unreliable addition to the food supply. Failure of the potato crop became a matter of the utmost importance, and after the Napoleonic war men lived 'in awful terror of its occurring.'[15]

Increased growing of potatoes had another consequence; it helped to extend the cultivated area. In many districts of the Highlands there was an internal frontier of cultivation, beyond which lay in most cases heathery moorland. From about the 1770s improving landlords, who had perhaps travelled and observed what was happening elsewhere, began to trench and drain such land, remove rocks and stones, enclose their property with double dry stone dykes, plant shelter belts and raise better crops. For a decade or two these activities were confined to the fringes of the Highlands. A typical improver was Lachlan MacIntosh of Raigmore who, having made a fortune in India, in 1776 bought lands near Inverness, containing many hundred acres of waste, and turned his estate into fertile fields. More commonly at first, waste ground was let, usually rent-free for some years or at a nominal rent for life, to poor cottagers known as mailers or mealers, who generally followed some labouring employment to keep them alive until the land should begin to yield a return. The mailer usually had no resources but his own labour and that of his family, although some landlords supplied free seed, wood or lime. On his small lot the mailer built his hut, and then spread on the ground

'his ashes, and the dung from his miserable animal of a horse, which he keeps for the purpose of bringing home his turf for fuel; and he generally commences with potatoes: when he thrives, he possibly acquires two horses, a few sheep, and perhaps a hog.'[16]

Such planting of potatoes on waste land seems to have been a common practice in the later decades of the eighteenth century—in Arisaig, for example, 'there were raised in the year 1763, no less than four hundred bolls of potatoes, all on land which had never before been in any culture whatever.'[17] Land thus reclaimed could later be used for grain-growing, or for the support of animals. It is impossible to say how many acres were affected, but the movement was an important one. In Islay by the 1830s there was 'a great extent of waste land reclaimed;'[18] near Loch Ness there were 'large tracts',[19] and in Skye 'a considerable quantity'[20] of once waste land was under turnips and clover. In Ross-shire and in some parts of Sutherland reclamation seems to have been on a particularly large scale. Much of this was the work of the humble mailers, who 'may be considered,' as Sinclair truly said, 'as the *aborigines* of improvement in this country.'[21]

Potato-growing was an innovation all the more remarkable because most other innovations were accepted so slowly and with so much reluctance. The two-horse plow, also known as Small's plow, was in general use

in the Lowlands by 1800 but was a novelty in the Highlands fifteen years
later, used only by gentlemen-farmers. Most men depended on the old
Scots plow, 'a very simple and feeble instrument',[22] so cumbersome as to
require the attendance of two men and four or five horses, so ineffective
that it had to be preceded by another instrument called a reestle, directed
by two men and pulled by yet another horse. In some places, such as North
Uist and Sutherland, the cascrome was still widely used. Much of this was
explained by the state of the land itself:

'When I commenced the improvement of the farm I now possess, three-
fifths part of it consisted of waste land, covered with furze, and so full of
stones as to be impervious to the plow. The remaining two-fifths, or
arable part, had been severely cropped some years before my entry, and
was much exhausted, and full of weeds; and the fields, if they could be
called so, were interspersed with patches of waste ground, composed of
cairns of stones, and covered with broom, etc. There was no inclosures,
and the office-houses were dispersed without any arrangement. In short,
everything was to be done before a regular course of cropping could be
adopted.'[23]

But the difficulties existed not only on the farms themselves. Bad roads, or
the absence of roads, for long drastically limited the scope of marketing and
exchange. Hence tenants had no motive to increase their output or improve
their efficiency. In many areas the use of wheeled vehicles was scarcely
known, even of carts. In the parish of Dingwall there were said to be only
twenty-four carts in use in the early 1790s, and carts were a novelty even
in a go-ahead place like Wick, where men depended on cassies made of oat-
straw and rushes: 'When a call comes to ship the master's victual, some
scores of the garrons or small horses . . . are sent out by the tenants, tied to
one another by the tail, with a cassie of meal or bear on either side of every
horse.'[24] Road building in the first quarter of the century altered the position, and carts came into general use in most of the Highlands, although in
a few districts, like Ardnamurchan, they were still a novelty in 1830.

Road building, however, changed not only the vehicles in use; it changed
everything: 'by these means we have learned that there is a world beyond
Glenelg.'[25] Men and ideas travelled north, and west, and commercial con-
tacts became numerous and closer. As a result, changes took place in almost every aspect of life. Those 'heavy and almost unlimited services',[26]
for example, which existed in so many highland parishes, and against
which every writer on agricultural improvement in the Highlands in-
veighed, began at last to disappear. They died slowly: in Harris, in the
1780s, they were actually on the increase.[27] In Sutherland, on the other
hand, they began to decline before 1785. Lord Reay's agent commuted
services for a money payment about 1790, and at the same time 'in a letter

to the minister of Tongue, reprobated, in very severe terms, any remnant
of such barbarity.'[28] But to many proprietors these services appeared
indispensable, given the existing mode of working the farms. Services
became less necessary only as farm management improved. Better implements, especially better plows, helped. Also, the spread of commerce and
the increase of productivity on tenants' land made it easier for tenants to
make money payments. The rotation of crops gradually began to be
practised, first on gentlemen's farms and then on tenants'. But again it was
a slow process. In easter Ross in the 1790s 'every rotation practised in the
South had been attempted by the gentlemen' but the small tenants still
sowed an endless succession of oats, barley and potatoes, 'no clover, no
turnip, no fallow, not a bit of what is called their *infield*, or old arable
grounds laid under grass. . . .'[29] Part of the difficulty was the ignorance and
poverty of the small tenant. In these respects landlords could and sometimes did help with seeds, and advice, and by example. By the 1820s rotations were fairly common in most parishes, although in many they were
still a novelty and in some, such as Laggan and Tiree, they were distinctly
uncommon and much of the ground was still 'in constant tillage.'[30]

Another aspect of the problem was that tenants-at-will, or tenants with
very short leases, had little motive to improve their land; and the vast
majority of tenants in the Highlands at the end of the eighteenth century
were tenants-at-will. It was usually stated that they were seldom removed
except for good reason; but the fact remains that they had no real independence, especially if they were liable for services. It was in the landlords'
power to alter this situation; but they on their side were often reluctant to
give long leases to men whose 'prejudices and attachment to old habits'[31]
were themselves an obstacle to improvement. A further difficulty was the
old custom of letting a farm, or 'toun', to a number of conjunct tenants,
who cultivated the farm in common and shared the produce. This system
gave each tenant a negative on the others, and meant moreover that the
enterprise of one man might receive no reward because of the idleness of
his fellows. Run-rig, still very general in the Highlands in the first decade
of the nineteenth century, worked in a similar way. Under this system,
tenants had a common pasture for their cattle, while the arable land was
divided among them in strips, 'by ridge and ridge alternately', each man
cultivating his own set of strips. Land was in many cases re-allocated annually, and the system was a source of much friction and frequent disputes.

Against all these impediments the use of long leases made slow headway.
Common on the larger farms and in marginally highland districts such as
Crieff and Blairgowrie at the start of the nineteenth century, they were
still in process of adoption in the 1820s. Seven year leases were in use on the

Sutherland estates in the 1790s. But in North and South Uist the elementary improvement of granting individual holdings was only introduced at the end of the Napoleonic War.

Holding land in common is the antithesis of enclosure. An enclosure movement in the Highlands had begun by the 1790s, but it seems doubtful if more than a tenth of the arable land was by then enclosed.[32] Yet 'trespass of cattle' was a powerful argument for enclosure, nowhere more so than in the Highlands, for the Highlands, especially the remoter areas, were cattle country. In Assynt, for example, it was said that the total arable area 'does not probably bear the proportion of one acre to an hundred, of what is hill pasture, moor and moss'.[33] In most other areas the proportion was not as low as this, but almost everywhere the cattle trade, for which the new roads were primarily being built, was both old and active at the beginning of the nineteenth century. In the Hebrides alone, in 1811, there were said to be over 100,000 head of cattle, of which one-fifth were exported annually 'to the British continent' at an average price of £5 each. It was on sales to the drovers, those intermediaries of the system, that most highlanders depended for payment of their rent:

> 'It is merely the number of black cattle, of three or four years old, annually sold off from every farm, that pays the present paltry rent, with sometimes a small overplus to the tenant. There is little else on the farm that brings any money. All the grain and the potatoes, all that is afforded from the dairy, all the sheep, the goats, and every other article the farm yields, serves only as a scanty maintenance for the farmer's numerous household. . . .'[34]

Cattle prices were rising, even before the war. Selling for a pound a head about 1750, black cattle doubled in price by the 1770s, almost doubled again by the 1790s, and rose further up to about 1805 or 1810; prices as high as £18 or £20 are occasionally mentioned. Yet these highland cattle were small, poor beasts, 'mostly in a starving condition';[35] and even the eighteenth century did not think much of them. Critics were agreed that cattle breeding was an art almost unknown in the Highlands—'provided there be a bull, the kind is little minded'[36]—and everywhere there was overstocking.[37] Tenants seem as a rule to have kept as many cattle as possible on the common pasture lands, paying little regard to the amount of winter feed which they could expect to have available.[38] By the end of the summer months the animals were in good, sometimes in excellent condition; but to survive the winter was not easy, and by the beginning of May they frequently 'could not rise from the ground without help, or walk to their pastures without staggering like a drunken man'.[39] Sinclair, at the end of the eighteenth century, reckoned that the system was uneconomic as well as technically backward: 'nothing can be more despicable,' he wrote, 'than the return made to the Highland farmer, who breeds cattle'.[40] Yet it was on kelp and cattle that the majority depended for their exiguous cash income.[41]

Besides cattle, there were, most notably, horses, goats and sheep. The tenant of a penny land—one twentieth or one thirtieth of a tacksman's farm—typically kept twenty or twenty-five head of black cattle, six or eight horses, and a few sheep. That the country was overstocked with horses was even more generally agreed than that it was overstocked with cattle. The highland horses were small, hardy and underfed. They were kept in large numbers for two reasons. First, they were required, if oxen were not used, to pull the cumbersome, inefficient plows which were still in use, four, five or even six horses to a plow. And secondly, they were needed to lead home the peat from the mosses. This was an essential task, for the vast majority of highlanders had no other fuel available through the long, cold winters. Yet the mosses were often distant; and, after centuries of use, it was becoming necessary to travel farther and farther afield to obtain supplies. The number of horses cannot now be known, but the reckoning of one horse for every five persons does not seem an overestimate. The corresponding grain requirement was a serious burden on a not very productive economy. Goats were not uncommon, but they were giving place to sheep, and were in any case disapproved of by landlords who were becoming interested in afforestation. On the hills roe and red deer were plentiful. In Perthshire in the 1790s the Duke of Atholl had 'a tract of 100,000 acres reserved chiefly for them, and it is computed that not less that 4,000 feed there constantly.'[42]

Sheep-rearing in the Highlands is less easily described. This is largely because, for many decades, it was the most dynamic component of the agricultural economy. Sheep were no novelty in the Highlands in the middle of the eighteenth century. Almost every tenant kept a few, although none kept many. These animals, the ancient, original breed, were, as Sir John Sinclair put it, 'of an inferior naughty size,'[43] or in the words of Walker,

'of a thin, lank shape. . . . The face and legs are white, the tail extremely short, and the wool of various colours; for, besides black and white, it is sometimes of a bluish grey colour, at other times brown, and sometimes of a deep russet, and frequently an individual is blotched with two or three of these different colours. In some of the low islands, where the pasture answers, the wool of this small sheep is of the finest kind, and the same with that of Shetland. . . .

Such is the original breed of sheep over all the Highlands and Islands of Scotland. It varies much indeed in its properties, according to the climate and pasture of different districts; but in general, it is so diminutive in size, and of so bad a form, that it is requisite it should be given up, wherever sheep farming is to be followed to any considerable extent.'[44] The management of these sheep was as primitive as the breeding of cattle was unknown. They were kept not for profit 'but merely as an article for the cloathing and sustenance of the farmer's family'.[45] Everywhere it was customary to milk the ewes. Over wide areas sheep could not be allowed to roam freely across the mountain pastures, because of predators; especially in Sutherland and Wester Ross, eagles and foxes were common, and in many districts these were hunted systematically only from about the beginning of the nineteenth century.[46] As a result, and also because so little arable land was enclosed, sheep had to be housed at night. Winter food was scarce for them as for all other creatures, and because of this they often died 'in great numbers'.[47]

Sheep-farming, as opposed to the keeping of a few sheep, was brought into the Highlands in the 1760s. Sheep farmers from Annandale, and other places in the south, took leases of farms in the highland parts of Dumbartonshire, Argyll and Perthshire, bordering on the low country. They gave a higher rent than had formerly been given for the farms when under black cattle, stocked them entirely with sheep, and soon found their enterprise a profitable one. The sheep came from the hills of Tweeddale, Annandale, Nithsdale and Clydesdale—the so-called black-faced or brockit sheep, or 'sheep of Linton market'. Later, Cheviots were introduced; although less hardy than the black-faced, requiring more in the way of turnips and hay for winter feed, their wool was more valuable. Gradually, sheep-farming spread north; through Perthshire; up the west coast into the Morvern and Ardnamurchan peninsulas, and on into the Spey valley and the Great Glen. By the 1790s sheep were replacing black cattle in parish after parish in the central and western Highlands. Parishes which had accommodated only a few hundred sheep in the 1760s or 1770s had now within their boundaries 20,000 or even 30,000 sheep. From about 1790 sheep-farming began to make its mark on the northern counties also. In 1792 Sir John Sinclair brought to his estate in Caithness 500 ewes from the Cheviot hills, and by 1800 his flocks had increased to 3,000. A little after 1800 black-faced sheep were introduced into Sutherland, where disease had almost exterminated the native breed, and about 1810 large flocks of Cheviots were brought to the county by farmers from Roxburghshire and Northumberland. Thus as early as 1808 it could be said that 'the sheep farming of the south of Scotland is now introduced, and in a manner established over all the Highlands'.[48]

Inevitably, this introduction of a new technology, changing land use over tens of thousands of acres, was bound to cause disturbance and friction in a country where, as Gray puts it, 'a network of grazing rights already spread over the land.'[49] The ratio of sheep to cattle changed dramatically. Where once it had been as one to one (tenants were sometimes restricted by their landlords, in the old days, not to exceed this ratio) it became ten to one in many parishes, in some—Balquhidder, for example— even twenty to one. The destruction of the foxes and the eagles was accelerated, and it began to be safe, even in the wildest country, to pasture sheep among the high rocks and hanging precipices where cattle were lost every winter. It should not be assumed that the number of cattle actually decreased. The food requirements of the two kinds of animal are different, so that ground grazed over by cattle may still be usable by sheep. Moreover, sheep can use country which is too steep or abrupt for cattle, and

> 'will thrive where cows and oxen would starve, and will go at all seasons
> of the year to such heights as are inaccessible to black cattle. . . . In a
> situation of this kind, the very wool of a flock would amount to more
> than the whole profit to be obtained by black cattle.'[50]

This, of course, is the crux of the matter: the motive to change was profit. Sir John Sinclair calculated that on his estate in Caithness 27,302 acres provided £322 in rent, of which £40 came from the salmon fishing. This left £282 for the land, or 2½d per acre. Eighty-six persons paid rent, and allowing six persons to a house ('which is not too high'),[51] this gave a total of 516 persons, all essentially dependent on cattle. But Sir John thought that the annual rental of a cattle farm could be doubled with coarse-wooled Tweeddale sheep, and multiplied four to ten fold if stocked with fine-wooled Cheviots. Little wonder that he concluded that the findings that sheep could live year in year out in the open, in the Highlands, and that even fine-wooled sheep could thrive there, 'are unquestionably among the most important discoveries, that ever have been made, for the advantage of a particular district.'[52]

But no technological innovation, however beneficial, is readily accepted by everyone; and few such innovations, if any, are to the advantage of all those who are affected. The introduction of sheep-farming into the Highlands was synonymous with the start of a very unequal struggle between the former possessors of land on the one hand, and the graziers on the other. The Earl of Selkirk, whose sympathies were perhaps almost as much with the peasantry as with the landowners, wrote what is probably a fair account of the decisive conflict of these decades:

> 'It would be difficult, perhaps, to quote an instance where the old tenan-
> try have been able to offer a rent fully equal to that which their competi-
> tors would have given. In many instances, indeed, the fear of such com-
> petition has induced them to stretch their utmost nerve, and to make
> offers, which left from the produce of the land a bare subsistence for
> themselves. The indulgence of the landlords has often induced them to
> prefer these offers, when they could certainly have procured higher; and

in these cases, the tenants have, perhaps, found their situation better than they had just reason to expect. The great and continual rise that has taken place [1805] in the value of every species of produce, and of none more than grazing cattle, has enabled them to pay their rent with tolerable ease, and even to accumulate some savings, though in no proportion to the profits of the sheep-farmers, during the same period.'[53]

But Selkirk could already see in 1805 that the new system of sheep-farming was bound to triumph throughout the mountainous parts of the Highlands, so well was it adapted to the natural circumstances of the country; this was already 'sufficiently proved by its rapid and continual progress.'[54]

In very many places, therefore, to compete against the graziers was to invite disaster, sooner of later. Increasingly, land once occupied by a number of tenants, herding cattle and growing their scanty crops, was taken over by a single sheep farmer. Sheep replaced men. As early as the 1790s the complaint was a common one: 'The principal cause of the decrease of population is the engrossing and uniting of several farms, and turning them into sheep-walks';[55] 'the engrossing of farms for sheep walks . . . has been introduced lately . . . and proved the occasion of reducing to hardships several honest families, who lived tolerably happy on the fruits of their industry and frugality . . . whole districts have been already depopulated by the introduction of sheep; so that, where formerly hundreds of people could be seen, no human faces are now to be met with, except a shepherd attended by his dog';[56] 'one man often rents a farm where formerly many families lived comfortably.'[57]

Yet the inevitability of this sequence is not obvious. The sheep were mostly on the hills, men lived in the straths and glens, or on the lower ground near the sea. Why could they not co-exist? And why could not the small tenants do collectively what the single sheep farmer did, and manage in a number of small flocks as many sheep as the grazier did in one large one?

The answers to these questions are partly technical and partly economic. As regards land use, there was a double difficulty. When the hills were given over to sheep, the cottars and subtenants could no longer send their cattle to the sheilings in summer time, but had to restrict them for the whole year to the grass immediately round their little settlements. This meant a drastic reduction in numbers. Secondly, although the sheep might spend a good part of their time on the hills, a reserve of winter pasture was indispensable, and of winter foodstuffs was at least desirable. It was reckless to build up flocks on the hills and not have in reserve some better pasture in sheltered situations for a retreat in winter; hence in many places when the sheep came 'all the haughs and holmes on the sides of the burns and rivers which were formerly under cultivation are covered with a sweet

25. Loch Lomond, 'The most beautiful of the Caledonian lakes.'
(Pennant)

Drawn by J.M.W. Turner R.A.   London, Published May 1, 1835 by J. Murray, Poultry.   Engraved by J. Heath.

LOCH-LOMOND.

and luxuriant herbage.'[58] Sometimes, also, a little of the lower ground was cultivated for turnips. Every successful sheep farmer in the Highlands wanted low ground for his flocks, as well as access to the hills; and it was in this area that he could be satisfied sometimes only at the expense of the small tenants.

But could the small tenants not protect their position by becoming sheep farmers themselves? To some extent they did try to do this. The pioneers of sheep-farming in the Highlands were incomers, men who rented land at little above the old valuations, made considerable profits, extended their capital, and re-invested it in sheep-farming. By the 1820s two partners in Sutherland had land for at least 10,000 sheep, while the famous—or notorious—Patrick Sellar operated with a similar stock. The greatest figure of all was Cameron of Lochaber, son of a crofter, who acquired his initial capital in droving and then went on to occupy eleven farms and to own, it was said, 60,000 sheep.[59] Such men were exceptional. But many farmers in Inverness, Perth and Argyle had holdings, by the first decades of the nineteenth century, of between 1,000 and 2,000 sheep. Some of these men were probably small proprietors of land who, having seen the success of the graziers, took the whole or the greater part of their estates into their own hands. Tacksmen too 'discard their superflous cotters and subtenants, and imitate the active industry of the strangers.'[60] And even some small tenants, if they did not specialize in sheep-farming, began to keep more sheep than cattle, to run the sheep with the cattle and still grow crops, and thus to introduce a new kind of mixed farming into some districts. Yet this response was a limited one.

There are several reasons why small men did not specialize in sheep-farming and why the business was dominated by large or medium to large graziers, each owning at least 500 to 1,000 sheep. Basically, sheep-farming is an activity which in several respects is more economically pursued on a larger than on a small scale; it offers, that is to say, a number of economies of scale. A shepherd, to be fully employed, has to look after not fewer than approximately 600 sheep. It is also desirable to have diversity of grazing, with different qualities and kinds of grass, at different altitudes, and with different aspects so as to suit animals of different age, and to suit the flock at different seasons and in varying weather conditions; this indicates a stock of the order of 2,000. Clearly, this means that the sheep farmer must have capital. If, in the Highlands in the eighteenth century, the native stock was not to be used, sheep had to be bought in the south, and at the end of the century it was calculated that a flock of 600 sheep would cost £376, and that the annual expenses, exclusive of rent, would be about £50.[61] A wedder stock of 2,000 animals, it was reckoned at the same time, would cost almost £1,200. These were large sums, but not nearly as large as were

26. The Gair Loch, Ross-shire, looking west towards Skye and the Hebrides.

employed in some instances—Atkinson and Marshall were said to have spent over £20,000 in stocking their Sutherland farms. Capital thus employed was at serious risk, as Walker pointed out:

> 'The storemaster, of all farmers, requires the greatest stock in money. In consequence of this, money is often borrowed to a great amount, and at a high rate, generally to his own prejudice, and always to the disadvantage of the landlord. A farmer's property in sheep, especially in a high country, is subjected to more risk and greater losses than any other. It is a stock liable at times to almost utter demolition, by intemperate seasons, and infectious diseases; both calamities having been often experienced'.[62]

Moreover, the competition for farms became in time excessive, and many farmers were so foolish as to offer rents which they could never pay, and many landlords were so greedy as to accept them. The early history of sheep-farming in the Highlands is strewn with failures—the winter of 1807–8, for example, taught many a tragic lesson. Another cause of difficulty was failure to realize that before land could be advantageously used for sheep it might be necessary to make extensive land surveys, to carry out costly schemes of drainage, to employ a woodman and to get rid of foxes and other predators. And finally, after all these difficulties had been overcome, there was the problem of marketing. In the early days,

> 'the farmer had no resource but to mount his pony and accompany his drove to Falkirk or the border markets; his wool in like manner he had to send on his own account to Hull or Liverpool where it was put into money by the commission broker.'[63]

For a small man, with a small stock, this was too much trouble, and too much waiting. But when marketing became organised, it was managed on a large scale by a handful of dealers, who bought and gave credit on the basis of samples, and who therefore preferred to deal with men of reputation whom they could trust:

> 'Five or six wool staplers and dealers in sheep from the north of England and the south of Scotland come to treat with three or four hundred respectable individuals; and such is the mutual confidence that bargains of wool and sheep to the amount of £150,000 and upwards are concluded without even a sample.'[64]

These considerations meant that it was virtually impossible to start in sheep-farming without capital, and very difficult to farm on a small scale and remain competitive. The dice were loaded against the small farmer, or small tenant; and it was almost always men of property, often coming from beyond the Highlands, who successfully exploited the opportunities offered by old land, new techniques, and new breeds of sheep.

The advance of sheep-farming thus required the redistribution of land. By 1800 this process had already gone far in the south-west and central

Highlands, and after 1800 it spread further north and into the islands. But it is a mistake to try to understand the great changes which took place in the Highlands in the first three or four decades of the nineteenth century simply in terms of the spread of sheep-farming. What happened embraced all kinds of agriculture and other occupations as well, and affected the economic and social relations of all classes of society in a variety of ways.

The position of the landowners, because of their social and economic domination of affairs, was of the first importance. They were, as Dr Johnson noted with some surprise, men of education—'I never was in any house of the islands, where I did not find books in more languages than one'[65]— they travelled abroad, and had some knowledge of the ways of life in Edinburgh, London, Paris, the Hague.[66] In the last three or four decades of the eighteenth century, as communications improved and the land became peaceful, their knowledge of the world beyond the Highlands must have increased; and that world changed rapidly. It was a world, as never before, of agricultural improvers, of engineers, of men of commercial enterprise. Inevitably, the tastes, interests and inclinations of the lairds moved like-wise. They began, tentatively, to raise rents and to reorganise their estates.

This movement accelerated over many decades. The landlord of the 'inn' at Anoch, who possessed a hundred sheep many goats and forty cattle, complained to Dr Johnson that his rent had been raised from five to twenty pounds in the preceding twenty-five years. In the late 1780s and the 1790s, a sharp rise in cattle prices was a stimulus to the engrossing of land, and eight or ten tenements might come to be occupied by a single tenant and his herd. Increasing commercial use began to be made of the forests. In 1783 the Duke of Gordon sold the forests of Glenmore in Abernethy to a merchant from Hull and the whole wood was cut down in twenty two years (leading, incidentally, to the establishment of shipbuilding at the mouth of the Spey 'where never vessel was built before'). From about 1795 cutting was stimulated by the high prices resulting from the reduction of foreign supplies due to war, and a peak was reached around 1813. North of the Great Glen the sheep came after 1800. Thus for several decades the opportunities for profitable innovation were good and landowners bene-fited. Improvements in the ordinary course of agriculture raised tenants' gross incomes; receipts from the sale of cattle rose as the price of cattle rose; there was the kelp boom; and sheep-farming provided a new source of income. Not uncommonly, rents increased three-fold, five-fold or even ten-fold between the 1760s and 1815. This more than took care of the rise in the general price level; and indeed there is evidence that landowners overplayed their hand, squeezing the tenantry to such an extent that it was impossible for them to rise above subsistence levels or to accumulate capital for 'home-made' improvements in agriculture. This was a consequence of what Gray has called a contradiction in the Highland aristocracy—'the attempt to live in emulation of the aristocracies of richer lands on the surplus of a poor peasantry struggling with what remained a barren environment.'[67] But part of the trouble was that money income in the Highlands in those years rose both fast and adventitiously. The increases in income were in a sense out of proportion to the constructive efforts made by landowners and tenants who were carried along by changes which frequently originated outside the Highlands, and to which they responded with what were sometimes ill-considered or reluctant adjustments of their own.

Such adjustments, being without precedent, caused much dissatisfaction; and the removal, in some cases, of tenants who refused to co-operate caused still further indignation. But the lairds were not disposed to call a halt. The increase of their incomes seldom kept pace with their growing taste for the elegance and luxuries of life with which they became increasingly familiar. Rents were 'continually carried out of the country,'[68] to be spent by the lairds in Edinburgh or better still in London—London which was already recognised in the eighteenth century to be 'a universal storehouse of whatever is pleasing to the eye and the senses, the centre of amusements, affording irresistible allurements for dissipating, in a fashionable style, the produce of their estates, and sometimes more'.[69] Thus, the landowners began to change their own character, to be no longer chiefs or chieftains of the clans, men who belonged to the Highlands although having some knowledge of the wider world, but to be strangers in their own country. Their point of view, and that of the tenants, now diverged: 'a man who has been accustomed to polished society, can find little to approve of, and much to blame, in the way of life followed by an uncivilized people. . . .'[70]

There were several ways in which landowners sought to raise the productivity of their estates. Sometimes they seem to have given increased power to the tacksmen, and to have demanded more from them. The tacksmen then responded by squeezing the subtenants 'without mercy,'[71] whose anger was much increased by the fact that previously they and the tacksmen had been, as a rule, on an almost equal footing as members of the clan. More often, the hereditary tacksmen seem to have been little interested in agricultural improvement, and the lairds therefore got rid of them. New men were brought in—not necessarily in connection with sheep-farming—men who shared the landowners' interest in technical change and profitability, and who were, essentially, professional farmers. In this case the effect on social relations was even more disastrous. Feelings of attachment to the chief gave way to feelings of disgust and irritation. Not only were rents raised, but orders were now given and probably further removals arranged by a stranger, one who 'taking the land at its full price, treats with the laird upon equal terms, and considers him not as a chief but as a trafficker in land. Thus the estate, perhaps, is improved, but the clan is broken.'[72]

The process was a gradual one. Those chiefs who had grown to manhood before 1745 were no doubt reluctant to sacrifice old feudal connections. But gradually power passed into the hands of a new generation, less interested in clan connections, less inclined to sacrifice the material advantages of landed property for the dignity of feudal position: 'The more necessitous, or the less generous, set the example; and one gradually followed another, till at length [1805] all scruple seems to be removed, and the proprietors in the Highlands have no more hesitation than in any other part of the kingdom, in turning their estates to the best advantage'.[73]

The shift to sheep-farming was a part of this process of agricultural change, and the need to remove tenants was of course most conspicuous where sheep were to be introduced. It is easy to declaim against the inhumanity of turning families out of their customary possessions, in order to make way for a solitary improving farmer, or for a shepherd and his dog. It is equally easy to regret the disappearance of the hereditary tacksmen, men often of culture and hospitality, turned by the force of events into common tenants or emigrants. But it is fair to recognise that landowners seem often to have delayed as long as they could. It was reported, for example, that McLean of Coll

'might let as a sheep-walk his large island of Rum, containing upwards of twenty thousand Scotch acres at a profit of several hundred pounds per annum, to two or three farmers, instead of the present three hundred and fifty inhabitants who possess it for a mere trifle, could he find any means of providing for these poor people consistent with his patriotism and humanity. But although he has been for some years looking out for eligible situations for these persons, who are more and more crowded every year, and consequently must gain by being removed from an island on which they cannot possibly raise a comfortable subsistence, yet he has not hitherto been successful.'[74]

What, after all, was the alternative to removal? To say that there were too many people trying to make a living in the Highlands is another way of saying that there was too little land or too little capital for them to work with. Those who simply kept their tenants and continued to parcel out their properties in tiny lots to people who, they knew very well, had neither the capital nor the skill to improve them, were merely perpetuating stagnation and starvation. But could the situation not have been saved by an injection of capital? It is doubtful if this was ever a realistic solution. Capital has to be provided in some specific form, and no one has yet discovered how to use capital in the Highlands so as to support 470,000 people. The road and canal building programs constituted capital injection by government on a pretty large scale, but these programs generated little continuing activity, and after them there was no prospect of further government assistance. It therefore fell to the landowners, who had themselves put considerable sums into road building, to solve the problem. Assuming that remunerative ways of employing more capital could have been found—an heroic assumption—the question that arises is whether the estates should have accumulated more funds in the days of prosperity than they did, so as to be able to reinvest them 'appropriately'. To decide this would require prolonged investigation of rents and expenditures.

On the face of it, however, it seems unlikely that different policies of estate management could have produced a very much better outcome. Economic circumstances changed so unpredictably, and the build-up of population was a serious drain on resources well before the end of the eighteenth century. Thus the removal of tenants was sometimes the only way to avoid the ruin of an estate, for if a famine occurred the landowners had to help, and thousands of pounds had to be spent on food supplies which, if not an outright gift, constituted a loan with very poor prospects of repayments. The result was severe financial pressure on landowners and tenants alike. As early as 1772 on the Sutherland estates £2,000 was spent to provide meal and seed corn for the tacksmen and small tenants. Starvation and emigration were checked, but the financial result was that arrears of rent which were around £2,500 in 1770 had doubled by 1773.[75] The giving of relief in this way became commoner in the Highlands in subsequent decades. Small wonder that so many estates changed hands between 1815 and 1840.[76]

In a few cases, removals took place on a large scale, and were sometimes resisted. The most famous of these 'clearances' occurred on the Marquess of Stafford's estates in Sutherland, where they were part of a long-term investment and reorganisation plan. Along with other landowners, the Marquess had co-operated with the Commissioners for Highland Roads in providing Sutherland with a road system. At the same time, he had conceived the idea of removing tenants from the poor, often boggy land of the interior, largely unsuitable for arable farming, and settling them on the more fertile coastal strips. The policy of removal was begun in 1807, and the Marquess's resolve was no doubt strengthened by the serious famines of 1812–13 and 1816–17. In 1813, in Kildonan, the tenants resisted removal, and there was resort to violence, and the same occurred in Strathnaver in 1814. When numerous tacks expired in 1818 and the two following years, the opportunity was taken to carry out an unusually large number of removals in the spring of 1819 and 1820. Some tenants co-operated with the policy, going to Strathy and Helmsdale, but in other cases there was bitterness and resistance. In many other parts of Scotland families were removed in the first decades of the nineteenth century, in Kintail, Glenelg, Loch Arkaig, Strathglass. In the 1830s there was trouble in Skye and in Harris, and as late as 1852 2,000 people were forcibly removed in North Uist. In all these cases many went peaceably and unrecorded; others resisted. Everywhere families clung to little holdings which they knew, and which were frequently almost all that they knew. When given notice to quit they did not quit, often because they had very little idea where to go. They clung to the land because it seemed their only guarantee of subsistence and of the continuity of life. These people were the remnants of a feudal system which had ebbed away, leaving them stranded in remote glens and straths. Landlords no longer counted their wealth in men, but, like everyone else, in money. And in terms of production these last retainers had staggeringly little to offer, as recurrent starvation showed.

Those who were removed had to go somewhere. A minority emigrated directly to Canada or Australia; others—especially those living already on the fringes of the Highlands—went south often to Glasgow, where work might be found. Others settled in little villages on the edge of the Highlands, some old and some new, villages such as Crieff, Blairgowrie, Granton-on-Spey; and these villages developed. In some cases dispossessed tenants were allowed to settle on the waste lands, planted potatoes, and paid a rent of a hen and a few eggs a year. But very many, in some districts and on some occasions the majority, were re-settled on the low grounds on or near the coast. In Sutherland in particular this was the policy. New small holdings were provided, some rent relief was allowed, free timber for new dwellings was made available. The cost to the estate was considerable, but so was the success. New hamlets sprang up and in a few instances new villlages were built, if not for these migrants at any rate in a way that helped them, as at Brora, begun in 1811, and Helmsdale, founded in 1814, and developed jointly by capitalists from the Moray Firth and further south, and by the Marquess of Stafford. Each of these was laid out on a regular rectilinear plan, and was provided, in time, with an improved harbour. Brora was linked to coal pits and salt pans by a small railway, and Helmsdale was planned as a herring fishing port, which by 1819 had a regular trade with Leith. But often a good deal less than this was done, and evicted tenants were left to wring a living as best they could from the coastal land or the sea. Thus sheep-farming not only led to emigration but also to a redistribution of people within the Highlands. Yet this redistribution as a rule did little to alleviate the already serious problem of land hunger among a growing population.

Pressure of population was already apparent in the last quarter of the eighteenth century. People increased, but resources did not, or at any rate not nearly as fast. In Tiree, for example, Cregeen notes that

'Whereas in 1776 roughly seventy or nearly half of the small tenants had sufficient animals to stock a four mail-land, in 1792 the chamberlain reported "the tenants in general are so very poor that it is not believed there are forty among them who could stock and manage four mail-land possessions".'[77]

Holdings, already small, were tending to become still smaller because of the ancient Celtic practice of sharing land with children or other near relations. This practice did not produce serious difficulties in the eighteenth century, and caused little comment. For a time, indeed, it was supported and its effects reinforced by the landlords themselves. This was chiefly because of the kelp trade. The landlords' attitude was made explicit by the Duke of Argyll in his Instructions to his chamberlain in Tiree in 1799:

'As you inform me that small tenants can afford to pay more rent for farms in Tiry than gentlemen-farmers, owing to the manufacture of kelp, this determines me to let the farms to small tenants which have been and are at present possessed by tacksmen who reside upon farms in Mull.'[78]

The kelp boom accelerated the disappearance of the tacksman. Farms previously held by a single tacksman, or occupied jointly by a number of small tenants, began to give way to the crofting system—small individual holdings, each worked by one family, with grazing rights held in common on wide stretches of moorland, and with reliance, often, on some other source of income such as fishing, spinning, or other employment off the croft. Landlords could thus retain, and increase, the labour force they needed for making kelp. What they could not do was to control the forces of population expansion which they thus provided for.

Finding that they had full employment for all who chose to settle upon their estates, they did not hesitate to croft out their farms. But the crofter was no less ready to divide his croft with his son when the latter married— and most married early; and if there was a daughter, and she married, then there was a further partition of the original croft; 'and this practice was continued till most of the crofts, originally intended for one family, had on them two or three, and sometimes four families.'[79]

Most evident on the kelp estates during the first two decades of the nineteenth century, this practice of subdivision, which was by no means new, took place wherever population was rising—and this meant all over the Highlands except in those inland areas where land was already given over to sheep-farming. On Skye, in the 1790s, it was reported that ten families inhabited where a generation before there were not above three. On Barra, where many families in the 1770s had possessed a whole penny of land, no tenant occupied more than a half penny twenty years later, and many had only a quarter or an eighth of a penny-land. Because of rising population

27. Dunrobin Castle, near Golspie, the ancient seat of the Earls of
Sutherland, before the Victorian extensions.

the Duke of Argyll was obliged to abandon his plans to create larger
farming units on his estates, and in 1803 issued instructions that

'different farms must be broke down into small crofts to accomodate the
people who are in want of possessions. Such as were formerly tenants to
have from 6 to 10 arable acres, and those who were only cottars and
tradesmen to have four arable acres, and both to have what accomodation
can be given in the article of summer grass.'[80]

No one believed that such subdivision was going to increase productivity.
Adam Smith had stated that 'the diminution of cottagers, and other small
occupiers of land, has in every part of Europe been the immediate fore-
runner of improvement and better cultivation,'[81] and in the Highlands as
elsewhere landlords realised that it was to their advantage to have their
estates divided into fewer and larger units of production. On the other
hand, they were usually reluctant to turn away people for whom they felt
themselves to be at least to some extent responsible, families who in many
cases had lived on the same estate for generations. The clan system had
gone; but it is a gross distortion of history to suggest that a mere cash
nexus promptly took its place. There was a struggle—for many landowners
a long and saddening struggle—between feelings of social obligation on the
one hand and mounting economic pressure on the other. Small tenants
paid very sma l rents and were often—increasingly often, as population
grew and hol ings became smaller and smaller—an absolute burden on an
estate. Gradually the pressure to remove the occupiers of minute portions
of land, those who could scarcely even in a good year produce enough for
their own survival, increased; but for several decades landlords resisted,
and did what they could to provide for their multiplying tenantry. In these
circumstances of economic dislocation and deadlock, it is not surprising to
find that subdivision and subletting sometimes took place without the
landlord's knowledge. Tenants who found themselves getting into difficulties took in a partner; others sub-let at a higher rent than they paid themselves, and pocketed the difference; others continued to hand over a portion
of the land to sons when they married, or to sons-in-law. 'They appeared
to have an idea, that so long as they paid their rent, they might do with the
land what they liked without asking leave of the proprietor.'[82] On large
estates it became virtually impossible to keep track of what was going on:

'Upon one estate in this neighbourhood I saw the gentleman who man-
ages the estate; he was on the spot with me, and showed me the arrangements that had been made not to allow the population to increase, I
remember one place where there were six settlements, and he said he had
made such arrangements that they were not to increase beyond that
number, I said to him, will you point out the six houses? because I
glanced over it, and I made seven residences. He counted them over. I

28. Coast of Caithness, the Ord, near Helmsdale. In 1769 Pennant saw
here 'numbers of seals floating on the waves, with sea-fowl swimming
among them with great security.'

said, What is that house there? pointing to another. He said, that is a barn. I said, Is it usual to have a glazed window in a barn? That made him look a little more particularly, and actually within about three weeks this barn had been converted without his knowledge into another residence. They had put in a window. They did not stand upon the ceremony of having a chimney, but they put in a window, and a new settlement was created without the knowledge of this gentleman, who would not have noticed it probably but for that accident.'[83]

By the 1830s subdivision and squatting had been carried to extreme lengths. Thousands of families—probably tens of thousands—lived on three or four acres of arable land, with pasture for a cow and a horse. All were inevitably on the verge of starvation. Near Tongue there were large numbers of

'mere cottars, having no land, in the majority of cases without any trade, and depending for their sustenance on a little day labour and on the kindness of their neighbours, who often give them patches of their own small crofts for raising a few potatoes.'[84]

On one estate 1,108 families paid a rent of £5,002, an average of £4 14s 5d. each; but it was reckoned that half the crofts were possessed by at least two families, and at five persons per family this gave an annual rental of 12s 7d per head.[85] No one supposed that families able to pay only so small a rent as this could survive for long. On Lord McDonald's estate in Skye in the late 1830s there were 1,200 families on the rental book, exclusive of Portree; but there were on the land, although not on the rental book, 1,300 families besides, mostly relatives of the tenants, and according to the factor, for every family on the estate who actually paid rent to the proprietor, there were two who paid no rent.[86]

A prolonged growth of population, lasting and possibly accelerating over several generations, was the foundation of these developments. This growth was itself a response to the appearance of increased food supplies— herring and potatoes, almost exclusively—and to the increased employ- ment opportunities which had become available largely as a result of the extension of the herring fishing and the kelp boom. On the west coast the herring fishing was declining after 1790, and the kelp boom was over by 1820. On a few estates, at least, landlords continued to employ tenants in making kelp even although prices soon became insufficient to cover costs. Even the cattle trade was in difficulties, for cattle prices fell steeply after 1815. Tenants responded by selling more cattle, but this merely depressed prices further and, besides, reduced the tenants' stock—the most valuable capital asset they had.

Gradually rural underemployment became chronic. It was notorious even in the later eighteenth century that the number of servants on a highland farm was twice as great as on a comparable farm in the lowlands, and that they were idle for a great part of the year.[87] As population grew and subdivision proceeded the situation grew worse. In 1811 it was stated that the sub-tenants in the Hebrides almost always supported a numerous family 'in a state bordering upon perfect idleness.' They preferred, it was said,

'having their children about them in the most miserable state imaginable, to the hardship, (or what they are pleased to call such) of driving them into service, either on their own island or any where else. It is a common sight, on entering the cottage of one of those subtenants, to find five or six grown individuals, half naked and savage-looking, around a peat fire, watching a pot of potatoes, (their sole food for nine months of the year) without any idea or wish of changing their manner of life . . .[88]

Many 'farms' became so small that the occupier could profitably spend only a little of his time on them, and was obliged as well to drive peat, to go to sea in the fishing season, to find work, if he could, on the larger farms, or to accept 'any other kind of employment that he can fall in with.'[89] On the mainland young men sometimes found work in the summer in making or repairing roads, in curing fish at the fishing stations, or, in the spring and autumn, as occasional hands on the larger farms, in their own or in other parishes. In Dunkeld, in the 1830s

'the labouring classes are principally employed in peeling oak, and in spring and summer work in some of the adjoining parishes. For the remainder of the year they are idle.'[90]

From Lochbroom young men went in the season to Wick or Peterhead and returned after the fishing with four or five pounds; but for the rest of the year 'there is no employment.'[91]

The result was, in the summer and autumn at least, that the Highlands contained what the minister of Kilmuir Easter called 'a fluctuating population . . . many of the people are always on the wing, shifting from one parish to another. . . .'[92] Some went south during the summer months, as the highlanders had done for many years.[93] From Skye

'almost all the young men leave the country annually, and resort to the south, in vast numbers, in quest of any employment which they may procure. In the same manner, many of the young women go to the Lothians in harvest to procure employment in reaping.'[94]

But this, too, was on the decline. Agriculture in the south was becoming more mechanised, and in many places the highlanders were driven out by Irish competition, which intensified as steamship services from Ireland improved faster than on the west coast and Irish workers began to come across to England for a shilling a head or less. For a time the Government's programme of road building, and work on the canals, had done something to alleviate the situation; but after 1820 these items, also, were diminishing,

and it came to be felt that the 'redundant population' ought not to be encouraged by 'a false humanity on the part of the landlords, allowing the
people to remain and take small patches of land.'[95]

The troubles and indeed the tragedies of the early decades of the century
thus owed their origins to a fairly long sequence of historical events. The
growth of productive capacity and of employment opportunities initiated
an increase of population with which productive capacity and employment
opportunities failed, after a short while, to keep pace. Fishing, in Caithness
and later on the east coast further south, became an established industry, and
it brought with it certain related activities—smoking, coopering, boat-
building, and the building of piers and harbours; but this could not by
itself solve the Highland's problems. Sheep-farming also endured; but
sheep-farming was labour saving and capital intensive. It invited the attention of rich men beyond the region, not of poor men within it. In the short
run it increased unemployment, and even in the long run it failed to give
rise to other kinds of employment within the region, for the woollen
manufacturing which Anderson had dreamed of did not appear in the
Highlands.

Yet it is important to realise that sheep-farming was not the fundamental
cause of the highlanders' difficulties. It was a new and, from the national
point of view, profitable way of using resources—although not human
resources. It improved the food supply for the growing urban population,
and produced more wool for the woollen industry. But it was the costs
rather than the benefits which were immediately apparent, and they were
borne in the Highlands. The shifts of population which sheep-farming
caused were drastic and were in some cases brought about in a heartless
and even ruthless fashion. It was irresponsible to suppose that poor tenants,
accustomed to a stagnant agricultural routine, could be dumped on the
sea-shore or on the shores of a sea-loch, without skill, experience or equipment, and successfully wrest a living from the sea as fishermen, with or
without the help of an acre or two of potatoes. Sir John Sinclair, himself
one of the chief progenitors of sheep-farming in the Highlands, protested
against the forcible removal of tenants who knew nothing but their customary way of life:

'It is one thing to build a village, to which people may resort if they
    choose it, and another to drive them from the country into villages,
    where they must starve, unless they change at once their manners, their
    habits, and their occupations.'[96]

The trouble was that the alteration required in the tenant's way of life was
so complete, his preparation for it so non-existent; that he resented and
resisted attempts to move him little by little towards a commercial life;
and that during the final phases of removing the tenantry, alternative em-

ployment opportunities were diminishing rather than increasing in the Highlands. The clearances, after all, did not come like a thunderstorm out of a cloudless sky; they were heralded—the more famous of them—by fifty years of remorseless and extensive change. But so isolated was the life of many districts that no preparations, no preliminary adjustments seem to have been made. In these circumstances, for landowners to have brought about a painless transition from the old order to the new would have been difficult, slow and costly. There would have had to be much planning and much expenditure. Tenants would have had to be persuaded of the desirability of change from their own point of view. It is fair to say that some efforts in this direction were made. But in other cases a struggle developed between landowners trying to bring about 'improvements' and tacksmen and tenants who wanted to preserve the *status quo*; and this struggle, in the course of which blows were from time to time exchanged, could be seen— and sometimes was seen—as a contest between authority on the one hand and on the other anarchy, or the assertion of simple human rights; depending on the point of view.

The clearances, to which so much attention has been paid in highland history, were important; but they were no more than the visible, breaking crest of a long-travelling, irresistible wave. Those who organised them and who later surveyed what they had done, found it good:

'Let any person, I don't care who he be, or what his prejudices. Let him view the inside of one of the new fishermen's stone cots in Loth—the man and his wife and young children weaving their nets around their winter fire. Let him contrast it with the sloth, and poverty, and filth, and sleep of an unremoved tenant's turf hut in the interior. Let him inspect the people, stock, cattle, horses, trees, and plants, in a stock farmer's possession, and compare it with the pared bottom from which turf in all ages had been taken, with the closely cropped roots of grass, and bushes and miserable lazy-bed's culture that surround a highlander's cabin, with the starved kyloes and scabbed ponies and sheep that stagger about his place, picking up half an existence; and, let him *believe*, if he can, that men are injured by civilization, and that, during the last ten years, a most important benefit has not been conferred on this country.'[97]

So wrote one of the greatest sheep farmers of the Highlands. But the changes which he so confidently surveyed were only a part of a general change of the same kind, taking place over a longer period and throughout the Highlands.

It is striking that as late as 1820 the old idea of civilizing the Highlands should still appear. Nowadays we speak—perhaps more evasively although it seems more precisely—about raising the standard of living. But changes took place in those years which were too deep-seated, too comprehensive to be included in the mere idea of a standard of living. Feudal servitudes declined and finally vanished, so that men became their own masters, no longer at the beck and call of a superior, although no longer under his protection; for better or for worse. Improved communications brought contact with the outside world, a world of change and, as it believed, of progress; different ways of thinking, and of living, were now in the highlander's ken; isolation and self sufficiency were at an end. The Gaelic language gave way to English, and more and more people learned to read and write—mostly in English. Illicit distilling, and smuggling, ceased to be common trades.

Most people outside the Highlands believed—perhaps most people still believe—that these were improvements. Few denied that they had been bought at a price. But as the world of new technology and urban industry and utilitarianism, of Whitworth and Telford, of Bentham and Malthus and James Mill became more firmly established, the calculation of loss and gain was increasingly made in what we would recognize as modern terms. In these terms, what had eighty years of development achieved?

The highland economy was more productive and less uniform than it had been in 1750. In the south-west there was a more varied agriculture, and some specialised dairy farming had developed in connection with the fast-growing Glasgow market. Fishing in the south-west, and especially in Loch Fyne, was important for the same reason. Because of the proximity of Glasgow and its commercial influences, some of these areas had almost ceased to be a part of the Highlands. Inverness had grown to be a town of about 14,000 inhabitants, the centre of a prosperous agricultural region and with an active coastal trade. Hemp and linen making had declined, but there were breweries, tanneries and distilleries in the town, shipbuilding was carried on, and there were even 'villas with gardens attached to them'. In Easter Ross, and in Caithness, grain growing had greatly expanded and was now carried on in ways of which an East Lothian farmer would not have been ashamed. Campbeltown, Stornoway and Wick were major fishing centres. In most areas sheep were important as well as cattle, potatoes were grown, and more modern techniques of cultivation, on enclosed land, were general. The isolation of regions within the Highlands had greatly diminished, and there was more trade between Highlands and Lowlands, as well as within the Highlands. Imports of food into the region were as necessary as ever. The local supply of potatoes, herrings, oatmeal and milk, greatly expanded as it had been, was not sufficient to keep the highlanders for more than perhaps seven or eight months in the year; for the rest, the people continued to depend on their earnings, mostly from the sale of black cattle, to buy from surplus-producing regions the bolls of meal which they required. These were carried into the hills from lowland

Perthshire, the Howe of the Mearns, Buchan, Morayshire, Easter Ross, or came from farther afield by sea; as early as the 1790s it was reported that Gairloch, 'and all the West coast, are supplied in the summer with meal, by vessels that come from the different ports at a distance; such as Caithness, Murray, Peterhead, Banff, Aberdeen, Greenock, etc.'[98] One third or a half, or in later years perhaps even more of a tenant's money income was spent in this way.

Because cultivable land, employment and food supply were increasing less fast than population, people were leaving the Highlands in increasing numbers. Most went south, to the Lowlands and to England, as they had always done; 'the Highlands are a nursery, for raising so many useful hands, for the countries below them. It is almost incredible to tell, what swarms leave the county every year, and go to the south for service'.[99] After the war, more emigrants than before went to Canada and Australia, especially, it seems, from the islands. Yet the highland population was larger in the 1820s and the 1830s than it had ever been. What was life like for those who remained? It is hard to generalize. Perhaps it would be safest to say that for the majority of people life was harder—in some instances a good deal harder—than it had been in the later eighteenth century. The mass of the tenantry lived on potatoes, herrings and oatmeal; wore clothing only of the coarsest materials; and lived in houses without chimneys which, often, they shared with their cattle. In some parishes life seems to have gone on more or less as it had always done. This was true of Lochbroom, for example:

'The language generally spoken is Gaelic; but it is evidently losing ground. The people are in general sober and quiet. . . . They are in general very poor. Their ordinary food consists chiefly of potatoes and fish; and it must be admitted that the strength of body, and daring spirit for which the Highlanders were once justly celebrated, are greatly on the decline. They cannot be entirely acquitted of poaching in game or salmon; nor is the country entirely free from the degrading and demoralizing practice of smuggling whisky'.[100]

In Assynt the picture was not dissimilar. The people there were said to

'live sparingly. Their chief articles of food are herrings and potatoes. Some attention has, of late, been paid to cleanliness and neatness about their dwellings, but very much remains to be done. Upon the whole, they may be said to be contented with their situations'.[101]

But these accounts are not typical of the west coast. There cannot have been much contentment in Glenshiel, for example, among a 'wretched poverty-stricken population',[102] nor in Portree, about whose inhabitants the minister wrote:

'No people on earth live on more simple or scanty diet than those in this parish. The great number of them subsist on potatoes of the worst kind, sometimes with, but oftener without fish.'[103]

These people had 'little either of day or night clothing . . . their children nearly approaching to absolute nakedness' and their huts 'smoky and filthy in the extreme'. Such conditions were not new in the Highlands. What was new was the report that things were getting worse. In the parish of Tongue the general standard was described as

'wretchedly low. No doubt a few of them are comfortable, but the generality seldom can rise above the commonest necessaries of life; and it is painful to think of how some eke out an existence. The consequence is, that poverty is gradually manifesting its baneful effects upon the intellects and morals of naturally a fine and generous people. The taste for music, dancing, and public games, is much on the decline. . . .'.[104]

Deterioration was especially noticeable in the islands. In Lewis, for example, the people were said to be 'much reduced in circumstances'[105] since the 1790s, and it was reported of Tiree and Coll that the people had once been 'happy and contented' but that 'of late years . . . poverty laid its iron hand upon them'.[106] In South Uist,

'The people in general are not alive to the benefits of education. This is partly owing to their poverty and consequent inability to pay the school-fees, and partly to the necessity of their employing the children at work, and herding cattle. Indeed, the poor children in general are so ragged and destitute of clothes and shoes, that in some districts most of them cannot attend school in winter, which is the season of the year when they could most conveniently attend. This destitution is very general. . . .'[107]

Along the fringes of the Highlands, on the other hand, in Argyll and in south and east Perthshire, there were signs of improvement—cotton cloth was sometimes bought at the nearest market, a little tea was drunk, and it could be said (as of Moulin) 'poor indeed is that family which does not rear a pig'.[108] Even in a parish like Kintail, where there had been much dispossession, it was reported in 1836 that

'strange as it may seem, in manners and dress, there is the greatest improvement. . . . The wages of the young people are raised. Cotton goods are cheap; and on Sabbath, the people are not only decently, but fashionable attired'.[109]

Improvement was probably most easily seen in the larger villages or little towns which were centres of trading, or fishing, or of an improved agriculture. The picture of Dingwall suggests the kind of change that was occurring in some places:

'The taste for amusements would seem to be declining here; even the Christmas and Newyear shinty matches, in which but recently, both old and young used to indulge with eager interest, are now abandoned. . . .

29. Dundarave Castle on the shores of Loch Fyne, a few miles east of Inveraray; once a principal seat of the Macnaughtons.

16

Although by no means filthy in their persons, [the people] are far from remarkable for cleanliness in their dwellings and domestic arrangements. But a marked change . . . is now taking place. More regard is now paid to neatness, at least in the exterior of their houses, and the dunghill, which used to disfigure the approach to them, is now pretty generally giving place to a flower-pot or shrubbery. The staple articles of food among the peasantry are potatoes and herrings, which, with oatmeal, form the subsistence of the poorer classes. Fresh fish . . . supplies them with a wholesome and agreeable variety. But the standard of living is exceedingly low. . . . Still, however, the people are social and contented, and enjoy the comforts of society in a higher degree than their slender circumstances would indicate.'[110]

There is, in accounts of this kind, a feeling of life and movement, of hope rather than of stagnation or decay, of poverty but not misery, of access to a wider world. Where this feeling existed it was generally agreed that the spread of education—in English—had played a major rôle.

The situation in the 1820s and the early 1830s was hardly a realisation of the great hopes which had been entertained in the 1780s. There were obviously still two worlds in Scotland, a poor highland world and a comparatively prosperous lowland world. Life in the former was dominated by the search for employment, and from time to time, increasingly, it became dominated by the search for food.

After 1820 it was common for many places to experience a food shortage, more or less, every summer before the harvest was got in. The situation gradually grew worse. 1835 and 1836 were remarkably cold, wet and stormy, and the crops failed. In 1836 the failure of the potato crop on the west coast was particularly extensive, and the herring fishing also failed. In Skye the crops were cut green, and so much rain fell that the people could not even secure their peats for the ensuing winter. Along the coasts of Argyll and Ross-shire, in the Hebrides and over large parts of Inverness-shire there was destitution and incipient starvation; worst, perhaps, in Skye, Tiree, and around Lochbroom. Not fewer than 50,000 people were in extreme distress. Relief was essential, and the government supplied £10,000, almost £70,000 more coming from private individuals in Edinburgh, Glasgow and London. Very little money was distributed; most of the relief was in the form of meal, potatoes and blankets. Proprietors did what they could to help, sometimes sending in supplies to the extent of several thousand pounds. But as a result of the collapse of the kelp trade, of falling agricultural prices after the war, of expenditure on roads and bridges and of extravagant living, many of the estates in the west of Scotland were encumbered with a great deal of heritable debt; many other places—the whole of Harris and South Uist and Barra for example—had newly

30. View from the Kyles of Bute, with Castle Toward; once the seat of the Lamonts, lords of Cowal; burned by the Campbells in 1646.

changed hands, and the new owners were not anxious to add to their recent outgoings; and on many estates there were large arrears of rent.

But in any case relief was only a temporary expedient; it kept the people from starving, but it left the economy in an unchanged state. Increasingly, landlords were coming to believe that the only solution was emigration. Gone were the hopes of yesteryear. Proprietors who had earlier opposed emigration, sometimes for selfish reasons, because they wanted to keep a labour force on their estates, sometimes from feelings of moral responsibility for the welfare of their tenants, began to assist families who wished to remove. From the middle of the 1820s there were many requests from landlords that the government should assist in sending tenants to the colonies. Feudal feelings lingered, but they weakened with every decade. The writings of Malthus encouraged the view that population growth could easily be a barrier to progress, that it was over-population rather than under-population that was to be feared. In 1826 a Select Committee on Emigration reported that in Scotland there were places where population was 'redundant', and that numbers of able-bodied should be removed to the colonies. In 1829 Edward Gibbon Wakefield began to spread the idea that assisted emigration was desirable. By the later 1830s the landlords were convinced that this was the answer to the problems which they faced.

Perhaps no man worked harder to build a modern economy with a variety of employment opportunities in the Highlands than the 5th Duke of Argyll. When his son appeared before the Select Committee on Emigration in 1841, the first question which he was asked was whether his estates were not 'very populous?', and he replied, 'very much so.' The second question was, 'has not that superabundant population arisen in a great measure in consequence of the measures adopted by your predecessor in granting crofts and subdividing the land?', and the Duke replied: 'Chiefly; it is that which had been productive of great evil. . . .' Later, in reply to a question about the fishing, he could only say that the people 'are exceedingly discouraged in that respect.' About manufactures, villages or improved communications nothing was said. The idea of building up the highland economy was over, and was not to be revived for more than a hundred years.

Postscript

The economic misfortunes of the Highlands, starting in the later eighteenth century and becoming more evident, more diverse and more intractable as time passed, were at bottom the outcome of changes going back to at least 1750. The various measures taken to promote highland development, relating to particular problems or to particular possibilities, were introduced into a situation in which the underlying trends were gravely unfavourable. The long wave of population growth; the rapidly increasing industrial advantages and agricultural efficiency of the lowlands and England; the incidence of war, and then peace, drawing men to the army and navy and then sending them back, suddenly raising and then even more suddenly lowering prices; the uncertain movement of the herring shoals—all these influences combined to counteract the steadying and beneficial effects of economic policy.

So much is quite evident. But to say this is not enough. Two questions evidently arise: first, did it have to be so? and second, must it always be so?

When the failure of policy came to be discussed in the 1830s and 1840s, there was one explanation which was popular in some quarters: failure was due, it was said, to the incorrigible idleness of the highlander. He would not make any effort to better his condition; he would not respond to incentives which sufficed for other men; he always preferred leisure to additional income above a minimum subsistence level. This explanation seems to have been most favoured by those who knew least about the Highlands. The experts' reply was to the effect that the highlander's indolence was the result of the situation in which he was placed. Minding cattle, it was argued, was not a strenuous occupation, and the return which could be got from unusual exertions in a remote country of poor soil and with a bad climate was derisory. There is certainly a great deal of truth in this argument. In a pastoral society the men are seldom great workers. There is some evidence, admittedly, that habits of idleness were perhaps carried rather further than could easily be justified—from a commercial point of view:

'Until a highland farmer gets his seed sown, he is as active as a man can be. When that business is over, he goes to sleep, until roused by the recollection that he must have some means of keeping himself warm during winter. He then spends a few days in the peat moss, where the women and children are the chief operators. He cuts the peats, and leaves them to be dried and piled up by his family. Whenever the peats have been brought home, another interval presents itself for repose, until the corn is ripe. During the winter, unless a good opportunity for smuggling occurs, a Highland farmer has nothing to do but to keep himself warm. He never thinks on labouring his fields during mild weather, or of collecting manure during spring. I cannot reckon how often I have seen Highland farmers basking in the sun on a fine summer day, in all the comforts of idleness. I have asked them, when I found them in such a situation, why they were not busy hoeing their potatoes —"O! the women and bairns do that", was the answer. I would then ask why they did not remove the heaps of stones, which I saw on their fields, or conduct away the water which rested on them. They would answer that they did not know where to put them; or, that they did no harm; or that they had been there so long, that it was not worth while to stir them; and that the water gave sap to the land; with many other answers equally absurd, and dictated by nothing but what must be considered constitutional sloth.'[1]

But the notion of constitutional sloth, applied indiscriminately to 300,000 people, is not one likely to carry much conviction in the twentieth century. The will to live better, as it has been called, is probably as universal as Adam Smith said it was, and experience in developing countries generally suggests that peasants and small farmers will respond to genuine economic incentives and opportunities, given security and a little time. Moreover, as was pointed out in the nineteenth century, many a highlander, on removal to a different environment, proved as enterprising and energetic as could be wished:

'Put a Highlander in the way of doing well, and there is no man who will continue at it with greater perseverance; there is no man who will live more soberly and quietly, and amass money. I have seen a great number of them who have come as poor boys to Glasgow, and yet have been able to retire from business with a competency.'[2]

Certainly the circumstances of highland life gave men habits of indolence; equally certainly, many of them shed these habits and adopted the behaviour appropriate to an acquisitive, competitive society when they settled in Glasgow, or Halifax, or Toronto. Their indolence may sometimes have seemed excessive, but perhaps this should be put down as much as anything to the depressing effects of the highland climate, so often destroying in a few days of rain and gale the work of a summer, and to the deadening effects of too long stagnation and too often disappointed hopes.

The nineteenth century was also inclined to argue that lack of education was at the heart of the highlanders' difficulties. To some extent this simply reflects the nineteenth century's faith in education as a solution to all sorts of problems. Also, it was easy to urge the advantages of more education as long as what constituted education was not too closely defined. A considerable number of highlanders could not read or write, and most of them could not speak English. There were schools, at least one in every parish, and literacy and English were spreading; but the schools were often very small, schoolteachers were always badly paid and sometimes ill-qualified, and many parents could not afford to pay fees or to do without their children's services in the fields or at the fishing. It is an appealing idea that more education would have helped; but in what ways and how quickly? Some supported the education argument on the ground that when they came to live in the big cities the highlanders were at a disadvantage because of their lack of education; others maintained that if they were educated they would no longer be content to stay in the Highlands.[3] Neither of these arguments suggests that more education would have helped the highlander in the Highlands—except by reducing total population; and this, of course, was what policy had originally set out to prevent. It is certainly true that literacy and the ability to speak English were bound, in the long run, to facilitate the adoption of new ideas and new attitudes—partly to be reflected, no doubt, in an increased rate of emigration. But it is not easy to see how more formal education could have helped a starving crofter working without capital on a poor soil; and all things considered it seems unlikely that additional investment in education in the Highlands—at least on any scale which might have been proposed—would have made much difference in the period under review.

Policy was not directed to providing more education: it was principally directed to helping the fishing industry (which proved very difficult to help), to providing better transport and, in the private sector, to modernising agriculture. This last was labour-saving; and the new roads and canals provided only temporary employment. As a result, the economic development which took place in the Highlands, instead of retarding the outflow of population, accelerated it. A conflict thus emerged between having the Highlands prosperous and having them populous. This conflict was recognised fairly early. In 1805, for example, Selkirk welcomed emigration as removing unproductive labour and enabling those who remained to produce a surplus for the support of industrial workers in other parts of the country.[4] A few years later, in 1810, Sir George Steuart Mackenzie put the matter quite explicitly:

'There exists a very strange contradiction in the opinions of many persons who have an interest in the prosperity of the Highlands. It is now uni-

versally admitted to be desirable to introduce a better system of rendering our numerous mountains more productive. Yet it has not in very
many instances been discovered, that these two desirable objects are
quite incompatible with the retention of the present number of people.'[5]
This was indeed a conflict of objectives. Landowners found it impossible to
develop an agriculture at once more productive and so labour-intensive
that it could employ all the available labour force. The fishing industry
could not support everyone. And manufactures failed to develop in spite
of much hope and a good deal of enterprise.

If it is granted that not much more could have been achieved *via* agriculture or the fishing industry, it becomes very important to ask why manufacturing industry failed to develop in the Highlands. The men of the
eighteenth century certainly thought that it could. They knew that industries tended to locate on the site of their raw materials; in the Highlands
the principal raw material for industry was to be wool. They also believed
that 'manufactures seldom prosper so well in large cities and royal
boroughs, as in country towns and villages' and it therefore followed that
the little highland villages—which could be increased in number—were
'exceedingly well calculated for the seat of Manufacturers.'[6] Finally,
Adam Smith had taught them that towns and villages were the meeting
place of enterprise of every kind, generating new activities and radiating
economic development throughout their region. The argument was complete. And it seemed, in the 1780s and 1790s, entirely reasonable.

As luck would have it, the drift of technology was against such plans.
The age of factory production, dependent first on water and then on steam
power and using iron machinery of a new complexity, was beginning; and
it produced a concentration of industry on coal beds and in industrial
towns which drained manufacturing activity out of country towns and
villages. Even those which seemed well established, with a skilled labour
force and good access to markets, suffered severely—places like Perth,
Forfar, or Blairgowrie. If these and others like them could not hold on to
what they had there was no hope for industrial development beyond the
highland line. And when manufactures failed to develop, the *raison d'être*
of the new highland villages partly disappeared.

It is tempting to speculate what would have happened if substantial
deposits of iron ore or coal had been discovered, or if the Highlands had
proved to be a first-class forest area. Forests alone would probably not
have done much to hold the population. Forestry tends to compete with
agriculture for the use of land, and in any case the amount of employment
provided per acre is small. There would also have been problems of access,
although the sea lochs would have provided useful loading points far inland and the Caledonian Canal might possibly have found a use sufficient

to justify its construction. Good ore or coal deposits would have made a greater difference. They would have provided primary employment, and it is likely that a certain amount of secondary industry would then have developed. If a constellation of reasonably good and varied resources had been found within one or two fairly small areas—coal or copper or iron along with forest land and sheep pasture—it is certainly possible that centres of economic activity might have grown up which would have come to support, at least in the course of time, a substantial part of the highland population.

What happened in the more northerly districts of Sweden is an instructive example of development in a remote area with an unfavourable climate, limited local markets, and no manufacturing tradition—but with resources superior to those of the Highlands. Extending from the sixty-second to the sixty-eighth parallel, and lying between the shores of the Gulf of Bothnia and the very sparsely inhabited mountains along the Norwegian frontier, Norrland has water power, ore fields, and seemingly endless supplies of timber. There is little scope for agriculture. Until about 150 years ago, settlement was almost entirely in isolated farms, and the density of population was extremely low. Then, in the 1840s, the steeply rising world demand for timber began to affect Norrland; saw mills were set up on the Gulf of Bothnia, and timber merchants began to penetrate inland to reach districts hitherto beyond the scope of trade. Towards the end of the century, rail transport began to supplement transport by sea—restricted due to the harbours being closed by ice in winter—and the large ore fields of Lapland became important.

The consequence of these developments was growth of population, with an inward movement that was especially noticeable in the 1840s. In the forty years after 1840 the population of Norrland doubled, and between 1880 and 1960 it almost doubled again. Norrland's share of Sweden's population rose from $8\frac{1}{2}$ per cent in 1860 to $12\frac{1}{2}$ per cent by 1910. But the pattern of settlement and the occupational structure are peculiar; and in recent years the population has begun to fall after increasing only slowly for several decades.

Most people live on the coast, in urban centres such as Sundsvall or Umeå. These coastal towns are based on saw milling and timber exporting, although there are also steel works, chemical works, and a variety of light industries. The rural population lives by agriculture, but not solely by agriculture. It has always been taken for granted that a farmer must have a considerable acreage in forest land, besides his fields; and in purely rural areas life depends on 'a combination of agriculture, livestock breeding, trapping, birdcatching and fishing, by which the inhabitants of the north traditionally lived. In the remote areas fishing, trapping and fowling might be the most important. The nomads, the Lapps, live by reindeer breeding, catching birds and small game, and fishing.'[7] But this traditional pattern of life is beginning to disappear, and occupational specialisation is taking its place. To some extent this is because the resources required for such a life have been reduced or pre-empted by firms or public authorities engaged in mining, forestry, or power supply. Also, it is increasingly difficult to combine farming with subsidiary employment in the 'new' industries. As a result small holdings are being joined together, cash crops are growing in importance, farm land is being turned over to forest, and forest workers, 'who formerly worked in the forest during the winter and farmed during the summer',[8] now work in forestry whole-time. Moreover, increasing occupational specialisation coupled with rising standards of living and the shift to a money economy has depopulated some districts and this has aggravated their marginal position as regards services. People no longer wish to live in areas where shops and schools are poorly provided; and thus these areas become still further run down. In 1950, 41 per cent of the population of Västerbotten was in 'agriculture and subsidiary occupations;' in 1960 the figure was 25 per cent.

Thus Norrland, with resources far superior to those of the Highlands, enjoyed for several generations both an increase in the number of inhabitants and a very great rise in the standard of living. But prospects for the future are not encouraging. Norrland is being industrialised and urbanised, and life in Norrland is becoming more like life elsewhere. Yet the population is smaller now than it was in 1960—although not very much smaller —and only the larger towns, those with a population of over 20,000, are growing in size; the smaller towns and villages are almost universally declining, some of them quite rapidly. Such changes give rise, in Norrland as in the Highlands, to resistance and regret. Some owners of small parcels of land cling to them, partly because—as ever—they provide at least the appearance of stability in a changing world, partly because the small landholder is his own master to an extent not common in the modern industry-state. But to behave in this fashion is to swim against the tide. The economic future of Norrland does not seem promising, and the old patterns of life are breaking up.

This last is for many people a matter for particular regret. There is nothing new in this either. Writing with reference to the year 1814, Elizabeth Grant of Rothiemurchus described the unfavourable reactions of a relative to the 'improvements' which were then taking place around her:

'She said it was all very proper, very necessary, quite inevitable, but not agreeable. She liked the Highlands as she had known them—primitive, when nobody spoke English, when all young men wore the kilt, when printed calicoes were not to be seen, when there was no wheaten bread to be got, when she and Aunt Mary had slept in two little closets in the old house just big enough to hold them, and not big enough to hold any of their property, when there was no tidy kitchen range, no kitchen even beyond the black hut, no neat lawn, but all the work going forward about the house, the maids in the broom island with kilted coats dancing in the tubs upon the linen, and the laird worshipped as a divinity by every human being in the place. The increase of comfort and the gradual enlightenment was all very correct, but it was not the Highlands.'[9]

What was passing away in 1814 has now passed away almost completely. Only the vestiges of a peculiar pattern of life remain. Yet the Highlands are still to some extent a distinctive region, socially as well as geographically, retaining in part at least some of their old economic and even social characteristics.

Because they are still recognised as a distinctive region, but not a prosperous one, the Highlands are the subject of distinctive policies. These policies must be judged in the first instance with reference to their objectives; and here there seems to be some conflict, or at least confusion of aims, which not everyone is willing to face. Three goals of policy are often mentioned or implied: the maintenance of numbers living and employed in the Highlands; the maintenance or raising of the standard of living; the preservation, to some degree, of a distinctive way of life. These three variables interact, and they may conflict. Many combinations of them are possible—that is to say, any one of them may be pursued with varying degrees of determination relative to the others—but some combinations are impossible; thus, if living standards were to fall relatively to those in the rest of the country, maintenance of numbers in the Highlands would tend to be increasingly difficult or even impracticable. If this is granted, the chief problem is as follows: is the principal purpose of policy to maintain population while raising living standards, or to preserve a familiar way of life? Population will not stay unless the standard of living is at least comparable with that in other parts of the country; but the traditional occupations, pursued in the old ways, will not provide such a standard of living, unless heavily subsidised. This dilemma was recognised by the Highlands and Islands Board at the start of its operations, and it came down fairly, if not quite squarely, on the side of retaining population: 'depopulation of the area is the central problem'; success would require, even, 'a substantial enough rise in numbers to give credibility to Highland regeneration'.[10] The Board recognised crofting 'to be a form of living and working which gives deep satisfaction to those who follow it',[11] but added that crofting could not survive without 'other employment support'. The crofter, in other words, was to be treated with respect, although he was not to be regarded as 'exempt from the ordinary laws of making a real livelihood'.[12]

But although the Board recognised that crofting was a problem and not a romance, it seemed to envisage that some new pattern of living could be created in the Highlands, neither the traditional highland nor the common contemporary pattern: the aim of the Board, wrote the Chairman, was 'the aim of adding another perfectly possible way of life to that in the great cities'.[13] What this way might be, one has to infer from the actions of the Board.

The policies which the Board has pursued since 1965 resemble quite closely those pursued in the late eighteenth and early nineteenth centuries—efforts to improve the fishing round the coasts, to provide (along with the central Government) better roads, to introduce new crops (for example, on the bulb fields of North Uist), to encourage (along with the Forestry Commission) afforestation, and to attract manufacturing industry. As before, it does not seem likely that fishing or forestry or agriculture, even in conjunction with better transport, will do very much to provide additional employment and prevent the continued loss of population from the region. Once again, it seems that what will matter will be the success or failure of the attempts to establish new industry.

The obvious difficulty is that the modern industrialist customarily prefers to locate his plant in or near a centre where manufacturing activity is already going on and where there is already a considerable concentration of population. His reasons for this are two-fold. He needs markets, and he must purchase inputs. A prosperous industrial area constitutes a market, especially for a manufacturer selling directly to final consumers, and it is also likely to be able to provide the labour, the specialised services and at least some of the intermediate goods which a modern plant requires if it is to operate efficiently. Because these goods and services are usually needed in considerable diversity and without much delay, the modern industrialist may hesitate to locate where population is scanty and industry little developed. And there is a further difficulty. Those conurbations in which, or fairly near which modern industry has so far chiefly developed, seem themselves to develop best within easy reach of one another, so that manufacturing industry tends to concentrate near the centre of all manufacturing industry—near London, Manchester, Rotterdam, the Ruhr—and not in the peripheral areas of Europe. These considerations militate against industrial development anywhere in the Highlands.

Not so long ago these would have seemed very serious obstacles. But recent experience suggests that industry has become more willing than it used to be to move away from the big centres of population and to locate in fairly small towns provided that there is an adaptable labour force, that houses have been or will be built for work people, and that there are amenities which will attract managerial staff to the area. Moreover, the

Highland's poverty of natural resources probably counts for much less than it did one hundred and fifty or two hundred years ago; more industry is 'foot-loose' now, not tied to natural resources, than was the case then. And the Highlands and Islands Development Board has sought as far as possible to counteract the disadvantages of the region by concentrating its efforts in the industrial field in two or three places—at Fort William, around Inverness and Invergordon, and, to a lesser extent, in the Wick-Thurso area. Such concentration of effort, which was not a feature of the old policies, increases the chances of success. There is still the problem of scale, for the selected centres of development are small and must for many years remain small, and they do not have that easy access to the commercial conveniences of a large city nearby which would offset their disadvantage of size. But the Inverness-Invergordon complex seems capable of overcoming the disadvantages of remoteness and small scale, and it may well prove sufficiently large, and sufficiently well endowed, to grow at a satisfactory rate. The success of the other two centres seems more doubtful because they are smaller and more remote.

It has been argued[14] that, even if the attitudes of industry had not changed, the drawbacks of a remote or 'lonely' location are not as serious as they used to be; that we live in an age when it is possible to overcome particular regional disadvantages by elaborate transport provision. This is perhaps technologically possible. The economic disadvantages of a small town, for example, might be overcome by means of sufficiently improved transport. There could be—if the idea does not seem too fanciful—a fast four-lane highway from Inverness to Ullapool. Or if it were to be decided that congestion elsewhere was becoming intolerable (and it is far from intolerable at present in what appear to be lower-cost locations such as the south of Scotland and the north of England), then there would not be any insuperable difficulties about establishing, for example, the linear city along the shores of the Moray and Cromarty Firths with a population of 300,000 of which the planners dream. All obstacles can be overcome by means of a sufficient injection of capital. But proposals of this kind run counter to what seems the national interest in having resources directed into those uses where their productivity is highest. As things stand, only a limited number of industrial enterprises can hope to be as productive or nearly as productive for a given cost by locating in the Highlands as by locating elsewhere. The disadvantages of a highland location could be overcome by sufficient financial inducements; or they could be reduced by the provision of better facilities. The best facility of all, however, namely the existence in the region of many other thriving industrial establishments, cannot be provided by a planning decision. A four-lane highway to Ullapool might be built, and, as Adam Smith said, 'By means of glasses, hotbeds, and hotwalls, very good grapes can be raised in Scotland, and very good wine can be made of them at about thirty times the expence for which at least equally good can be brought from foreign countries'.[15] It is not necessarily worthwhile to do whatever could be done. The problem is to discover a policy that would provide reasonable prosperity in the Highlands at an acceptable cost in terms of subsidy from the rest of the community. Economic policy is always a question of balancing benefits against costs.

Finally it may be argued that the shores of the Moray and Cromarty Firths hardly belong to the Highlands proper; that a thriving city there would not much change the situation in Assynt or Ardnamurchan. This is perhaps not quite fair; Inverness has always been recognised as a highland town, although it is on the very edge of the Highlands; and if it were to grow, it is at least possible that this would produce 'spread' effects in other parts of the region. What seems likely to happen is that one or a few urban centres will grow—those already the larger, as in Norrland—and population elsewhere will decline. The Highlands as a whole will remain unindustrial and thinly populated. This is, to most people, although not always to those who live there, their main attraction; and it is ironical to see the Board, which is committed to a policy of economic development, proclaiming with evident pride that theirs is 'the last great unspoilt region'. Because of this, tourism, on which the Board has laid considerable emphasis, is already an industry of some importance—the possibilities were mentioned by Knox in 1787.[16] But tourism is not a high-wage industry and over most of the Highlands it must be seasonal; it will not do more than keep the region ticking over, although it may destroy—and indeed it has already gone a considerable way in this direction—its unspoilt and impressive character.

Thus a new pattern of life in the Highlands is indeed emerging. The region is not being 'preserved' for crofting or for any other activity, but is being developed so as to retain, if possible, at least its present population. This requires the growth of small-town industry, as far as that can be contrived (and rather as the eighteenth century had wanted), along with increased activity in forestry, fishing and tourism. Some progress along these lines has been made, and as a result the Highlands are already a somewhat different place from what they were even ten years ago. Development means change. Economic development, especially if it involves increased competitive efficiency, cannot be achieved without changing character. To give priority to economic development is to set aside status, and tradition. Whether the new Highlands will make the same appeal to loyalty and imagination as did the old Highlands, either of the eighteenth century or of the nineteenth century, remains to be seen; but it is unlikely. For it has been the peculiar excellence of the Highlands that they were grand, and different. They did not submit to the ordinary kinds of human exploitation. For long they preserved a culture of their own and an independent way of life. For longer still they have remained, like northern Norway and Sweden, like parts of Arizona and New Mexico, remote from the great centres of industry and population, little affected by man and modern technology; and it may be that it is this and not their potential for being refashioned in the image of Lanarkshire or Midlothian, that has given them their highest value in the modern world.

Chapter One

1. S. Johnson *A Journey to the Hebrides* in *Works* IX (Oxford 1825) p.24.

2. *Dictionary of National Biography*, 'Pennant'.

3. Thomas Pennant *A Tour in Scotland and Voyage to the Hebrides, 1772* I (London 1776) p.367.

4. Boswell *Life of Johnson*, 12 April 1778.

5. Naturally there is a problem of definition: it is not quite clear what should be included within the Highlands and what should be left out. For present purposes, the Highlands are taken as consisting of six counties: Caithness, Sutherland, Ross and Cromarty, Inverness, Argyll and Perthshire. This is obviously not an ideal definition. Much of Caithness is not highland in character. Neither is south-east Perthshire, particularly the Carse of Gowrie, and the country south of the River Earn below Crieff. On the other hand, it is hard to deny the description 'highland' to the western part of Aberdeenshire and to the remoter uplands of Angus and Banff. (It is significant how Gaelic place-names become increasingly more common as one travels inland towards the higher hills in any of these counties.) But for ease of definition, and particularly because the county boundaries are convenient for the collection of data, especially statistical data, the definition given will be adhered to, with occasional adjustments when it seems likely to distort the truth too much.

6. Jorevin de Rocheford (1661?) in *Early Travellers in Scotland*, ed.P.Hume Brown (Edinburgh 1891) p.217.

7. Thomas Morer (1689) in *Early Travellers* p.268.

8. Fraser Darling *Natural History in the Highlands and Islands* (London 1947) p. 30.

9. John Knox *A Tour through the Highlands of Scotland and the Hebride Isles in 1786* (London 1787) p.lxxxiv. John Knox (1720–90) was for many years a bookseller in the Strand. He retired with a large fortune in 1764, and thereafter interested himself in promoting manufactures and fisheries in Scotland. Between 1764 and 1775 he made sixteen tours through Scotland, and was a prominent member of the British Fisheries Society from its inception in 1786. His *Tour* was probably his best known work.

10. James Watt, Third Report from the Committee appointed to enquire into the State of the British Fisheries (1785) App. 22, pp.279–80.

11. The first frosts of winter begin in inland areas around early September, on the east coast in late October or early November, and in the Inner and Outer Hebrides not until about the beginning of December.

12. Fraser Darling notes the interesting fact 'that the heights above 2,000 feet are grazed by deer almost exclusively' when clear of snow 'because they are the only hoofed animals with sufficient mobility to get up and down between the recurrent bad spells of gales and rain.' Fraser Darling *West Highland Survey* (London 1955) p.158.

13. The most famous of these is the narrow Gulf of Corrievreckan between Jura and Scarba, where there is a whirlpool coupled with reverse tidal effects caused by a strong tide from the Atlantic being funnelled through a narrow strait with an uneven floor. The current can run extremely fast, and the passage and its vicinity are generally dangerous.

14. Those who have visited the west coast only in fine weather are likely to underestimate its dangers. Violent storms, mists and sudden squalls make these waters very hazardous. An Englishman who lived for many years in South Uist before 1914 and who discovered how many tragedies took place at sea, even for a small community, wrote as follows: 'I now began to understand a little of the attitude of the people, Uist-born and others, towards the sea. I often spoke to them of bathing and swimming in its clear waters, and expressed wonder at their not indulging in these pleasures. These remarks were always met with a slow shake of the head, or a threatening fist stretched out towards the sea—their feeling regarding it seemed a mixture of awe, fear and anger. . . . Yet these Uist men are the bravest and the most daring of all fishermen, and make the finest sailors in the world . . .' F.G. Rea *A School in South Uist* (London 1964) pp.84–5.

15. W. Croft Dickinson *Scotland from the Earlier Times to 1603* (London 1961) p.276.

16. Dickinson *Scotland from the Earlier Times* p. 8.

17. The arrangement just before the '45 was as follows: 'A garrison of regular soldiers, with General Clayton as Commander-in-chief, occupied the line of the present Caledonian Canal, between Inverness and Fort William. These were reinforced by a "body of disciplined Highlanders, wearing the dress and speaking the language" of the region, in a word, the old independent companies, now regimented. Not only could they do the work of cavalry in difficult country among bogs and mountains where cavalry were useless, but as intelligencers, they could bring to their leaders secrets circulating among the native population.' G. Menary *The Life and Letters of Duncan Forbes of Culloden* (London 1936) p. 191.

18. Quoted in Menary *Life and Letters* p. 9.

19. S. Johnson *A Journey to the Hebrides* in *Works* IX (Oxford 1825) p. 82.

20. Ibid.

21. J. Home *The History of the Rebellion in 1745* (London 1802) pp. 9–10.

22. A. Allardyce, ed. *Scotland and Scotsmen in the Eighteenth Century, from the MSS of Ramsay of Ochtertyre* II (Edinburgh 1888) p. 393.

23. E. R. Cregeen *Argyll Estate Instructions 1771–1805* (Edinburgh 1964) p. xxxix.

24. John Walker *An Economical History of the Hebrides and Highlands of Scotland* I (London and Edinburgh 1812), pp. 51–2.

25. Seventh Duke of Argyll *Scotland as It Was and As It Is* (Edinburgh 1887) p. 267.

26. The Earl of Selkirk *Observations on the Present State of the Highlands of Scotland* (London 1805) p. 15.

27. Selkirk *Observations*, pp. 13–14. This story is to be found in Home *History of the Rebellion* p. 20. The story is told of McDonald of Keppoch, who was killed at the Battle of Culloden.

28. Selkirk *Observations* pp. 16–17.

29. Allardyce *Scotland and Scotsmen* p. 408.

30. Adam Ferguson *An Essay on the History of the Civil Society*, ed. Duncan Forbes (Edinburgh 1966) p. 194.

31. Ferguson *Essay on Civil Society* pp. xxxviii to xl.

32. Walker *Economical History* I, p. 79.

33. Ibid., p. 47.

34. W. Marshall *General View of the Agriculture of the Central Highlands*. (London 1794) pp. 30–1. Life on the hills was more important in some districts than in others. In Glenelg, for example, it seems to have been the dominant feature of life before 1745. 'As there were extensive sheallings or grasings attached to this country, in the neighbourhood of the lordship of Badenoch, the inhabitants in the beginning of summer removed to these sheallings with their whole cattle, man, woman and child; and it was no uncommon thing to observe an infant in one creel, and a stone on the other side of the horse, to keep up an equilibrium; and when the grass became scarce in the sheallings, they returned again to their principal farms, where they remained while they had sufficiency of pasture, and then, in the same manner, went back to their sheallings, and observed this ambulatory course during the seasons of vegetation; and the only operations attended to during the summer season was their peats or fuel, and reparing their rustic habitations. When their small crops were fit for it, all hands descended from the hills, and continued on the farms till the same was cut and secured in barns, the walls of which were generally made of dry stone, or wreathed with branches or boughs of trees; and it was no singular custom, after harvest, for the whole inhabitants to return to their sheallings, and to abide there till driven from thence by the snow. . . . The cultivation of the country was all performed in spring, the inhabitants having no taste for following green crops or other modern improvements.' Sir John Sinclair *The Statistical Account of Scotland* (Edinburgh 1791–9) XX, Boleskine and Abertarf, pp. 24–5 (hereafter referred to as *O.S.A.*).

35. 'The first time potatoes were planted in the Hebrides, or in the Highlands, was in the year 1743, and in the island of South Uist. In the spring of that year, old Clanronald was in Ireland, upon a visit to his relation, Macdonnel of Antrim; he saw with surprise and approbation, the practice of the country, and having a vessel of his own along with him, brought home a large cargo of potatoes. On his arrival, the tenants in the island were convened, and directed how to plant them; but they all refused. On this, they were all committed to prison. After a little confinement, they agreed at last to plant these unknown roots, of which they had a very unfavourable opinion. When they were raised in autumn, they were laid down at the chieftain's gate, by some of the tenants, who said the Laird indeed might order them to plant these foolish roots, but they would not be forced to eat them. In a very little time, however, the inhabitants of South Uist came to know better, when every man of them would have gone to prison, rather than not plant potatoes.' Walker *Economical History* I, p.251.

36. Ibid., p.121.
37. Marshall *Central Highlands* pp.37–8.
38. A. Lang, ed. *The Highlands of Scotland in 1750* (Edinburgh 1898) pp.60–1.
39. Ibid., pp.62–4. See also *Anecdotes and Egotisms of Henry Mackenzie* (Oxford and London 1927) p.13, and Pennant *A Tour in Scotland 1769* (London 1773) pp.187–8.
40. Argyll *Scotland As It Was* p.262. According to the government agent already quoted, 'Donald of Lochiel about twenty years ago made some Attempts to bring his People from Theft and Idleness; but some of his Neighbouring Chiefs prevailed upon him to allow his People to Continue in their Old way, as it was absolutely necessary for his men to be kept in the use of Arms if he intended to Contribute to the Glorious Cause of restoring the Stuart Family'. Lang *Highlands of Scotland* p.84.
41. Cregeen *Argyll Estate Instructions* p. xii.
42. Ibid., p.xi.
43. Lang *Highlands of Scotland* pp.39–40.
44. Sir James Fergusson 'Scottish support for the Forty-five' in *Common Errors in Scottish History* (Historical Association 1956).
45. Marchmont Papers, I, 131.
46. J. Fergusson *John Fergusson 1727–1750* (London 1948) p.176.
47. 'Letters from Archbishop Herring' *English Historical Review* XIX (London 1904) p.726.
48. In Edinburgh 'not one of the mob who were so fond of seeing him ever asked to enlist in his service'. Lord David Elcho *A Short Account of the Affairs of Scotland*, ed.E. Charteris (Edinburgh 1907) p.261.

49. Quoted in Menary *Life and Letters* p.239.
50. Fergusson 'Scottish support for the Forty-five.'
51. Home *History of the Rebellion* pp.44–5.
52. Letter from William Corse, dated 15 February 1746, quoted in Menary *Life and Letters* p.264.
53. Lang *Highlands of Scotland* p.xxxv. It should be added that Forbes did his utmost after the Battle of Culloden to secure justice and clemency for those who had been involved in the rebellion.
54. *Culloden Papers . . . including . . . Memoirs of The Right Honourable Duncan Forbes* (London 1815) p.298.

Chapter Two

1. Home *History of the Rebellion* p.2.
2. P. Hume Brown *History of Scotland to the Present Time* III (Cambridge 1911) p.261.
3. This Act 'was so badly put into force that the most disaffected clans remained better armed than ever. By the Act, the collectors of taxes were empowered to pay for the arms delivered up; but none were given in except such as were broken and unfit for use, which were valued at a price far beyond what they were worth. Not only so, but a brisk trade appears to have been carried on with Holland and other countries in broken and useless arms, which were imported and delivered up to the commissioners at exorbitant prices.' Ed. J.S. Keltie *A History of the Scottish Highlands* I (Edinburgh and London 1879) p.496.
4. Hume Brown *History* p.261.
5. Allardyce *Scotland and Scotsmen* II, p. 396.
6. The Lovat estate was restored in 1774, the others in 1784. The funds left in the hands of the Barons of Exchequer were subsequently devoted to public works, for example, the building of the Crinan Canal, and of Register House in the New Town of Edinburgh.
7. Report by the Commissioners to the King, 3 March 1763 (E723/2).
8. *O.S.A.* VI, Kilmuir Easter, p.189.
9. Report of Drs Hyndman and Dick, Ecclesiastical Documents (1760) SRO CH8/212, p.82.

10. The transhumant agriculture practised by many highlanders made the problem more difficult. One group living 'about three measured miles from the school at Finnart and having about thirty young ones who are not able to Travel the Distance backwards and forwards in the Winter' asked for a new school, but added, 'The petitioners beg leave to inform your Lordship that during the summer season they live in the hills at such Distance that though their Children were not otherways employed at herding they coud not attend the School at Finnart.' E783/63, 29 January 1763.

11. E783/60, 5 March 1784.

12. Forfeited Estates E730/2/2.

13. The rules of 1762 were subsequently printed, with minor alterations and additions, in 1765, 1773 and 1774.

14. Forfeited Estates E730/1/1. 'Instruction for the Factors upon the annexed Estates.'

1. That they shall make regular circuits twice a year through the corn farms, converse with the Tenants about their method of culture, observe whether they follow the directions given by the Commissioners and instruct them where they go wrong.

2. That they survey their labouring instruments and give the Tenants Instruction about the best kinds.

3. That they look to the Cattle whether in good or bad order and to give instructions about their management.

15. On being informed that there was 'Idleness and Disorder, occasioned by too great a number of Change-houses' in the Highlands, the Commissioners began an enquiry, which revealed, among other things, that on the estate of Monaltry there were three change-houses kept by 'the Miller, the Smith and the Boatman; which the Factor is of opinion, are Sufficient.' Below this entry there is a note in another hand, probably written by one of the Commissioners, 'Would not one public house be sufficient for 140 Inhabitants?'

16. Forfeited Estates E730/39.

17. This company bought some 60,000 trees for charring purposes about 1730. Ore was brought all the way from the Lecht beyond Tomintoul on pack ponies. The 'iron mill croft', half a mile above

Nethybridge, was still to be seen at the start of the present century. The company collapsed before 1740 but taught the local people how to make rafts of trees; these were made at the mouth of the Nethy and floated down the Spey to Garmouth.

18. E783/58 21 February 1757.

19. Lang *The Highlands of Scotland* p. 34.

20. Forfeited Estates E730/15.

21. Forfeited Estates E746/111.

22. Forfeited Estates E730/25.

23. Report on Coasts and Central Highlands (1803) p. 4.

24. *Scots Magazine* (November 1754) 529–30.

25. Forfeited Estates E730/20.

26. Ibid.

27. Lang *The Highlands of Scotland* pp. 67–8.

28. Forfeited Estates E730/20.

29. Forfeited Estates E777/221.

30. Forfeited Estates E730/25.

31. Ibid.

32. Forfeited Estates E730/38.

33. Forfeited Estates E730/25.

34. Ibid.

35. Forfeited Estates E730/32.

36. Lang *The Highlands of Scotland* p. 52.

37. Forfeited Estates E730/25.

38. Cregeen *Argyll Estate Instructions* pp. xii–xiii.

39. 'I will fall on some proper way of showing my displeasure to such as are refractory and to encourage those who do as I direct. I'm resolved to keep no tenants but such as will be peaceable and apply to industry. You'l cause intimate this some sabbath after sermon.' MS 'Instruction to the Chamberlain of Tiry', 1756, quoted in Cregeen *Argyll Estate Instructions* p. xix.

40. Ibid., p. xx.

41. Pennant *Tour 1769* p. 103.

42. Ibid., p. 233.

43. The Argyll Estate Instructions contain the following entry for 1786: 'My chamberlain of Mull continues to complain of the abuses committed on my woods by the people of Tiry and says that in a few years they will utterly destroy the woods. I insist that you take measures for preventing their getting a single stick without your order and your knowing what use it is for. ...' Cregeen *Argyll Estate Instructions* p. 7.

44. Pennant *1769* p.92.

45. Edward Burt *Letters from a Gentleman in the North of Scotland* . . . (London 1815) p.35.

46. Pennant *1772* I, p.261.

47. Quoted in ed. M. M. McArthur *Survey of Lochtayside* I (Edinburgh 1936) p.xxx.

48. Pennant *1769* p.115.

49. Cregeen *Argyll Estate Instructions* p.xii.

50. Pennant *1769* p.101.

51. See John Home *Survey of Assynt* ed. R.J. Adam (Edinburgh 1960) p.lii.

52. Pennant *1769* p.107. 'The first thing the Highlanders did when they went to the hills, was to bleed all their black cattle; and, boiling the blood in kettles, with a great quantity of salt, as soon as the mass became cold and solid, they cut it in pieces, and laid it up for food.' Home *History of the Rebellion* p.6.

53. Before 1746, when the Highlanders could still carry arms and still preserved their independence, they were able to supplement their meagre food supplies by fishing and hunting, 'free to people of all ranks, in a country where the rivers and lakes swarmed with fish, and the hills were covered with game.' Home *History of the Rebellion* p.7.

54. Pennant *1769* p.115. It is fair to add that the passage ends with the words: 'I never saw so much plainness among the lower rank of females: but the *ne plus ultra* of hard features is not found till you arrive among the fish-women of Aberdeen'.

55. Pennant *1772* I, p.261.

56. Burt *Letters* II, p.180.

57. Pennant *1772* I, p.365.

58. Adam *Survey of Assynt* p.xxvii.

59. McArthur *Survey of Lochtayside* p.lxxii.

60. Cregeen *Argyll Estate Instructions* pp.xxii–xxiii.

61. Ibid., p.xxiv.

62. Pennant *1769* p.168.

63. Ibid., p.187.

64. It is true that Dr Johnson expressed disappointment: 'We came thither too late to see what we expected, a people of peculiar appearance, and a system of antiquated life.' What he did not see was the clan system in its hey-day; but the Highland which he describes are very far from a replica of London life to which the Doctor was accustomed.

65. *Scots Magazine* (1771) 325.

66. Ibid., 500.

67. Ibid. (1772) 395.

68. Ibid., 515.

69. For an assessment of Webster's performance see A.J. Youngson 'Alexander Webster and his Account of the Number of People in Scotland in the Year 1755' *Population Studies* XV, no.2 (1961).

70. Walker *Economical History* I, p.25.

71. It is worth noting that in his list of Gaelic speaking parishes Walker includes Strathdon and Kincardine O'Neill, both in Aberdeenshire.

72. *Scots Magazine* (1771) 325.

73. Ibid. (1772) 395.

74. Pennant *1772* I, p.354.

75. Quoted in Pennant *1769* p.191.

76. Pennant *1769* p.191.

77. Quoted in Adam *Survey of Assynt* p.xxxii.

78. Cregeen *Argyll Estate Instructions* p.xxviii and Walker *Economical History* II, p.401.

79. Quoted in Adam *Survey of Assynt* p.xxvi.

80. Pennant *1772* I, pp.365–6.

81. Quoted in Adam *Survey of Assynt* p.xxv.

82. *Scots Magazine* (1772) 515.

83. Ibid. (1771) 500.

84. The matter was stated by Walker in 1808 in the following terms: 'This emigrating spirit commenced about the year 1770, when some considerable proprietors resolved to raise their rents. The tacksmen refused to comply with the offered terms; upon which the lands were let to the inferior people, who had been their subtenants. It does not appear that these tacksmen were induced to leave their country from any wanton desire of change or any deliberate plan of enterprize; but they found themselves uneasy at home, by alterations in the state of property, to which they had not been accustomed, and to which their minds and views could not correspond; being men of substance and influence, they have power to persuade numbers of their servants and dependents to accompany them to the wilds of America.' Walker *Economical History* II, p.406.

85. *Scots Magazine* (1772) 628.

86. Quoted in Adam *Survey of Assynt* p.xxxi.

Chapter Three

1. Adam Smith *The Wealth of Nations* ed. E. Cannan, I (London 1904) p.19.
2. Ibid., p.81.
3. Charles Davenant *Discourses on the Public Revenues* II (London 1698) p.262.
4. Sir Joseph Child *A New Discourse of Trade* (London 1690) p.87.
5. Charles Davenant *An Essay upon . . . the Balance of Trade* (London 1699) p.53.
6. Smith *Wealth of Nations* II, p.111.
7. David Loch *Essays on the Trade Commerce, Manufactures and Fisheries of Scotland* I (Edinburgh 1778) p.140.
8. Ibid., p.142.
9. David Hume *Essays Moral, Political and Literary*, ed. T.H. Green and T.H. Grose, I (London 1882) p.293.
10. The quotations in this and the following paragraphs are from the Preface to James Anderson *Observations and the Means of Exciting a Spirit of National Industry* (Edinburgh 1777) pp.v–x. James Anderson (1739-1808) was a practising farmer, latterly at Monkshill in Aberdeenshire. He was actively interested in many aspects of contemporary policy, and wrote a good deal on miscellaneous subjects in the fields of agriculture, economics and politics. He corresponded with both Bentham and George Washington. In 1777 he published an essay on the Corn Laws in which he is supposed by some authors to have anticipated Ricardo's views on rent.
11. Hume *Essays* I, p.303.
12. Sir William Petty *Economic Writings* ed. C.H. Hull, I (Cambridge 1899) p.274.
13. W. Letwin *The Origins of Scientific Economics* (London 1963) p.41.
14. Sir Henry Pollexfen *A Discourse of Trade* (London 1700) p.47.
15. F. Fauquier *Essays on Ways and Means* (London 1756) p.18.
16. Josiah Tucker *A Brief Essay . . . with regard to Trade* (London 1750) p.46.
17. E.S. Furniss *The Position of the Labourer in a System of Nationalism* (New York 1920) ch.VI.
18. Malachy Postlethwayt *The Universal Dictionary of Trade and Commerce* (London 1766) p.14.
19. Ed. Sir Walter Harris *Remarks on the Affairs and Trade of England and Ireland* (London 1691) p.53.
20. Sir William Temple *Works* III (London 1814) p.12.
21. Sir William Mildmay *The Laws and Policy of England Relating to Trade . . .* (London 1765) p.3.
22. Davenant *Essay* p.123.
23. Child *New Discourse*, Preface.
24. John Cary *A Discourse on Trade* (Bristol 1745) p. 145.
25. Thus the possibility of varying the price of provisions led to confusion: 'The balance-of-trade is against us in almost every country in Europe, because of those countries who rival us in manufactures and commerce by living cheaper and paying smaller wages, undersell us in most of the foreign markets. Our governors should, therefore, use their warmest endeavours to find out effectual methods to reduce the prices of provisions, such a measure would be an effectual means of relieving the distresses of our fellow creatures.' John Powell *View of Real Grievances* (London 1772) p.281.
26. Anderson *Observations* p.5.
27. Ibid., 6–7.
28. John Knox *A View of the British Empire, more especially Scotland . . .* (London 1785) p.127.
29. Hume *Essays* I, p.297.
30. Davenant *Essay* p.24.
31. Anderson *Observations* p.287.
32. Sir William Temple *Observations upon the United Provinces of the Netherlands*, ed. G.N. Clark (Cambridge 1932) p.93.
33. William Petyt *Britannia Languens* (London 1680) p.153.
34. Temple *Observations*, p.xi.
35. Knox *View of the British Empire* p.xlviii.
36. Child *New Discourse* p.192.
37. Thomas Mun *Englands Treasure by Foreign Trade* (London 1664) p.12.
38. Temple *Observations* p. xi.
39. Ibid., p.52.
40. Ibid., p.76.
41. Ibid., p.128.
42. Temple *Observations* pp.129–30.
43. Ibid., p.131.
44. Ibid., p.132.

45. Ibid., p. 135.

46. Ibid.

47. Ibid., p. 140.

48. Hume *Essays* I, p. 300.

49. Ibid., p. 176.

50. 'Tis always observed, in years of scarcity, if it be not extreme, that the poor labour more, and really live better, than in years of great plenty, when they indulge themselves in idleness and riot. I have been told, by a considerable manufacturer, that in the year 1740, when bread and provisions of all kinds were very dear, his workmen not only made a shift to live, but paid debts, which they had contracted in former years, that were much more favourable and abundant.' This appeared in the text of all editions published between 1742 and 1768.

51. Hume *Essays* I, p. 325.

52. See above pp. 56–7.

53. Hume *Essays* I, p. 357. The passage quoted by Hume appears above on p. 57.

54. Ibid., p. 176.

55. Ibid., p. 299.

56. Ibid., p. 298.

57. For example, Hume also emphasises the importance of foreign trade (ibid., p. 298) and the close connection between economic development and the maintenance of law and order.

58. The only other English writer referred to by Hume is Mandeville, who is accused of inconsistency or 'a contradiction in terms' (ibid., pp. 308–9).

59. The following quotations are from the essay 'Of Commerce' in ibid., pp. 289 ff.

60. Ibid., p. 294.

61. Ibid., p. 293.

62. This is a summary of an already compressed argument. It may be restated as follows:
It was Hume's achievement to clarify, sometimes to dispose of earlier ideas. In his essay 'Of Commerce' he took the popular view that the foundation of wealth is a surplus, obtained through foreign trade, and, working in real and not in money terms, explained just how and why a surplus was likely to be beneficial. He began by restating the popular view: 'The greatness of a state, and the happiness of its subjects, how independent soever they may be supposed in some respects, are commonly allowed to be inseparable with regard to commerce; and as private men receive greater security, in the possession of their trade and riches, from the power of the public, so the public becomes powerful in proportion to the opulence and extensive commerce of private men. This maxim is true in general. . . .' *Essays* I, pp. 289 ff. But, Hume adds, 'it may possibly admit of exceptions'. His argument is, briefly, that when technology in agriculture reaches such a level that a part of the population can be maintained without having to work on the land, these 'superflous hands' can either 'apply themselves to the finer arts' and thereby 'add to the happiness of the state', or they may be drafted into 'fleets and armies, to encrease the dominions of the state abroad, and spread its fame over distant nations'. It follows that if the 'proprietors and labourers of land' are content with a simple way of life, the superfluous hands have no motive to become 'tradesmen and manufactures', and are available for the support of 'fleets and armies to a much greater extent, than where a great many arts are required to minister to the luxury of particular persons'. The 'ambition of the sovereign must entrench on the luxury of individuals'.

Hume then asks whether 'the sovereign' should not therefore limit the expenditure of individuals so as to build up the power of the state. His answer is that little can be done in this way, because 'that policy is violent, which aggrandises the public by the poverty of individuals'. Sovereigns 'must take mankind as they find them', and it is only in exceptional circumstances that men will work for the state without direct benefit to themselves. If superfluous hands were not employed in industry they would not be employed at all; indolence would become the rule; and if at any time 'the public exigencies require, that great numbers should be employed in the public service', there would be found a shortage of skill, application and food. Foreign commerce is important not because it yields treasure, but because it provides employment and 'materials for new manufactures'. Where it exists, 'a greater number of laborious men are maintained, who may be diverted to the public service'. This is how 'a stock of labour' may be 'stored up against any public exigency'; this is how the nation becomes 'more powerful, as well as richer and happier'. In other words, what matters is not treasure. It is not even a question of the surplus of production over consumption. Public greatness and private riches are reconciled by the transferability of skills and resources from private to public use. Hume does not rely in any way on mystical ideas about the state, and he puts much more emphasis on art and industry and less on mere numbers than previous writers had done. Both for the greatness of the state (an idea which he does not reject) and for the happiness of individuals Hume emphasises skill, enterprise, and the stimulus and opportunities of foreign trade. This is an analysis on an altogether higher level than had ever been achieved before. Hume thinks like a modern economist; although he still accepts some of the objectives and limitations set by his predecessors, he acknowledges that individuals have rights, and are not to be simply manipulated for the good of the state.

63. Sir James Steuart *Principles of Political Oeconomy* I (London 1767) pp. 25–6.

64. Ibid., p. 34.

65. Ibid., p. 35.

66. Ibid., p. 40.

67. Ibid., p. 43.

68. Ibid., p. 44.

69. Ibid., pp. 44–5.

70. Ibid., p. 157.

71. Ibid., p. 91.

72. Smith *Wealth of Nations* II, p. 396. Adam Smith also refers with approval to Hume's argument that commerce and manufactures promote order and good government—'by far the most important of all their effects' (*Wealth of Nations* I, p. 383).

73. Smith *Wealth of Nations* I, p. 148.

74. Ibid., II, p. 358.

75. Ibid., I, p. 325.

76. Ibid., p. 346.

77. Ibid., p. 357. This passage, as Cannan observes, may have been suggested by a reading of Cantillon's *Essai*, written about 1730 and published in 1755.

78. Smith *Wealth of Nations* I, p. 357.

79. Ibid., p. 355.

80. There was to be a canal from the Thames to the Severn, linked to the Trent, 'and so from that to the Rivers Humber and Tine, and, by Degrees, to go Northwards, with these or such other Canals, crossing and joining Branches of the Rivers Tweed and Forth, and the Lake called Lochlomond,' and so on into the Highlands. Sir Alexander Murray of Stanhope *The True Interest of Great Britain . . .* (London 1740) p. 40.

81. Knox *View of the British Empire* p. 143; Lang *Highlands of Scotland* pp. 143–4; Loch *Essays* II, p. 120.

82. Anderson *Observations* pp. 204–5.

83. Dr Johnson's view of the highland climate was as follows: 'Their weather is not pleasing: half the year is deluged with rain. From the autumnal to the vernal equinox, a dry day is hardly known, except when the showers are suspended by a tempest. Under such skies can be expected no great exhuberance of vegetation.' *Journey* (1825) p. 74.

84. Knox *View of the British Empire* p. 141. He also wrote of the Highlands as 'a country where soil and climate have been so niggardly of their favours' (p. 434).

85. Ibid., p. 142. See also p. 142n.

86. Anderson *Observations* p. 199.

87. Knox *View of the British Empire* p. 149

88. Anderson *Observations* p. 198.

89. Child *New Discourse* p. 192.

90. Anderson *Observations* p. 287.

Chapter Four

1. Walter Bagehot *Economic Studies*, ed. R. H. Hutton (London 1880) p. 154.

2. Adam Smith *The Theory of Moral Sentiments* ed. Dugald Stewart (London 1853) p. 265.

3. G. E. Davie 'Hume, Reid, and the Passion for Ideas' in *Edinburgh in the Age of Reason* (Edinburgh 1967).

4. J. Viner in *Man versus Society in Eighteenth-Century Britain* ed. J. L. Clifford (Cambridge 1962) p. 23.

5. *Third Report from the Committee appointed to enquire into the State of the British Fisheries* (1785) p. 52.

6. Knox *Tour through the Highlands* p. cliii. The net revenue from the coal duties in the 1750s was officially stated to be not much over £1,000 per annum.

7. Ibid., p.cxlxix.

8. Sir John Sinclair *General Report of the Agricultural State and Political Circumstances of Scotland* . . . II, Appendix (Edinburgh 1814) pp.410–11.

9. Anderson *Observations* p.18.

10. Ibid., pp.412–13.

11. Ibid., p.17.

12. Ibid.

13. Ibid., pp.412–14.

14. Sinclair *General Report* II, Appendix, p.394.

15. Quoted in ibid.

16. *Third Report on Fisheries* (1785) p.91.

17. Anderson *Observations* p.15.

18. Ibid., p.16.

19. Ibid., p.22.

20. Ibid.

21. Ibid.

22. Ibid., p.23.

23. Ibid., pp.34–5.

24. Ibid., p.26

25. Ibid., p.57.

26. Ibid.

27. Ibid., p.47.

28. Ibid.

29. Ibid., p.48.

30. Anderson depicted the drovers as monopolistic exploiters, men who 'on account of the difficulty of travelling in that country, which prevents access to strangers, have in some measure an entire monopoly of the sale of cattle, and there-fore give almost what prices they please; and thus in a short time amass more wealth, and live in greater splendour than many of the ancient chieftains themselves can do. And as these drovers are usually considerable graziers themselves, when at any time the demand for cattle slackens a little, it is but natural to suppose, that they will then sell only their own; so that every other person is then reduced to the most pinching want.' (*Observations* p.49). This statement of the drovers' position does not seem to be supported by any evidence.

31. Ibid., p.176.

32. Ibid., p.48.

33. Ibid., p.192.

34. Defoe, quoted in ibid., p.195.

35. Anderson *Observations* p.198.

36. Ibid., p.203.

37. Ibid., p.206.

38. Ibid., pp.204–5.

39. Ibid., p.428.

40. Ibid., p.430.

41. See ibid., p.431.

42. Described in *Third Report on Fisheries* (1785) Appendix II, pp.148–9. This Appendix is by Anderson.

43. *Third Report on Fisheries* (1785) p.71.

44. Ibid., Appendix II, p.151.

45. Ibid., p.153.

46. Ibid., p.154.

47. Ibid., p.179.

48. See Smith *Wealth of Nations* IV, ch. VIII.

49. *Third Report on Fisheries* (1785) pp. 48–9.

50. Ibid., Appendix II, p.153.

51. Ibid., p.167.

52. These ideas Anderson no doubt derived from the *Wealth of Nations*. In discussing what he called 'the natural progress of opulence,' or as we would say, the normal course of economic development, Adam Smith had written as follows: 'The inhabitants of the town and those of the country are mutually the servants of one another. The town is a continual fair or market, to which the inhabitants of the country resort, in order to exchange their rude for manufactured produce.' (vol. II, p.357, Cannan's edition). Adam Smith does not labour this point, but it is essential to his historical argument, and there is a small chapter entitled 'How the commerce of the towns contributed to the improvement of the country.' This chapter deals chiefly with the effects of commercial activities upon feudal servitudes and connections.

53. *Third Report on Fisheries* (1785) Appendix II, p.201.

54. Ibid., p.203.

55. Ibid., p.204.

56. Ibid., p.206.

57. Ibid., p.207.

58. Ibid.

59. Ibid., p.168.

60. Ibid.

61. Ibid., p.171.

62. Detailed proposals for such a town are to be found in Appendix x 'Hints for the Civil Police of a Town . . .' in James Anderson *An Account of the Present State of the Hebrides* . . . (Edinburgh 1785).

63. *Third Report on Fisheries* (1785) Appendix 11, p. 169.
64. Ibid., p. 169.
65. Ibid., p. 170.
66. Commenting on his Report, Anderson produced a different calculation. Boat and gear were to cost £18, and the land given to each family was put at £1; a total cost of £24 for establishing six fishing families, or 16s per person. Non fishing families would cost one pound each (for the ground), or 4s per person. Thus if the two groups were equal in number the average cost would be 10s per person. Therefore £5,000 plus £3,500 for premiums would provide for 10,000 persons. 'This continued for twenty years would amount to 200,000 Persons, not to take into the Account the Encrease by natural Procreation.' *Third Report on Fisheries* (1785) p. 70.
67. Ibid., Appendix 11, p. 161.
68. Ibid., p. 160.
69. Ibid.
70. Ibid., p. 174.
71. *Third Report on Fisheries* (1785) p. 64.
72. *Third Report on Fisheries* (1785) Appendix 11, pp. 181–2.
73. Letter from Minister of Fodderty, dated 20 June 1783 (Forfeited Estates E746/86).
74. 'The year 1782 was remarkably cold and wet, the crops over great parts of Europe were more or less injured, and the northern climates experienced a scarcity, amounting to a famine. The scanty crops in the Highlands of Scotland were green in October, when a fall of snow attended with frost, prevented every species of grain from arriving at maturity . . . Potatoes, which in bad seasons had proved a substitute for grain, were this year frost-bitten, and rendered entirely useless . . . During this distress at home, no relief could be obtained from abroad . . . Thus deprived of every resource . . . many hundred persons languished and died through want of sustenance. The husband and parent, unable to behold these scenes of distress without endeavouring to relieve them, set out, amidst frost and snow, upon the long and almost im-practicable journey to Inverness, where they expected to purchase a little grain with the produce of their cloths or

furniture . . . Several of those who had engaged in this generous enterprise, fell a sacrifice to hunger and cold, in their way to the market. They were found dead on the roads, in caverns and amongst thickets where they had taken shelter from the inclemencies of the weather, while the small, emaciated horses, the com-panions of their distress, could scarcely stand or walk'. Knox *View of the British Empire* (1784 ed.) pp. 78–9.
75. Ibid., p. i.
76. Ibid., p. v.
77. Ibid.
78. Ibid., p. lx.
79. Ibid., p. x.
80. Ibid., p. xiii.
81. Ibid., p. xxviii.
82. Ibid., pp. xxix–xxx.
83. Ibid., p. xxxii.
84. Ibid., p. xlix.
85. Ibid.
86. Ibid., p. xlviii.
87. Ibid., p. li.
88. Ibid., p. 17.
89. Ibid., p. 18.
90. Ibid., p. 19.
91. Ibid., p. 22.
92. Ibid., p. 25.
93. Ibid., pp. 26–7.
94. Ibid., p. 38.
95. Ibid., p. 41.
96. Ibid., p. 42.
97. Ibid., p. 63.
98. Ibid., pp. 64–5.
99. Ibid., p. 48.
100. Quotations in this paragraph from Knox (1784) pp. 67–77.
101. Knox (1785) pp. 241 and 251.
102. Ibid., p. 434.
103. Ibid., pp. 438–9.
104. Ibid., p. 440.
105. Ibid., p. 441.
106. Ibid., p. 421.
107. Ibid.
108. Ibid., p. 422.
109. Quotations in this paragraph from Knox (1785) pp. 671–92.
110. Anderson *An Account of the Hebrides* pp. lvii–lviii.
111. Knox *Tour through the Highlands* pp. cii–cxii.
112. *Loch Essays* III, p. 106.
113. Ibid., I, p. 9.
114. Ibid., p. 24.

115. Ibid., p. I.

116. Ibid., II, p. I79.

117. 'It is the interest of the landed gentle-men to promote Manufactures: For Manufactures cause a brisk circulation of money; money enables the manufacturer to marry; marriage augments population; population increases consumption; consumption enriches the farmer; and the farmer, by a due cultivation of his lands (the value of which increases proportionally), fills the coffers of the landlord . . .' *Loch Essays* II, p. I48.

118. Ibid., p. 22.

119. Ibid.

120. Dempster was a lowlander, an im-proving landlord who was chiefly interested in Scottish agriculture and fisheries. Born in Dundee in I732, he was educated at St Andrews and Edinburgh and was for many years MP for Forfarshire. He had a seat at Dunnichen, in Angus, but in I786 purchased an estate at Skibo in Sutherland. He died in I8I8.

121. *Letters of George Dempster to Sir Adam Fergusson 1756–1813*, ed. J. Fergusson (London I934) p. I38.

122. Ibid.

Chapter Five

1. Johnson *Journey* p. 84.

2. Knox *View of the British Empire* (I784) p. 43.

3. Pennant *1772* I, pp. 373–4.

4. *Third Report on Fisheries* (I785) Appendix I4, p. 245.

5. Pennant *1772* I, p. 370.

6. M. Gray *The Highland Economy 1750–1850* (Edinburgh I957) p. I08.

7. *Third Report on Fisheries* (I785) Appendix I4, p. 232.

8. Ibid.

9. Smith *Wealth of Nations* (Canaan's edition) II, p. 2I. It is only fair to add that the system of giving a bounty per barrel of fish had been tried without much success, having 'opened a Door for Fraud, Perjury, and all the Tricks which Ingenuity could invent to rob the Public; Some Barrels were partly filled up with Stones or Rubbish; others, on which the Bounty had been paid, were re-loaded, and again presented for a Bounty'. *Third*

Report on Fisheries (I785) p. 97.

10. *Third Report on Fisheries* (I785) p. 80.

11. Ibid., p. 97.

12. Ibid., Appendix I4, p. 234.

13. Ibid., Appendix 40, p. 342.

14. Ibid., p. IIo.

15. Ibid., Appendix II, p. 2Io.

16. Smith *Wealth of Nations* II, p. 22.

17. According to Pennant, there were in Loch Broom 'as in most of the lochs, a few, a very few of the natives who possess a boat and nets; and fish in order to sell the capture fresh to the busses.' (*Tour 1772* I, p. 376). But Pennant appears not to have known that this practice, if it existed, was illegal.

18. *Third Report on Fisheries* (I785) Appendix I4, p. 235.

19. Pennant *1772* I, p. 37I.

20. *Third Report on Fisheries* (I785) Appendix I4, pp. 236–7. By the I780s there were sometimes eighty or a hundred busses in Loch Broom when the herring shoals 'came upon the coast'.

21. Knox *Tour through the Highlands* p. IoI.

22. *Third Report on Fisheries* (I785) Appendix II, pp. I5I–2.

23. 'The Bulk of the Inhabitants are more or less employed in fishing as well as farming, every Farmer being obliged, by the Tenor of his Holding, to be a Fisher himself, or to hire One, whose Fish, and other Produce arising from his Labour, by Sea or Shore, his Landlord claims an exclusive Right to, at a stipulated Price, and obliges the Fisher to buy of him, at his own Price also, all his Fishing Necessaries, etc., and so far this is obligatory, that upon the Fisher's Breach of it, by disposing of his Fish or other Produce to the highest Bidder he forfeits his Lease, which is only Verbal . . .' *Third Report on Fisheries* (I785) p. 29.

24. 'The seeker of credit usually pledged an unplanted crop to pay for a loan of unstipulated amount at a rate of interest to be determined by the creditor.' C. V. Woodward *Origins of the New South, 1877–1912* (Baton Rouge I95I) p. II.

25. See *Third Report on Fisheries* (I785) Appendix Io, p. I38.

26. Ibid., Appendix II, p. I55.

27. So, at least, it was said by the Collector of Customs at Isle Martin, Loch Broom. *Third Report on Fisheries* (I785) Appendix 2I.

28. Ibid., Appendix 40, p. 349.

29. J. Anderson *Observations on the Effects of the Coal Duty* (Edinburgh 1792) p. 22.

30. *O.S.A.* IV, Fearn, Ross-shire, p. 297.

31. Ibid.. Fintray, Aberdeenshire, p. 238.

32. Ibid., Kirkhill, Inverness-shire, p. 122. Turf in this context means heather sods, which can be used to produce a miserable smoky fire.

33. David Stewart *Sketches of the Character, Manners and Present Situation of the Highlands of Scotland* (Edinburgh 1822) p. 197. Burt, writing in the 1720s, found highland ale little to his liking: 'This liquor is disagreeable to those who are not used to it; but time and custom will make almost any thing familiar. The malt, which is dried with peat, turf, or furzes, gives to the drink a taste of that kind of fuel; it is often drank before it is cold, out of a *cap* or *coif* as they call it: this is a wooden dish with two ears or handles, about the size of a tea saucer, and as shallow, so that a steady hand is necessary to carry it to the mouth, and, in windy weather, at the door of a change, I have seen the liquor blown into the drinker's face. This drink is of itself apt to give a diarrhoea; and therefore when the natives drink plentifully of it, they interlace it with brandy or usky.' (Burt *Letters* I, p. 151).

34. Pennant *1772* I, p. 221.

35. *O.S.A.* XVII, Killearnean, p. 352.

36. 'How many workmen are employed in your neighbourhood to work a forty gallon still?—I keep two men attending my Still, while I work night and day, and an extra hand in the hurry of making my Malt to assist them.' *Report from the Committee upon the Distilleries in Scotland* (1798) p. 333.

37. *Report on Distilleries* (1798) p. 376.

38. Ibid., p. 319.

39. Evasion was facilitated by the practice of siting distilleries 'in distant parts of the country, often on eminences surrounded with high walls and gates, and as far as possible removed from towns or places where the officers can have their residence'. *Report on Distilleries* (1798) p. 461.

40. Distillers had reason to complain, as they did, of 'the local situation and disadvantages of the Highland districts, in respect to the face of the country hilly, and of bad roads, with access and bridges for transporting their Grain, which they must carry over difficult paths and extended morasses, where no cart can approach, and sending their Spirits to market, that is, to the consumer's door, which the distiller must disperse in small quantities over the face of the country'. *Report on Distilleries* (1798) p. 501.

41. *First Report from the Committee appointed to enquire into the Illicit Practices used in Defrauding the Revenue* (1783).

42. *Report on Distilleries* (1798) p. 336.

43. One remarkable but not uncharacteristic eighteenth-century anomaly deserves mention; the case of the lands of Ferrintosh. Duncan Forbes of Culloden was proprietor of the lands of Ferrintosh, and in the reign of James II he 'was one of those who stood up in the defence of the religion, laws, and liberties of their country, and at a very great expence, as well as risk of his life and fortune, zealously engaged in promoting the late happy Revolution'. As a result, the enemies of the house of Hanover laid waste the barony of Ferrintosh, 'whereon he had an ancient brewery of Aqua Vitae', and in recompense Culloden obtained an Act of Parliament in 1690 which farmed to him and his heirs the yearly excise of the lands of Ferrintosh on payment of the sum of £22 2s 5d per annum. In 1695 another Act confirmed this, but added that the sum should be adjusted in proportion to what additional excise was or should be imposed by law upon the whole kingdom. As a result of these adjustments, the sum payable reached £72 18s 11d by 1781. In 1703 the privilege was declared by Parliament to be restricted to spirits made from barley at Ferrintosh, but to this restriction Culloden paid no attention, 'bringing into the district of Ferrintosh large quantities of grain from the neighbouring and even distant countries', and the Commissioners of Excise, although they complained frequently, were unable to take any effective action. The result of all this was, as the Commissioners rightly remarked, that 'Mr Forbes distilled in a manner duty free'; and output soared. By the early 1780s the quantity of spirits made at Ferrintosh exceeded 100,000 gallons per annum, on which the duty would have been of the order of £20,000. Culloden continued to pay £72 18s 11d 'and thereby undersold and ruined his neighbours as effectually as if he had a monopoly, and prejudiced the revenues of the country to a very considerable extent'. Ferrintosh was good whisky, and it was sold throughout Scotland and England, including London, where in 1780 a public warehouse was built to handle the large and growing consignments. Loyalty to the government was rewarded, and trade was good. Quotations from *Second Report on Illicit Practices* (1784) Appendix 1.

44. There was a good deal of variety in the methods of production and in the final product. Highland distillers, especially, were individualists — craftsmen, although perhaps not as that term is usually understood. At Stonefield, for example, near Oban, there was a distillery managed by 'an old Highlander, whose Whisky bore a high character in the country', and who was found to work in the following manner:
'he had no coolers: he kept his Wort in barrels, each of which had an old sack thrown over its mouth; his fermenting tuns were barrels of the same kind, and so clotted with dirt and yeast both within and without, that when I put my stick to this coating of filth, it peeled off in layers; and while I was standing by, he took up another dirty vessel that contained the sediment of his last fermentation, and going to his fermenting barrels, he poured, with impartiality, into each its portion. I asked him, with some surprise, why he did so; for dipping my finger into a little of what remained, I found this sediment sour as verjuice. He nodded significantly, and would not tell. I next enquired why he kept his vessels so filthy. He said, that tho it was against him, as the law now stood, to stop his work and clean his vessels, yet whatever others might do, he had always made a point of making everything sweet and clean once a year, in spring. This conversation took place in October . . .'
The still was very old fashioned, and the working very slow. On being told how rapidly stills were now worked in other parts of the country 'he burst into tears, and said that his customers had sometimes been telling him of these things, but he never would believe them; for he thought

they wished only to vex him, and to get his whisky cheap'. *Report on Distilleries* (1798) pp.723–4.

45. Ibid., p.684.

46. Ibid., p.456. The Statistical Account for Campbeltown said the same thing slightly differently: 'When a man may get half an English pint of potent spirits, or, in other words, get completely drunk for 2d. or 3d., he may well not be sober.' *O.S.A.* x, p.557.

47. When this Act was passed an Aberdeenshire minister 'saw several of these illegal stills carried upon the carts of carriers through the borough of Inverury in noon day, and I was informed that two and twenty had passed through in one week'. *Report on Distilleries* (1798) p.336. These men were presumably on their way to the hills, for renewed or extended operations.

48. Ibid., p.461.

49. The ordinary customs officers, or guagers, received a salary of only £33 per annum. This had not been altered since 1726, although prices had risen. On the other hand, the customs officers usually shared in the proceeds when illegal stills or stocks of spirit were confiscated. All this makes it easier to understand their known, if intermittent, connivance at illegal distilling.

50. Ibid., p.751.

51. The system of taxing according to the capacity of the still was worked by issuing a licence in respect of the sum paid.

52. Ibid., p.754.

53. Ibid., p.461.

54. 'In this country [Caithness] the officers and I have often experienced, that after going all night to place where we have had an information against, and good cause to suspect that illicit distillation was carried on, and after all our searches found nothing, those concerned being in the practice of shifting the still from one place to another, that it is almost impossible to make a detection: and the persons that have been detected in this Collection are poor creatures that have nothing to lose, if the Justices were inclined to make examples.' Letter from Commissioner of Excise for the Caithness District, printed in *Report from the Committee upon the Distilleries in Scotland* (1799) p.666.

55. The person fined was often a member

of a 'combination', who, being 'nowise capable of paying the penalties was chosen by his comrades for the active and apparent smuggler in case of detection'. *Report on Distilleries* (1799) p. 667.

56. Stewart *Sketches of the Highlands*, p. 197.
57. This is stated in the *First Report on Illicit Practices* (1783) p. 231.
58. Ibid., p. 228.
59. Ibid., p. 230.
60. *Report on Distilleries* (1798) p. 335.
61. Ibid., p. 459. Evidence given in 1784 to a Committee of the House of Commons.
62. Sea battles off the Ayrshire coast were not uncommon. For example, on 1 October 1783, a 16 gun revenue cutter with a crew of 50 engaged the *Thunderer*, laden with tea and spirits, mounting 24 guns and with a crew of 70. The battle began at sunset and continued until dark, when the ships became separated. The revenue cruiser sustained extensive damage in the rigging, and as a result of two shots on the waterline there were three feet of water in the hold when the engagement was broken off. The *Thunderer* subsequently landed her cargo.
63. Ibid., p. 351.
64. Ibid.
65. Ibid., p. 352.

Chapter Six

1. *O.S.A.* XIII, Barra, p. 336.
2. Ibid., VI, Edderachylis, p. 305.
3. Quoted in Jean Dunlop 'The British Fisheries Society 1786–1893' p. 188 (unpublished PH.D. thesis, University of Edinburgh.)
4. In the following pages I have relied heavily on the work of Dr Jean Dunlop, referred to in the preceding footnote.
5. Knox *Tour* p. lxxviii.
6. The aim of the founders was 'to form a Society that might prove beneficial to the Highlands' but its objects were mainly literary and artistic. It did, however, between 1778 and 1786 offer premiums for the best method of curing herring after the Dutch manner and for good catches by deep sea fishing.
7. Dunlop 'British Fisheries Society' p. 161.
8. Pennant *1772* I, pp. 362–3.
9. Ibid., p. 369.

10. Henry Beaufoy, speech in the House of Commons, quoted in Dunlop 'British Fisheries Society' p. 161.
11. Argyll MSS Papers, I, quoted in Dunlop 'British Fisheries Society' p. 61.
12. Dunlop 'British Fisheries Society' p. 64.
13. *O.S.A.* X, Lochbroom, p. 465.
14. It is interesting to note that Robert Mylne had a hand in the design both of the warehouse and the inn.
15. Perhaps the Society was too ambitious. In 1810 it was argued that the buildings were 'on a scale rather more extensive than the infant state of the colony required, or the prospects of success warranted'. Sir G. S. Mackenzie *General View of the Agriculture of the Counties of Ross and Cromarty* (London 1810) p. 264.
16. Quoted in Dunlop 'British Fisheries Society' p. 83.
17. Dunlop 'British Fisheries Society' p. 83.
18. *O.S.A.* X, Lochbroom, p. 464–5.
19. Dunlop 'British Fisheries Society' p. 132.
20. *O.S.A.* XIV, Kilninian, pp. 146–7.
21. Ibid., XI, Kilmore and Kilbride, p. 133.
22. Ibid., V, Inveraray, p. 294.
23. Ibid., XIX, Stornoway, p. 244.
24. Ibid., p. 242.
25. The details of these schools are interesting. One was a parochial school, the other was founded by the Society for the Propagation of Christian Knowledge. The two masters were paid £25 per annum and £17 per annum respectively, and their assistants £15 and £8; in addition, the parochial master had 'a dwelling house and garden rent-free, and some land'. Fees per quarter varied in the parochial school from 2s 6d for English and writing to £1 1s for navigation. Book-keeping was taught, for a fee of 5s per quarter. Charges at the SPCK school, which was subsidised by the Earl of Seaforth, were lower, ranging from 1s 6d for reading to 10s for navigation. See *O.S.A.* XIX, p. 243.
26. Ibid., XVI, Portree, p. 158.
27. A. R. B. Haldane *The Drove Roads of Scotland* (Edinburgh 1952) p. 107.
28. *O.S.A.* XVI, Assint, p. 173.
29. Selkirk *Observations* p. 97.
30. Dunlop 'British Fisheries Society' p. 47.
31. Quoted in ibid., pp. 46–7.
32. Selkirk *Observations* p. 100.

33. The Earl of Kinnoul, quoted in Dunlop 'British Fisheries Society' p.104.
34. This is according to the Fisheries Society's agent at Lochbay, summarized in ibid., p.239.
35. *O.S.A.* xx, Thurso, p.495.
36. Ibid., p.529.
37. Ibid., p.520.
38. Ibid., x, Wick, p.10.
39. Ibid., pp.11–12.
40. Ibid., p.10.
41. Quoted in Dunlop 'British Fisheries Society' p.82.
42. The figures given are as follows (*O.S.A.* xix, Stornaway, p.247):
Barrels of herring despatched

1791	4,592
1792	6,163
1793	10,945
1794	6,739
1795	4,395
1796	1,753

43. Ibid., xi, Kilmore and Kilbride, p.133.
44. Dunlop 'British Fisheries Society' p.253.
45. Agent's Report (1811), quoted in ibid., p.254.
46. Agent's Report (1811), quoted in ibid., p.256.
47. Dunlop 'British Fisheries Society' p.270.
48. Agent's report (1832), quoted in ibid.
49. *New Statistical Account of Scotland* xiv, Lochbroom, p.86 (hereafter *N.S.A.*).
50. Ibid., Portree, p.230.
51. *O.S.A.* xvii, Shapinshay, Orkney, pp.233–4.
52. *O.S.A.* xiv, Kilfinichen and Kilviceuen, p.182.
53. Figures accordingly to the Duke of Argyll's Chamberlain of Mull, quoted in Cregeen *Argyll Estate Instructions* p.188.
54. *Report of the Select Committee on Emigration (Scotland)* (1841) Appendix 1.
55. *O.S.A.* vi, Edderachylis, p.281.
56. *Report on Emigration* (1841) Q. 793.
57. *N.S.A.* xiv, Inverness, p.194.
58. *O.S.A.* x, Harris, p.360.
59. Gray *Highland Economy* p.135.
60. *Report on Emigration* (1841) Q. 2053.
61. *O.S.A.* xiii, North Uist, pp.310–11.
62. *Report on Emigration* (1841) Q. 794.
63. Ibid., Q. 2628.
64. Ibid., Q. 33.

65. Ibid.
66. *Inverness Courier*, 19 September 1822.
67. *Report on Emigration* (1841) Q. 10.
68. Although in one way a novelty, this was in accord with the common practice of tenants paying their rents, at least partly, in kind. Cregeen notes that a hundred women were said to be employed in spinning flax on Tiree, either at home or in the spinning school. The Duke had hopes of establishing linen factories both on Tiree and in Morvern. See MSS instructions to his Chamberlain in Tiree, 1756, quoted in Cregeen *Argyll Estate Instructions* pp. xviii–xix.
69. *O.S.A.* xi, Kildalton, Islay, p.288.
70. Ibid., Kilchoman, p.280.
71. Sir John Sinclair *General View of the Agriculture of the Northern Counties and Islands of Scotland . . .* (London 1795) p.64.
72. *O.S.A.* xi, Tain, p.464.
73. Ibid., xv, Avoch, p.620.
74. Ibid., ii, Blair-Atholl and Strowan, p.469.
75. *Third Report on Fisheries* (1785) Appendix 22, p.278.
76. Ibid., p.284.
77. Ibid., p.285. He also states that on the north passage it was 'not uncommon for vessels to be detained six weeks to two months. . . . In the Winter Season the Risque of Shipwreck in those boisterous Seas is very great . . . and Insurances are High'. (p.279)
78. Ibid., p.285.
79. Ibid., p.287.
80. Ibid., p.282.
81. Ibid., p.288.
82. Ibid., p.279.
83. Telford's *Survey and Report* (1803).
84. Letter dated 1802, quoted in A.R.B. Haldane *New Ways through the Glens* (Edinburgh 1962) p.32.
85. Telford's *Survey and Report* (1803).
86. *Third Report of the Committee on Highland Roads and Bridges* (1803).
87. See Telford's *Survey and Report* (1803 p.8.
88. Quoted in Haldane *New Ways* p.80.
89. *Reports of Commissioners, Highland Roads and Bridges, Second Report* (1805).
90. Letter from Telford, 1812, quoted in Haldane *New Ways* p. 83.
91. *Papers of the Commissioners for the Caledonian Canal*, M.T.1./207.

92. *Report of the Caledonian Canal Commissioners* (1812).

93. Quoted in Haldane *New Ways* p. 81.

94. *Report of the Caledonian Canal Commissioners* (1812).

95. Haldane *New Ways* pp. 145–6.

96. Quoted in Haldane *New Ways* p. 149.

97. *Report of a Select Committee on the Caledonian and Crinan Canals* (1839) p. 11.

98. *Report of the Caledonian Canal Commissioners* (1827).

99. Ibid.

100. Ibid., p. v.

101. See above, p. 84.

102. *Report on the Caledonian and Crinan Canals* (1839) p. ix.

103. *N.S.A.* x, Perthshire, p. 999.

104. General Mackay, quoted in Haldane *New Ways* p. 9.

105. *O.S.A.* xvi, Glenelg, p. 274.

106. Ibid., vi, Kintail, p. 244.

107. Ibid., iii, Dingwall, p. 14.

108. Ibid., Bracadale, p. 249.

109. Ibid., xiv, Kilfinichen and Kilviceuen, p. 206.

110. Ibid., xvi, Assint, p. 198.

111. Telford's *Survey and Report* (1803) p. 5.

112. Ibid., p. 7.

113. Secretary to the Commissioners, to Telford, 1805, quoted in Haldane *New Ways* p. 110.

114. Two particularly interesting bridges for which Telford and the Commissioners were responsible were the beautiful bridge over the Dee at Potarch, and the striking and unusual iron bridge over the Spey at Craigellachie. Neither of these, however, lies within the Highlands as here defined. They were completed in 1813 and 1815 respectively.

115. This works out at rather more than one bridge per mile.

116. Government contributed more than half the total cost because it alone paid for surveys and the expenses of general management. In 1821 the Commissioners had another £80,000 on offer from landowners, which they refused to match with public money; the proposals they thus rejected were for roads to Assynt, to Loch Maree and Ullapool, and to John o' Groats.

117. R. Southey *Journal of a Journey in Scotland in 1819* (London 1829) entry for 1 September.

118. *N.S.A.*, xiv, Inverness, p. 115,

119. Ibid., Dingwall, p. 229.

120. Ibid., x, Dunkeld and Dowally, p. 991.

121. Ibid., xiv, Ross and Cromarty, Lochbroom, p. 86. The Dingwall–Ullapool road, which when it was built in the early 1790s 'astonished the natives not a little', found small favour in the 1830s—'the line chosen was so absurd, and the execution so wretched, that the road has been, for many years back, not only useless, but dangerous . . . and to wheel carriages almost impassable.' p. 89.

122. Quoted in Haldane *New Ways* p. 185.

123. Southey *Journal* p. 157.

124. Ibid., p. 41.

125. John MacCulloch *The Highlands and Western Isles of Scotland* 2 (Edinburgh and London 1819) pp. 182–3.

126. Southey *Journal* p. 157.

127. Quoted in Haldane *New Ways* p. 137.

Chapter Seven

1. *O.S.A.* xiii, Barra, p. 332.

2. Ibid., p. 312.

3. *O.S.A.* xii, Kilmuir Wester and Suddy, p. 262.

4. The Argyll estate papers contain more detailed information for the island of Tiree

Year	Population	
c. 1750	1509	(Webster)
c. 1765	1793	(Dr Walker's *Observations*. Probably an over estimate)
1768	1676	(Surveyor's list, farm-by-farm enumeration)
1776	1997	(Farm-by-farm estate census)
1779	1881	(Farm-by-farm estate census—men absent at the war)
1787	2206	(Minister's catechist list)
1792	2416	(*O.S.A.*)
	2443	(Farm-by-farm estate census)
1802	2776	(Chamberlain)
1808	3200	(MacDonald's *Agriculture in the Hebrides*)
1811	3186	(Census)

These figures are in Cregeen *Argyll Estate Instructions* pp. xxviii–xxix. They support the contention that population growth was no novelty in 1800. Sources of information are in parentheses.

5. *O.S.A.* xx, Thurso, 503.

6. Ibid., xvi, Assint, p.207.

7. *N.S.A.* xiv, Inverness, North Uist, p.176.

8. Walker *Economical History* i, p.212.

9. *O.S.A.* xiii, North Uist, p.304.

10. See above, p.204, n.35.

11. *O.S.A.* xx, Boleskine and Abertarf, p.30.

12. Ibid., vi, Tarbat, Tain, p.421.

13. Ibid., Kintail, p.248.

14. Ibid., Edderachylis, p.289.

15. *Report on Emigration* (1814) Q. 805.

16. Sinclair *Northern Counties* p.58. These mailers were extremely poor, and the progress which they made in improving the land was sometimes very slow. 'I know of one instance of a crofter who was settled on a very good land and took fifteen years to improve three acres.' (Mackenzie *General View* p.84).

17. Walker *Economical History* i, p.188.

18. *N.S.A.* vii, Argyll, p.665.

19. *N.S.A.* xiv, Inverness, p.415.

20. Ibid., p.309.

21. Sinclair *Northern Counties* p.59.

22. Sinclair *General Report* ii, Appendix, p.400.

23. Quoted in Mackenzie *General View* p.91.

24. *O.S.A.* x, Wick, p.23.

25. *N.S.A.* xiv, Inverness, p.144.

26. *O.S.A.* x, Wick, p.17.

27. See John L. Buchanan *Travels in the Western Hebrides from 1782–1790* (London 1793) pp.52–3.

28. *O.S.A.* iii, Tongue, p.528.

29. Sinclair *Northern Counties*, p.98.

30. *N.S.A.* vii, Argyle, p.210.

31. Sinclair *Northern Counties*, p.52.

32. In the Hebrides, as late as 1811, it was said that 'None of the islands, excepting five or six of the more southerly, and a few farms in Skye, are furnished with anything which merits the name of inclosure'. James Macdonald *General View of the Agriculture of the Hebrides . . .* (Edinburgh 1811) pp.163–4.

33. *O.S.A.* xvi, Assint, p.187.

34. Walker *Economical History* ii, p.46.

35. *O.S.A.* x, Tiree, p.412.

36. *O.S.A.* vi, North Knapdale, p.281.

37. See, for example, Sinclair *General Report* ii, Appendix, pp.398–9; Walker *Economical History* i, pp.56–7; *O.S.A.* iii,

p.177, and vi, p.261; Mackenzie *General View* p.81.

38. 'During winter and spring they receive no dry or artificial provender, and have nothing to support them but the decayed gleanings of the herbage of the former summer.' Walker *Economical History* i, p.381.

39. Macdonald *General View* p.436.

40. Sinclair *Northern Counties* pp. 112–13.

41. The calculation of a typical tenant's income in North Uist in the 1790s was as follows: 'A tenant possessing half a penny lands, if he has any grown up children to assist him, will, by manufacturing kelp, make about £6 Sterling yearly. He has 6 cows, that is to say, as many great and small as will be equal to 6 grown up cows. Three of them will probably be milch cows. One of their calves will be killed, in order to have 2 of the cows coupled, another may be supposed to die by accident, or through want, before the time it should be fit for the market, so that this man has only one cow yearly to dispose of, for which he may be allowed to draw £2 8s at an average, and which, added to the £6 above mentioned, will amount to the sum of £8 8s. This is his whole yearly income, having nothing else that he can turn into money. On the other hand, this man pays £5 4s rent including public burdens. As he must keep 6 horses, he will be under the necessity of buying one every second year, at the average price of £3 10s which makes £1 15s a-year. Though in an extraordinary good year, his lands may supply his family with meal, yet he is for ordinary obliged to buy that necessary article; so that matters are not exaggerated, when it is said, that he buys 1 boll a-year, at the average price of 17s. From this statement, this tenant has only a balance of 12s in his favour, for the purpose of buying all his other necessaries; such as timber for keeping his houses, implements of husbandry, and perhaps boat, in repair; for buying iron, tar, spades, flax, and several other articles that a tenant has occasion for throughout the year. This man, therefore, will either fall in arrears to the proprietor, or become indebted to those from whom he buys his necessaries; so that if the proprietor's chamberlain should be rigorous in taking up the rents, and other in exacting their lawful debts, many such would find themselves much distressed'. *O.S.A.* XIII, North Uist, pp.310–11.

42. *O.S.A.* xx, Dowally, p.470. The Duke also experimented in keeping 'rein deer', but this was not a success.

43. Sinclair *Northern Counties* p.14.

44. Walker *Economical History* II, pp.69–70.

45. Ibid., p.47.

46. In Skye, however, according to Walker, a premium for the destruction of foxes was offered as early as 1764, and as a result no fewer than 112 foxes were killed in 1765 in the district of Trotternish alone. (Walker *Economical History* II, p.360). By 1773, according to Johnson, foxes in Skye had become so scarce that the reward for killing one had been raised to a guinea (Johnson *Journey* p.57). But there were still plenty on the mainland.

47. Sinclair *Northern Counties* p.197.

48. Walker *Economical History* II, p.68.

49. Gray *Highland Economy* p.87.

50. Walker *Economical History* II, p.66.

51. Sinclair *Northern Counties* p.184.

52. Ibid.

53. Selkirk *Observations* pp.30–1.

54. Ibid., p.31.

55. *O.S.A.* VI, Ardchattan and Muckairn, p.178.

56. Ibid., x, Lochbroom, p.470.

57. Ibid., XVI, Glenelg, p.269.

58. James Loch *An Account of the Improvements on the Estates of the Marquess of Stafford* (London 1820) p.145.

59. See Loch *Improvements* Appendix VII, p.57; and J. Mitchell *Reminiscences of My Life in the Highlands* I (Chilworth 1883) p.335.

60. Selkirk *Observations* p.32.

61. See James Robson *General View of the Agriculture of the County of Argyll* . . . (London 1794) pp.45–7.

62. Walker *Economical History* II, p.408.

63. Loch *Improvements* Appendix VII, p.65.

64. Ibid., p.66.

65. Johnson *Journey* p.50.

66. They also lived comfortably, as did some of the greater tacksmen, at any rate in the eighteenth century. 'The tacksmen,' remarked Buchanan, writing of the Hebrides in the 1780s, 'from a large and advantageous farm, the cheapness of every necessary, and by means of smuggling of every luxury, rolls in ease and affluence.'

(Buchanan *Travels* p.39.) Dr Johnson likewise remarked of the lairds, 'Their trade is unconstrained; they pay no custom, for there is no officer to demand them . . .' (Johnson *Journey* p.52.).

67. Gray *Highland Economy* p.149.

68. Anderson *Observations* p.15.

69. Knox *View of the British Empire* (1784) p.lv.

70. Anderson *Observations* p.15.

71. Buchanan *Travels* p.49.

72. Johnson *Journey* p.91.

73. Selkirk *Observations* p.23.

74. Macdonald *General View* pp.104–5.

75. See Adam *Survey of Assynt* p.xxix.

76. 'At the end of the eighteenth century the chief proprietor in Morvern had owned land there for 125 years; there had been MacLeans in uninterrupted possession of their territories for more than twice as long; and no Lowland Scot or other *sasunnach* held an acre of land in the parish. Yet in the twenty-five years from 1813 to 1838 every single property of Morvern changed hands, and by 1844 there was scarcely a proprietor left who had any traditional or lengthy association with the parish, or (in most cases) with anywhere else in the Highlands either.' Philip Gaskell *Morvern Transformed: a Highland Parish in the Nineteenth Century* (Cambridge 1968) p.23.

77. Cregeen *Argyll Estate Instructions* p.xxix.

78. Quoted in ibid., p.xxxii.

79. *Report on Emigration* (1841) Q.33.

80. Quoted in Cregeen *Argyll Estate Instructions* p.73.

81. Smith *Wealth of Nations* I, p.225.

82. *Report on Emigration* (1841) Q.3262.

83. Ibid., Q.437.

84. *N.S.A.* xv, Tongue, Sutherland, p.177.

85. *Report on Emigration* (1841) Q.104.

86. Ibid., Q.951.

87. See Sinclair *General View* II, Appendix, pp.398–9; Walker *Economical History* I, pp.82–3. Walker states 'that more than double the number of horses and men servants are employed in the north of Scotland, on a farm of the same description and extent, than in the south . . . there are few farms in the North Highlands but might be managed and equally well cultivated with one third of the number of servants.'

88. Macdonald *General View* p. 79.

89. *N.S.A.* xv, Wick, Caithness, p. 150.

90. Ibid., x, Dunkeld, p. 989.

91. *Report on Emigration* (1841) Q. 3248.

92. *N.S.A.* xiv, Ross and Cromarty, Kilmuir Easter, p. 312.

93. 'They had the entire cutting down of the crops in the low country, with the exception of a very few farm servants; they went in my earliest memory, and long before that, in great crowds to cut down the crops, and I have met with old women in the Highlands who could give me a very excellent account of the rich fields in England to which they used to come . . .' *Report on Emigration* (1841) Q. 817.

94. *N.S.A.* xiv, Sutherland, Strath, p. 308.

95. *Report on Emigration* (1841) Q. 548.

96. Sinclair *Northern Counties* p. 135.

97. Letter from Patrick Sellar to James Loch, dated 1820; quoted in Loch *Improvements* Appendix VII, pp. 56–7.

98. *O.S.A.* iii, Gairloch, p. 90.

99. Ibid., ii, Fortingal, p. 459.

100. *N.S.A.* xiv, Ross and Cromarty, p. 84 (1835).

101. Ibid., xv, Assynt, Sutherland, p. 113.

102. Ibid., xiv, Ross and Cromarty, p. 210.

103. Ibid., xiv, Inverness, p. 226.

104. Ibid., xv, Sutherland, p. 177.

105. Ibid., xiv, Ross and Cromarty, Lochs, Lewis, p. 157.

106. Ibid., vii Argyle, p. 209.

107. Ibid., xiv, Inverness, p. 196 (1837).

108. Ibid., x, Moulin, Perthshire, p. 653.

109. Ibid., xiv, Ross and Cromarty p. 180 (1836)

110. Ibid., xiv, Dingwall, Ross and Cromarty, p. 223 (1837).

Postscript

1. Mackenzie *General View* p. 150.

2. *Report on Emigration* (1841) Q. 689.

3. See, e.g., ibid., Q. 533 and 686.

4. 'After all the declamation that has been excited by the depopulation of the Highlands, the fact in reality amounts to this: that the produce of the country, instead of being consumed by a set of intrepid but indolent military retainers, is applied to the support of peaceable and industrious manufacturers . . . the result is ultimately favourable to population, when we take into account that of the whole kingdom, balancing the diminution in one district by the increase in another.' Selkirk *Observations* p. 77.

5. Mackenzie *General View* p. 295.

6. Loch *Essays* p. 131,

7. Gerd Enequist 'Geographical changes of rural steelment in north western Sweden since 1523', Meddelanden från Uppsala Universitets Geografiska Institution Ser A No. 143, p. 17.

8. Ibid., p. 19.

9. *Memoirs of a Highland Lady: the autobiography of Elizabeth Grant of Rothiermurchus* ed. Lady Strachey (London 1898) p. 241.

10. *First Report of the Highlands and Islands Development Board* (1967). paras. 12, 24.

11. Ibid., para. 25.

12. Ibid., para. 14.

13. Ibid., para. 6.

14. See, e.g. E. Nevin in *Three Banks Review* (December 1966).

15. Smith *Wealth of Nations* i, p. 423.

16. See Knox *Tour* p. cxliii.

LOCH BOISDALE in SOUTH UIST
Sketched without measurement
6 Sept 1784 by AA

EXPLANATIONS

ORKNEY ISLANDS

THE HEBRIDES

CAITHNESS

SOUTHERLAND SHIRE

THE MINCH

THE ATLANTIC OCEAN

ROSS SHIRE

SKYE

THE MINCH OR

MURRAY FIRTH

ABERDEEN SHIRE

MURRAY SHIRE

MEARNS

INVERNESS SHIRE

ANGUS SHIRE

WESTERN

PERTH SHIRE

FIRTH OF TAY

ISLES

MULL I.

Icolmkill I.

FIFE SHIRE

KINROSS

STIRLING SH.

FIRTH OF FORTH

DUMBARTON SH.

HADDINGTON SHIRE

RENFREW SH.

GLASGOW

LITHGOW SH.

EDINBURGH SH.

BERWICK SHIRE

LANERK SHIRE

PEEBLES SHIRE

SELKIRK SHIRE

AIR SHIRE

ROXBOROUGH SHIRE

BUTE SH.

ARRAN SH.

DUMFRIES SHIRE

PART

A NEW MAP
of
SCOTLAND;
The
Hebrides and Western Coasts.
in particular.
being carefully laid down
from the best Authorities
corrected
by late Observations
1785

WIGTON SHIRE

KIRKUDBRIGHT SHIRE

OF

ENGLAND

PART OF IRELAND

WIGTON BAY

SOLWAY FIRTH

1 Deg. West from Edinburgh